Daughter of the Drunk at the Bar

Michelle O'Neil

Chapter One

Chink! Clang! Chink!

A whoosh of metal comes so close it fluffs the hair on the side of my head as it passes by. Next thing I know, Daddy has me by the neck of my shirt, and he's in my face screaming at me. "If one of you kids gets hit with a horseshoe, I'm not ruinin' my day takin' you to the God damn ER. You got that?"

I nod and Daddy lets go of my shirt but keeps glaring at me.

"You'll be shit outta' luck," he says, before picking his beer up off a stump by the horseshoe pit. He turns away from me and takes a long drink before getting back into the game with his friends from The Rusty Nail.

Daddy's name is Butch and he's got black hair and brown eyes and really strong muscles in his arms and legs. He wears jeans and t-shirts, and on his feet he wears steel-toed work boots, even in the summer.

Walking away from Daddy I'm wondering why he only yelled *at me*. Hilary and Adam were running near the horseshoe pits too. It isn't fair.

Our yard is full of microphone stands, a drum set, guitars and people. All the instruments are plugged into big extension cords running from the house and some of Daddy's friends from The Rusty Nail are playing music really loud. We just moved back to upstate NY after trying out Florida for a year and we're having a party in our new house to celebrate!

There's a big metal bin, with a black hose and a spout. Beer comes out when you squeeze the knob. It's hot outside and I keep going over to the beer bin for pieces of ice. Daddy cooked hamburgers and chicken on a great big fire pit he made out of cinder blocks in the middle of our yard. He used a sledgehammer to set up the horseshoe poles. When someone throws a ringer, all the men get happy and yell, and I like the sound the heavy horseshoe makes when it swirls around the metal pole before clunking into the dirt in a poof of dust.

Mommy comes over to me and leans down to tell me something. "I don't want you over near those horseshoes again, okay?"

I look up at her and she smiles and I can see I'm not really in trouble. Mommy's name is Diana. She is skinny, and has long brown wavy hair. She's the prettiest lady at our party and everyone is always telling her,

"You don't look old enough to have three kids!"

She is old enough though. She's got Hilary who is eight, and Adam who is four and I am almost six. Mommy is 26.

Mommy asks me to run inside to get more mustard and ketchup and I veer *way* around the horseshoe pit to get across the yard.

Our new address is 1227 Centerville Highway. Our house has dark brown shingles on the outside, and inside, there's dark brown wooden trim along the doors and ceilings. The living room has dark wood floors mostly covered by a grass green carpet and the ceiling is sky blue, like a robin's egg. The front wall has a big window that's covered with plastic and Mommy says it's to keep the cold air out come wintertime. The back wall has a door to Mommy and Daddy's bedroom. It also has a big lightening bolt crack in the plaster that goes from one corner almost down to the floor. The sidewall has shelves Mommy made out of cinder blocks and big thick boards. They're three stories high and loaded with Daddy's record albums, toys, bags of clothes for Gramma Bonner to mend, a Bible, and the encyclopedias.

Encyclopedias are big black books, and when I pull one out and open it, I stick my nose inside and smell the good smell before looking at the pictures. Daddy likes to look up stuff he doesn't know in the encyclopedias.

The living room is connected to the dining room. In the corner of the dining room is a big black wood stove that heats our house. It squats on some cinder blocks stacked up off the floor. The wood stove worries me. Mommy says we'll have to be careful around it in the winter, 'cause if you stand too close it will melt your nightgown right onto your legs. The table is in the middle of the room and there's a big window up front and a small window on the sidewall. There are exposed wooden beams and electric cords dangle down between the dining room and the kitchen and you're not allowed to touch them.

The kitchen has no walls, just brown paper bag looking stuff with pink fluff sticking out the sides. Mommy says it's called insulation. There are dark grease stains on the brown insulation paper behind the stove where Mommy cooks.

The steps to get upstairs are off of the kitchen. At the bottom of the steps is a doorframe but no door. My bedroom is right at the top of the stairs. It has sloped ceilings and curves around like an L shape leading into Hilary's nook. Hilary's half of the room is small and it faces out toward the front yard. She's got three little windows that swing open like tiny doors. My half of the room faces our neighbor, Mr. Parson's yard.

Adam has to go through mine and Hilary's areas to get to his room. Mommy says our rooms used to be an attic. Our bedrooms have real walls and Mommy painted them light brown. I would have liked pink, but light brown is still better than no walls, better than insulation.

The bathroom is off the kitchen and it also connects to Mommy and Daddy's room. It has no tub so we're learning to take showers now. When we lived in Florida we took showers to get the sand off after we went to the beach, but now we wash our hair and everything. The backdoor is right by the bathroom and it leads to the covered back porch with the rickety stairs down to the basement.

We also have a front porch. When I stand on it, I look down at all the cars going by on the highway and feel big! We can sit on the front porch, but we're not allowed to play in the front yard because it's too close to the highway. That's okay though, because our back yard is huge.

Running back outside I give Mommy the ketchup and mustard, veer around the horseshoe pit again and head back to the edge of the yard where Adam and the other kids are playing. At the edge of our back yard, right before you get to the hill with the woods, there's a little ditch. Me and Adam love the ditch because there are frogs' eggs and tadpoles in it. Adam is holding up a long slimy string of frog eggs on a stick and the other kids are all gathered around to look at it and touch the slime. Hilary won't touch slimy things. She's back by Mommy, pretending she's big and not a kid. The rest of us run around all day, catching tadpoles in our hands and watching them squirm before putting them back in the water.

A giant weeping willow stands in our backyard and a tire swing hangs from a thick high branch. It's not just a plain old tire swing either. Daddy made it special by using his knife to carve a seat with big circle handles. You can sit on it and swing really high. You can have someone turn it around and around and when they let go you get a fast, spinny ride. You can even *stand* on it, hooking your feet in the bottom of the handles and using your arms to pull the ropes sideways. You never have to worry about smacking into the tree because Daddy put the swing way out far on the branch. You can go as high as the sky on the swing Daddy made. All the kids at our party wait in line for their turn over and over, all day long and into the night.

By the time it's dark, our yard is jammed full with people. Mommy and her friend Fran are helping all the kids roast marshmallows and make s'mores. Hilary is handing out the marshmallows and acting like she's the boss. Mommy is in a good mood and we can all have two s'mores each. The band is playing *Taking Care of Business*, loud and fast, and there are lots of people dancing. Holding my stick over the fire, I see Daddy through the orange flames. He drank a lot of beer tonight and he's dancing crazy and wild. Lots of people are around him, moving, but he's alone. His legs are bent and his head is down and he goes faster and faster, like a wild Indian hoping to bring down the rain. It's spooky. His eyes are shut tight like he's praying, but he *can't* be praying 'cause Daddy says there's no such thing as God.

7

Chapter Two

Mommy and Gramma Bonner say there *is* a God. On Sundays Gramma Bonner runs her bony pointer finger below the words in the hymnal at St. Benjamin's Episcopal Church. When we sing, I lean in close and listen. Gramma's voice is high and shaky and I love being here with her. After singing, I sit in the pew, holding her hand. Gramma Bonner is skinny and her hands have big blue veins. She doesn't mind if I roll her veins side to side with my fingers, as long as I sit quietly.

Our priest is Father Duncan, but I think he secretly is Jesus. He's small, and thin with a long sad face just like Jesus on the cross up in front. Father Duncan is married and his kids go to Sunday school with us. I pretend we're lucky Jesus actually runs our church. Every other week, we go up to the altar and the grown-ups drink from the shiny gold cup. We kneel around the wooden bar and the grown-ups put out their hands and get a wafer, and they drink one sip of blood. Kids don't get wafers and I'm glad I'm not old enough to drink blood, but when Father Duncan gets to me, he stops and looks right at me. He takes his thumb and puts it on my forehead, two times, making a cross and he says, "May the Lord bless you and keep you."

You can tell he really means it, and it does feel like the Lord is blessing me and keeping me, right then and there. I love Father Duncan.

Today at church, I'm not feeling so good. I think it's because of my real father. Daddy doesn't believe in God and he doesn't ever come to church. He spends most of his time at The Rusty Nail. I wish Daddy would come to church though, because lately home feels like a mean headache and it smells like old beer and cigarettes. My tummy is always upset.

"Mommy, I feel sick," I whisper. She leaves Hilary and Adam in the pew with Gramma Bonner and takes me outside on the steps of the old stone church. We sit in the warm morning sunshine and Mommy puts her arm around me. She talks gentle to me and rubs my back. She strokes my hair. Mommy looks pretty in the sunshine. She smells like Prell shampoo. I like Prell because it's bright green and comes in a clear tube with a bubble in it. Now matter how you tip it, the bubble always floats to the top. She doesn't make us go back inside and this is the best church morning ever.

After church we get a donut in the reception hall and then drop Gramma Bonner off at her apartment. When we get home, Daddy stomps around, yelling, "Brainwashing them is what you're doing!"

He walks back and forth in the kitchen and Mommy pretends she doesn't hear him. He takes Hilary by the arm and says in a voice that means he's picking on her, "So what did you learn today at *Sunday school*?"

When she starts to tell him he says, "What a load of crap" and "You believe that bullshit?"

Sometimes Mommy tells him to stop, but mostly she just sits on the living room floor, reading the Sunday paper, pretending like she doesn't hear him.

When Daddy asks me, I tell him we learned "Our Father, who art in heaven."

Daddy takes my shoulders and yells, "*I'm* your father. Do you hear me? *I'm* the only *father* you got."

Looking across the room for Mommy, I see her slowly flip another page and I'm so mad at her for not helping us.

***

Just because someone doesn't believe in God, doesn't mean they're a bad person. Sometimes Daddy is nice. When we go to The Rusty Nail with him, he buys us each a coke, and gives us change so we can play the jukebox and foosball. All his friends say what a great guy he is, and how much he helps them, giving advice, and sometimes even loaning them money.

Today he's taking me to the movies, for no reason! Hilary stayed over at a friend's house and Adam went to Gramma Bonner's so I get to be the only one going with Daddy. I love the movies and I hope we get popcorn. So far I've seen *Bambi* and *Herbie the Love Bug*. Daddy says we're going to a grown up movie he's been wanting to see, and I say that's okay because it will still be fun to have popcorn and to have Daddy all to myself.

You smell the popcorn as soon as you open the doors to the mall. Daddy buys two tickets and the skinny boy behind the counter in the maroon vest takes a long look at me and raises his eyebrows. "You are aware this is an *adult* movie, Sir?" The boy in the vest has metal on his teeth and freckles on his face.

Daddy gives him a look that tells him to *mind his own damn business* and I give him a look that says *mind your own damn business* too. The boy looks me up and down, shrugs, and gives Daddy the tickets.

Daddy says we have time to look in the pet store next door. The puppies are so cute! There are little white fluffy ones and also some hotdogs and a beagle. They're behind glass so you can't pet them. Someday when I'm big I'm getting a dog *and* a cat. When I'm big I'll have all the puppies and kittens I want.

When we get to the bunnies, Daddy asks the lady if I can hold one. The bunny I get to hold is white and has ears that flop down. Daddy smiles at me and I know he's sorry about what happened to our neighbor's bunny in Florida. What happened to that bunny is too awful to mention.

Back at the theater Daddy says, *yes* we can get popcorn. When we sit down my seat folds up on me three times before I figure out how to sit on the front edge of it better. Daddy lets me hold the popcorn and it's yummy, all buttery and salty and warm. Holding the popcorn makes me proud.

"Daddy, thank you for the popcorn," I say.

He smiles at me like I'm extra cute and says, "Now you see? Your sister would never even think to say thanks."

Daddy doesn't ever say something nice about one kid without saying something bad about another one.

As the lights start to dim, he leans over and whispers, "You are welcome, Janie."

My tummy braces itself when the music for this movie comes on. I lower my head and lean back in my seat. On the screen is a girl named Reagan and she's sick and making all kinds of yucky noises and throwing herself around. Leaning toward Daddy, I hand him the popcorn and sit back, wiping the grease on my pants. My seat folds up on me again, but this time I keep it that way and try to squeeze into the crack of it to hide.

Reagan has spooky eyes and now her voice is low and grumbly and she's saying bad words. The priest comes to help her but she's *really* bad to him. She floats in the air over the bed and things are crashing. Closing my eyes, I sit sideways in my folded up seat, facing Daddy. Covering my ears with my hands I start to rock forward and back. Even though my ears are covered I still hear Reagan's mean monster voice. I turn my head and open my eyes to slits and Reagan's face is all scratched and yucky. Shutting my eyes tight, I start a high hum inside my head to block out this very bad movie.

"Hmmm…..hmmm……hmmmmmmm."

Leaning in toward Daddy I whisper, "I want to go home."

He puts his arm around me but that just makes my body turn to face the screen so I squirm out from him and do my sideways rocking and humming in the crack of my seat. Opening my eyes I stare at Daddy's face. The shadows and light flicker on him and I'm praying to "the only father I got," *Daddy, please take me home… please.*

Next, there's a horrible monster noise and Daddy crinkles his nose and goes, "Ughhhhh!"

His cheeks puff out and he brings his hand up over his mouth and turns his head toward me. When he sees me there rocking, he looks surprised. Like he forgot I was right there with him. I peek at the screen and it looks like Reagan threw up green stuff all over the place. I start rocking and humming again. Daddy touches my shoulder and says, "We better get you out of here."

We walk out before the movie is over and I'm sad when we get in Daddy's pick up truck because I forgot my popcorn.

At home,"You took her to see *what?*" Mommy yells.

Daddy holds his hands up, palms facing the ceiling. "What? I told you, *we left*. I really wanted to see it but I *walked out*. How was I supposed to know it would be so bad?"

"She's barely s*ix years old!*" Mommy says gritting her teeth together. Then she just stops talking to Daddy at all. She does the dishes with quick jerky motions and she's mad at me and Daddy for seeing such a bad movie.

Every night after that I wake in the dark and lay in bed worrying about Reagan, hoping my eyes never get all spooky and gross. I see her face and her green throw up. Her deep yucky voice says naughty words at me. Almost every night I run downstairs with her chasing close behind. I'm not safe until I crawl into Mommy and Daddy's bed and even then, she floats in the air in the corner of the room, legs folded in her arms, smirking at me with her white gray eyeballs.

Daddy and Mommy don't like me in their bed, so I lay right at the foot and don't move a muscle. Most of the time they don't notice I'm there until morning. Sometimes they make a lot of moaning noises and it's hard to sleep.

One morning, Mommy is already gone when I wake up. I scoot over to Daddy and wriggle into the crook under his shoulder, flopping my arm across his chest. He gives me a squeeze. Daddy is warm and naked. He says, "What are you doing in our bed again?"

I shrug my shoulders and nuzzle in.

It's so cozy with Daddy. I run my finger nails across his chest and around his boobies just like Mommy does. One time Daddy sucked on Mommy's boobie right in front of me.

"Ewwww!" I said, and Daddy said,

"If you don't like it, get the hell out of our bed."

Daddy and Mommy don't know I *have* to be in their bed. They don't know about Reagan chasing me in the night.

Daddy opens one eye and looks at me and then closes it again. I keep rubbing his chest with my fingernails and then Daddy's pee-pee pops up and it looks so funny. Not little like Adam's at all. Daddy suddenly opens both eyes and barks at me, "You get out of here."

He draws his legs back and then pushes them forward, kicking me off the bed. With a thunk, I land hard on my bottom on the floor. I feel like I'm in trouble. Like I did something bad, but why is it okay for Mommy to do it?

Later, Mommy tells me, "You are about to start second grade. You are too big to sleep in our bed."

So at night, I squeeze my eyes shut as tight as I can to make Reagan go away. What I find out is this...if you really concentrate, you can go away, and if you do, it's almost like *nothing is wrong*.

Chapter Three

My tummy does a nervous flip as I step into my second grade classroom. Looking around I see a hat, a bonnet really. Making my way toward the girl wearing it, I see the bonnet goes with a dress and the dress has an apron. She is like Laura Ingalls, Holly Hobby, and the girl on the raison box all combined. I *dream* of dresses like this and decide right then and there she's going to be my friend. We paint on easels right next to each other and I ask, "Can I try on your bonnet?"

She looks me up and down and taking it off says, "Only for a minute, because it's *mine,* and I want it back."

She hands it to me and I put it on my head and smile.

Her eyes are so dark you can't tell the difference between the colored part and the black part. She has a little dent in her chin. Her wavy hair is down to her shoulders and it's dark brown. She sees me checking it out and running her fingers through it says, "My daddy says my hair is chestnut brown."

Taking off the bonnet, I hand it back to her. "Mine is dirty blonde."

"Ew! Your hair is dirty?"

She squinches up her nose and checks her bonnet.

"No, that's just what they called it, even if I took a bath," I shrug.

"Oh," she says, looking over my hair and putting the bonnet back on her head.

"My name is Janie," I smile.

"I'm Sophie," she says, grinning back at me.

The second week of school Sophie Sheinmel invites me over to her house to play. Sophie's living room has no furniture. They've got a piano, a stereo, and huge cushions on the floor. The piano has teeth marks on it where Sophie bites it when she gets mad because she hit the wrong note. The speakers to her mom's stereo are as tall as me. Mrs. Sheinmel listens to music called Steely Dan, and she plays it loud. Over the stereo is a great big painting with bright colors and it's weird because the people in it have no faces.

Sophie's mom has tanned skin, long black curly hair, and she wears dark lipstick. She's skinny and wears cool hippy clothes. She also talks funny.

"We're from LAWNG Island," she says and I picture them, Sophie and her parents, like the castaways on Gilligan, only *their* island is very long and not a circle. They stand on the beach smiling and waving at the boats sailing off in the distance. There are palm trees behind them. One day I hope I'll get to see Long Island too.

Sophie's mom tells me to call her "Lydia," but I can't. It feels too weird calling a grown up Lydia. Whenever I say "Mrs. Sheinmel," she rolls her eyes.

Mrs. Sheinmel lies on the cushions in the living room, reading her books and her big dogs Dalia and Starr lie all over her. They're German Short Haired Pointers and Sophie got to name Starr herself. The dogs are speckled gray and black and white and have short stubby tails. Starr is wearing boy's underpants and her tail sticks out the pee-pee hole because she's "in heat." I don't know what that means but dogs in underpants sure look funny.

Sophie also has a cat named Poncho and I love him. He follows us around and lets me hold him. He purrs real loud when I scratch behind his ears. I wish I could have a cat of my own, so bad.

The Sheinmels are weird. They eat things called falafels and tofu. They save garbage in a pile in their backyard and call it compost.

"We're Jewish," Sophie says, shrugging her shoulders.

"Oh," I say. I never met anyone Jewish before, and I guess that explains things.

Her mom fixes us snacks and gives us apple juice in empty yogurt containers. We've never had yogurt at my house and I think it's neat to drink out of a yogurt cup. After we eat, we go downstairs to play.

In the rec room, there are big sliding glass doors leading into what Sophie calls the breezeway. We can see ourselves in the doors when we dance to Sophie's records. There are lots of pictures of Sophie on the walls. Holding Sophie's cat, I walk around the room, looking at all the pictures. In one, she's a baby and the picture is almost as big as a real toddler. She's so cute with her pigtails. There are no pictures of me or Hilary or Adam on our walls at home.

Sophie has a dollhouse with a Barbie, a Ken, and a little sister Skipper. She takes Barbie and gives me Skipper. After a while she says I can be Ken instead.

"How about we pretend they go to bed?"

"Okay, " I say.

We walk Ken and Barbie into the bedroom of her dollhouse. They lay down. Sophie puts a Barbie sized blanket over them, and they go to sleep.

"Now they get up," she says.

"Okay." I sit Ken up.

Sophie says, "Now Ken has to say, I have something to tell you."

In a low Ken voice I say, "I have something to tell you." I wait for what I'm supposed to say next.

"Now Ken has to say…Last night……. while we were sleeping," she says.

"Last night…..while we were sleeping….," I say…all low, just like Sophie said it.

"I…er…..well. I got you…..pregnant," she says.

"I got you…pregnant," I say.

Barbie goes crazy. "WHAT! HOW *COULD* YOU! WHAT ARE WE GOING TO DO? HOW WILL I EVER FINISH COLLEGE?"

I don't know what I'm supposed to say next, but it doesn't matter because Mrs. Sheinmel is yelling down the stairs, "Janie! Your mom is here!"

Giving Poncho one last nuzzle, I head upstairs to go home.

***

Me and Sophie are both born in October. I am twenty days older than her and she can't stand how I'm turning eight while she is still seven. I love it. I'll always be older, and there is nothing she can do about it.

On my birthday, when I get home from school, Mommy greets me at the door and tells me to close my eyes. She holds my hand and when we get in the living room she lets go.

"Open your eyes!" she says.

On the floor is a box, and inside it is a tiny fuzzy kitten. Mommy takes her out and puts her on the floor.

The kitten is black and white and orange and gray and she steps around with clumsy legs on the carpet. My mouth opens. My eyes go big. I look at Mommy and she nods. Biting down on my bottom lip, I drop to my knees in front of the little ball of fur.

"She's a calico," Mommy says.

Running my finger down her back, she's so soft. When I pick her up I can feel the teeny bones in her sides and it seems like she'll break if I squeeze too hard. Gently, I hold her to my shoulder and she lets out a tiny, "Meeew." I look at Mommy and grin.

"Is she mine?"

Mommy nods. "Happy birthday," she smiles.

My throat gets tight and there's a warm feeling in my heart. I thought I loved my Baby Tender Love doll but that was *nothing* compared to this. Kneeling next to me, Mommy hugs me hard.

"What will you name her?" she asks.

"I get to name her?"

"She's yours, so you get to name her," she says.

Holding the kitten out in front of me she meows again and on account of this warm feeling in my heart I know what I'll call her.

"I'm going to name her Sunshine."

Mommy smiles and says, "That's a really good name."

At school, I can't wait to get home to my kitty. Sunshine is so fun to play with. She lets me carry her around over my shoulder like a real baby. She lets me put doll hats on her head. We tie old socks in knots and hold them over her and she stands on her back legs to bat at them. She lets me put her on the couch on her back, cross her bottom legs and put her front paws behind her head just like a person. Mommy can't believe she stays like that for me and she snaps a picture with the Polaroid camera. Her fur is long and soft and I love all her colors. At bedtime Sunshine helps me feel God. She purrs next to me and if I really concentrate, it's almost like *nothing is wrong.*

***

A couple of weeks after my birthday, Mommy is standing at the front door talking to three men. They all keep saying the word, "repossess." Mommy tells me, Hillary and Adam to go on, away from the door. We do, but I peel back a loose piece of plastic on the front window so we can see. Outside now, in the front yard, Mommy is shrugging her shoulders and shaking her head. She's smiling but something isn't right. She looks worried. Finally she comes in, closes the door, and leans against it with her eyes shut. We hear the men in the driveway outside and me and Adam peek out the front window again. The gravel is crunching loud under their feet as the men start hooking up chains to Daddy's black Jeep. Just like that, they lift the front of it up in the air and pull it away with a big truck. Me and Adam look at each other with our mouths open wide. Hilary goes over to Mommy, worried.

"Mommy, what does repossess mean?" I ask.

She flips her head toward me and with her eyebrows crunched together like she's mad says, "It means your father didn't pay the bills, and the bank came and took his Jeep away."

"They can't just take it, can they?" I ask. Feeling mad, I look out the window again, even though the Jeep is already gone. Hilary and Adam are quiet. They don't make a peep.

"It wasn't his. He wasn't making the payments. Yes, they *can* take it and they did."

Then she hisses, "But your father is too much of a coward to be here and deal with the embarrassment of it all."

Poor Daddy got his Jeep taken away and I don't know why Mommy has to be so mean? Daddy *loved* that Jeep. I think of him, sitting down the road at The Rusty Nail, and I wonder who's going to tell him? Or maybe he already knows, and he's sad.

The first day he brought the Jeep home he pulled off the top and took us kids for a ride. Adam started to put his seatbelt on, but Daddy called him a sissy, so he dropped the belt and never did buckle up. Adam *isn't* a sissy. He's littler than me but his body is all muscles like Daddy. He's strong. He sat there in the back seat in his husky Tough Skin jeans, his brown straight hair hanging in front of his eyes.

My seatbelt was buckled, but Daddy didn't call me a sissy because I'm a girl. I ran my fingers over the plaid cushions and he showed us how he could work the steering wheel with just one pinky.

"Power steering," he'd said, with a big smile. Hilary was in the front, and me and Adam sat in the back.

Our hair blew wild in the wind as we went faster and faster. When Daddy took the corners, Adam's body leaned way over into mine. It felt just like the rides at the Centerville Field Days. When I get big, I'm going to buy Daddy an even nicer Jeep and no one will ever take it away.

***

Since she can't count on Daddy to pay the bills, this year Mom is going to school to be a nurse. She does not like things being repossessed. When Mom is at school, Hilary is in charge. She's almost 12 now and she's supposed to be watching us for just a little while until Dad gets home, but lots of times Dad doesn't come home at all.

I can't remember why we started fighting, but me and Adam have been rolling and tumbling through every room in the house. At first we were just horsing around but now we're mad. *Really m*ad. Punching, scratching, hitting and screaming at each other.

Hilary's mad too, because she wanted to go next door to her friend Misty's house but she *can't* because she has to watch us. Misty is someone I can't stand. Hilary never likes me. She acts like I'm stupid and annoying, but if Misty's around, she's even meaner than usual. Since she can't go next door, Hilary and Misty stand in the windows looking at each other, talking on the phone.

Now, me and Adam are upstairs on his bed and I have him in a headlock. If I let go he's going to kill me so I squeeze harder. His face is turning red and then he kicks my shin hard. I let go, but then grab him again, shoving his face into the mattress, once, twice, again, and now he's crying.

Adam is a fighter. He never cries. Dad won't let him. *I'm gonna be in so much trouble.*

Adam rolls over and pulls his dirty sheet up over his head.

"Adam, what happened? Are you hurt?" I ask. *I hope he doesn't tell on me.*

22

He doesn't say anything.

I pull down his sheet. He's not crying anymore. He's glaring at me and it's the first time I've ever, in my whole life, felt hated. It makes me shiver. His face is red and blotchy. He whips the sheet back up over his head and flips over toward the wall.

"Adam, I'm sorry."

This time I really am.

"Are you hurt?" I ask.

He won't talk.

"Adam please *tell* me. What's wrong? Why won't you answer me? Tell me!" I beg, trying to pull down his covers again. He yanks them back up over his head.

"Big boys don't cry. Tough guys don't cry." That's what Daddy says. That's why he's hating instead.

Leaning back against his bed, I sit on the floor and quietly cry for him.

I look at the clock, waiting for Mom to get home from school. She comes in at 9PM like she said she would, but Dad never does come home from The Rusty Nail. Not 'til after we're all in bed.

The next morning, Mom is on the phone talking about how one of Daddy's friends got killed at The Rusty Nail last night. This is what I hear:

"A beer brawl."

"It happened right after Butch left."

"He was hit over the head with a bottle."

"Head injury."

"Never woke up."

Mom shoos me away when I try to ask questions. She plays with the long curly phone cord as she talks. Her cereal sits in a bowl on the table in front of her, getting soggy.

Late in the afternoon, when he gets home from work, I bury my face in Dad's chest and smell the wood chips on his scratchy wool lumberjack shirt. Dad's job is cutting down trees. His belly is getting fat. His hair is long around the collar and greasy. He hugs me back, then lets go, but I still cling to him. "Daddy, please don't go."

"C'mon," he says, peeling me off of him.

He's going back to The Rusty Nail. Even after someone was killed there last night. I can't believe it.

All day I've been imagining Dad's dead friend. The one with the red hair and the red beard. He had a wife, and a little baby. In my mind, I see him with his skull cracked and off kilter, blood dripping down his face.

Lunging forward, I cling to Dad again. I look up to meet his eyes. If I can just keep his eyes he won't go. If he sees how much I love him, he'll stay home.

Keep looking at me Daddy.

He looks right at me and then turning away he takes my shoulders and shoves me aside.

Standing in the kitchen between the wooden beams and the electrical cords dangling down, I watch him walk out the back door. Mom comes over and tries to hug me, but I just stand with my arms flat to my sides. Looking blankly at the insulation on the kitchen walls I blink back tears and think to myself, *"If only I were more lovable."*

There might be a way to get Dad to stay home. Gramma Bonner bought us a piano and starting next month, I'm gonna take lessons from Mrs. Stone. She's the organ lady at church. For now, I'm sitting at the bench, using my pointer finger to figure out a song for

Dad. I want to cheer him up about his Jeep. Maybe then, he'll come home in the evenings when Mommy is at nursing school.

Maybe, if I can figure out this song…. and play it real pretty, and sing it really nice, Dad will realize how much he loves us and everything will change. Maybe he'll realize how wrong it is to pee all our money away at The Rusty Nail, and maybe he'll stay home and be nice to us. We'll forgive him for being so grumpy all the time, and we'll just be a regular, normal, family. Maybe he'll even realize how special I am.

Adam is out back with Mommy. She's mowing the lawn and he's on the swing. Hilary is next door at Misty's. It isn't often I get any time alone with the piano. Usually when I start to play it, Hilary and Adam tell me to shut up because they can't hear the TV.

Mom told me Dad really liked this song. It's John Denver.

I'll walk in the rain by your side.

Plunk, plunk,plunk.

The piano sits in front of the big dining room window, facing the highway. Looking out, I see the blue sky and yes, Dad *will* love me. I know he will. Everything is going to be different. Earnestly I sing, *I'll cling to the warmth of your hand.*

Me and Dad are holding hands.

I'm the apple of his eye.

Plunk, plunk, plunk.

The wind is whispering my name to me.

Plunk.

I'm really into it, singing loud now.

Daddy and I are walking through a sunny meadow.

We pass through a tree tunnel, and smile.

The leaves are bowing down to us as we walk by.

My voice cracks on the high note, and suddenly, I hear,

"Haaaaaaaaaaaaaaaa! Ha!"

My whole body clenches.

Hilary and Misty are standing there. They have their hair curled like Farah Fawcett and they're wearing *short* shorts and Dr. Scholl's sandals. I didn't hear them come in.

Misty puts her nose up in the air and sings high and silly, cracking her voice on purpose to make fun of me.

Hilary stands there, smirk on her face, hands on her hips, but finally she says, "Okay Misty, knock it off."

My throat is tight and my face is hot and I run from the dining room, through the kitchen and up the stairs.

Nope, nope, nope. I won't let them see me cry, I won't. Under my covers the tears come and I wipe my nose on my bed sheet. Curling myself up into the tiniest ball, I can't believe I even thought about singing for Dad with my stupid ugly cracky voice. I'm so dumb. No wonder he never wants to come home.

Chapter Four

Sophie says her dad comes home every night, at 7:00 on the dot. I've been to her house lots of times after school, but tonight is the first time I get to stay over. She has *two* beds that make an L-shape, and her own TV in her room! When her dad comes home from work, Sophie runs down the hall yelling, "Daddy!" and jumps all over him. He scoops her up and swings her around, giving her a kiss on the head. He turns to me and kneels down, looking me in the eye and I feel shy because I never met her dad before.

"Who's this?" he smiles. He's thin and he has dark wavy hair like Sophie. He's got the same dark eyes as her and the same dent in his chin as she does. Sophie calls it a cleft. His shirt is white with buttons and he's wearing a tie. He's very handsome.

"This is Janie," Sophie answers him. "She's spending the night."

Sophie has her hands on her hips and she's hopping from the heel of one foot to the heel of her other, in a little jig. It's *happy* when her dad gets home.

He puts his hand out and I give him mine. He shakes my hand gentle and smiles, "It is *very* nice to meet you Janie."

He walks us back to Sophie's room and then stands in the doorway, watching us play for a minute. He's still smiling, but he looks a little sad too, like he's thinking of something far away.

"*Dad,*" Sophie says, "We're *trying* to play."

Mr. Sheinmel laughs and says, "Sorry Sweetie. Didn't mean to cramp your style."

He comes back in the room, gives Sophie a tickle and a kiss and then leaves.

At dinner, Mr. Sheinmel teaches me how to eat an artichoke. After they steam it, you pull out a leaf and dip it in melted butter. Then you put the leaf facing up in your mouth and scrape out the meat with your top teeth as you pull it forward. Artichokes are yummy. Sophie's mom talks about a dog show she's getting ready for. Delia and Starr are show dogs and Mrs. Sheinmel trains them. She has ribbons and trophies and everything. At bedtime, Mrs. Sheinmel tucks us in and gives Sophie a hug and a kiss and then gives me a kiss on the cheek too. It's weird to get a kiss from someone who isn't your own mom, but it's nice. Me and Sophie stay up giggling for a while but then she falls asleep. Lying there, I wish I had my own room with plaid curtains, a TV, and two beds. I wish my Dad ate artichokes.

In the morning Sophie is still sleeping but I have to pee. Quietly, I step out of her bedroom and there's her dad, walking down the hall toward me in nothing but a pair of tiny purple underwear. He says, "Morning kiddo," as he passes, and goes back in his room.

Without answering, I scoot into the bathroom and shut the door quick behind me.

When Sophie wakes up I tell her, "I saw your Dad in the hall and he was wearing ladies' underpants. Purple bikinis."

"They aren't for *ladies* dummy. He wears Speedos. They're for men."

"Oh," I say, pulling the covers back up to my neck. I never heard of underpants called Speedos. They must only be for Jewish men.

Later, Mr. Sheinmel takes us hiking on a nature trail and Sophie isn't very happy at all. Every time her Dad talks to me she gets mad. Then, she starts fussing about her shoes.

"Daddy, I hate my shoes! I want shoes like Janie's!"

"You don't need new shoes, kiddo. Yours are brand new."

Looking down at my feet, my shoes *are* pretty cool. Gramma Bonner took me downtown to get them. We had to walk a long way from her apartment, and catch a bus. We looked all day and were about to give up when the salesman at Franklin's department store brought these out. They're kind of like saddle shoes, but instead of black and white, they're all brown. Gramma Bonner says they're a more grown up version of saddle shoes. Gramma Bonner always makes sure we have at least one good pair of shoes. No one else has shoes like mine and I puff up my chest proud because Sophie likes them so much.

Sophie cries and carries on for the whole hike. She's acting like such a baby! My dad would *kill* me if I behaved like that. Mr. Sheinmel ends up carrying her piggyback and I follow behind them, thinking about purple Speedos and my cool shoes. Why does Sophie care about *my shoes* when she already has everything? Her Nana in Florida buys her clothes all the time. I look up at the blue sky and smile. It sure feels good to have something she wants.

At school on Monday, Sophie's wearing shoes just like mine. Gramma Bonner says if you don't have something nice to say you aren't allowed to say anything, so I'm quiet, but inside I'm piping mad. Sophie's dad spoils her rotten.

Chapter Five

My Dad doesn't spoil anyone but himself. He has a brand new pick up truck that all of us can barely fit in. Dad is driving and we're all squished together in the front. Adam is on Mommy's lap. Me and Hilary are in the middle. Hilary keeps elbowing me and giving me dirty looks, but I can't help it. There's no room. It's Christmas Eve and it's snowing and I'm trying to ignore Hilary by pretending we're in one of those snow globes you shake. Dad is smiling, steering the truck with just his pinky. We're going to Gramma Shea's house. Gramma Shea is Dad's mom.

Gramma Shea lives a half-hour from us, in a town called Orion. From the highway, you turn down a gravel road, pass a trailer park, and her house sits at the bottom of a hill. Behind her house is a huge field that small airplanes use for taking off and landing. On the other side of the airstrip is the Susquehanna River. In New York, everywhere you go, the Susquehanna River is right there. I like saying Susquehanna. It's an Indian name.

Gramma Shea is short and her skin is dark, kind of like an Indian squaw. We learned about Indian chiefs and squaws and papooses at school for Thanksgiving. Gramma Shea has curly black and gray hair and she wears red lipstick. Her laugh sounds like a witch's cackle. Gramma Shea has a boy named Patrick who's a year older than me, but he doesn't look it because he's retarded and very little. Gramma Shea says they used to call people like Patrick mongoloid, but that it isn't a very nice thing to say, so we should just say retarded, but we *never, ever* should call him a "retard."

Patrick's real mommy died when he was a baby and Gramma Shea lives with Patrick's Daddy, so she's his mommy now. Clyde is like our Grampa. Clyde is tall and bald and he has a big belly. He doesn't talk much, but when he does he sounds like a cowboy because he's from Texas. He greets us with a big smile like he loves us and he always tells me I'm real good with Patrick.

At Gramma Shea's the grown-ups are happy and we get lots of good things to eat. She has Hershey Bars and Reese's Cups in the kitchen cabinet and we can help ourselves to as much candy and soda as we want.

Mom drinks soda. Gramma Shea drinks 7 & 7's. Daddy, his brothers, and Clyde drink beer.

The grown-ups sit at the table in the dining room and Gramma Shea gives Daddy and his brothers a hard time and everyone laughs. She's nice even though she doesn't go to church and sometimes she picks on people too much. She's always saying "Jesus Christ, Patrick!" when he's too loud or when he interrupts, but Patrick just laughs and puts his head on her shoulder because he knows she loves him and he isn't afraid of her. I am afraid of her though, a little.

Gramma Shea's house is clean and nice. It has carpet and thick shiny polished wood furniture. Last year they put on an addition that's now the living room. Everyone likes to sit in the addition because it's really pretty with its huge windows that look out onto the airstrip. Tonight you can see big icicles hanging down from the windows outside. There are two recliners in the addition. One for Gramma, and one for Clyde. Some of the magazines in the racks next to the recliners have naked ladies in them.

Dad and my uncles read them right out in the open which is funny because at home Dad's naked lady magazines are hidden under his bed. The ladies in Dad's magazines have flat tummies and big boobs. They're really pretty, but it's kind of gross the way they show their privates all the time.

Patrick has a record player and all us kids dance when he puts on "Ba-ba-ba, Ba-Barbara Ann," by the Beach Boys and, "Knock Three Times," by Tony Orlando and Dawn. Patrick loves being the DJ and he laughs when we dance to his music. He sits on the floor by the record player with his legs twisted up crisscross, both feet pointing to the ceiling. He puts two thumbs up in the air, smiles, and says, "Aaaaaye!" pretending to be Fonzie. We all try to sit like Patrick but none of us can do it for very long.

Gramma Shea made a yummy dinner with ham and potatoes and gravy and rolls. After, the grown-ups sit around the dining room table drinking and talking as it starts to get late. Mom sips her soda and she's the only one out of all of them that isn't glassy-eyed and loud.

After a while it's time to go. Gramma Shea gives us presents to take home and unwrap tomorrow. Mom asks Dad if he wants her to drive and my stomach drops when he yanks the keys from her saying, "I'm *fine*." She knows he always drives, I don't know why she's trying to make him mad.

When we step outside, the wind whips my face and I shiver as we crunch over the snow on the sidewalk, making our way to the truck. Some snow goes up my pant leg and I shiver again.

In the truck Adam wants to sit next to Daddy. Hilary is in the middle. I know I'm too big for it, but I sit on mom's lap, and lay the back of my head against her chest. I feel my mother's breath on my neck as I look out the window. The world looks beautiful but also lonely with a perfectly white round moon shining down on the snow. Everything looks bluish, like we're in outer space.

Dad lights a cigarette, then pulls on the lever that sticks out of the steering wheel. We wave as we pull out of Gramma Shea's driveway and as we start up the hill, the truck wiggles. Dad says, "I should have put the chains on the tires."

He flicks on the radio. No one says anything. We're all tired.

No other cars are on the road tonight. The choir on the radio is singing Christmas carols as we head home. Going down the big hill, by the IBM plant, the truck starts to zigzag back and forth. Mom screams and holds me tight and Dad puts one arm across Hilary and Adam. The truck spins around and when it stops we're in a ditch.

"Fuck! Shit! Fuck!" Dad says, hitting the steering wheel with both hands.

"Is everyone okay?" Mom asks.

We're all okay and Dad gets out and kicks the truck. Then, he disappears, walking into the blue white night. We stay in the truck, huddled together and after a while Clyde is there, hooking chains up to the truck. We get out and wait in the freezing cold while they pull Dad's new truck out of the ditch. No one breathes a word as Mom drives the rest of the way home.

Chapter Six

Richie Cunningham and Fonzie went on a double date with Laverne and Shirley tonight but it was *me* who fell in love. Happy Days is the highlight of my week. Just when I thought it couldn't get any better, it did.

"God bless Mom and Dad. God, please let Dad be killed in a drunk driving accident, but please make it a one car crash so no one else gets hurt. God, please let him die quickly without feeling any pain. God bless Hilary and Adam, all my aunts, uncles and cousins. God bless all our friends and relatives and God....please...PLEASE...let Laverne and Shirley come back on Happy Days again."

Not only were they on again. They got their own show!

Thank.
You.
God.

Tuesday nights, right after *Happy Days,* Laverne & Shirley count in time as they *"schlemiel, shamozzle"* arm & arm down the sidewalk in front of their apartment. I take my place on the floor in front of the TV, dreaming of the fun of one day working in a brewery. Laverne's monogrammed sweaters have me secretly wishing my name began with an *L*. Laverne winks when she says "Vodio-do-do" and I *know* it means something sexy. Shirley's boyfriend Carmine protects her and I wish someone loved *me* like that. Laverne and Shirley are best friends, there for each other, through and through. They have *the life*. I don't love the characters Lenny and Squiggy always hanging around. In my opinion, they are *beneath* Laverne and Shirley.

One night halfway through the first season, Dad comes home all mean. He's always nasty if he hasn't stopped at The Rusty Nail first. He paces around the house in his steel-toed work boots, *tha-dump, tha-dump, tha-dump*. He's getting fatter and fatter and his belly pushes at the buttons on his plaid lumberjack shirt. I try to ignore him. My show is starting and I'm not going to let him bother me and wreck it. Hilary is on the blue couch, lying on her side, propped up on her elbow. Adam is sitting Indian style at the other end of the couch. I'm up close to the TV so I can still hear if they start talking. My feet are resting in their usual spot at the base of the TV stand, hands folded behind my head on the floor. Suddenly, Dad is there holding the pliers in his big fat hairy hand. He squeezes them to the metal post where the knob is missing and starts flipping through the TV channels.

Jumping up off the floor I yell, "HEY! WHAT ARE YOU DOING?"

"I'm seeing what else is on," he barks. Dad stands there in his dirty jeans, mud caked onto the front of his thighs. His black hair looks wet from sweat or grease and his face is round and angry. He's got a dark beard now and it's scraggly.

"I was watching that! *We* were watching that!" I say, glancing back at Hilary and Adam, hoping they'll back me.

Hilary sits up and Adam scooches closer to her. They sink back, deep into the couch, their eyes big. Neither one says a word.

My fists clench. My jaw clenches. I can't believe he's making me miss my show.

I hate him.

I hate him.

I hate him.

Glaring at Dad I say, "We were watching that! It's my favorite show! It's the only show I care about!"

He ignores me.

My throat gets tight and I try not to cry.

He gets in my face and I see he's really sweating now. The little holes in his skin look big and black. His beard is all wiry, grey hairs mixed in with the black. He stinks like old beer.

"It's *my* damn TV. *I* paid for it. *I'll* watch whatever the fuck *I* want to watch," he yells.

Turning back to the TV he runs through the stations two more times with the pliers and starts going around a third.

Wild energy rushes through me and *that's it.* Some things are just worth fighting for.

"YOU'VE GONE AROUND THE CHANNELS TWICE! YOU DON'T EVEN HAVE ANYTHING ELSE YOU WANT TO WATCH! YOU JUST WANT TO BE MEAN! YOU ARE A MEAN *AWFUL* PERSON! YOU DON'T CARE ABOUT US AT ALL! YOU...YOU...YOU... *PECKER*!"

My hands fly to my mouth. It's one of Dad's words. How did it come out of *me?* He draws his hand back like he's going to crack me across the face but he stops just before my right cheek. My face feels the heat of his palm, hanging in the air for a second. Then he drops it.

Shaking his head Dad says, "Little fuckin' spoiled brat," as he takes the pliers and flips back to *Laverne & Shirley.* We've already missed a whole bunch of it. He grabs his keys out of his pocket and it's the sound of his boots, *tha-dump, tha-dump, tha-dump* out the back door. Then, his truck is tearing out over the gravel driveway.

Hilary and Adam stare at me from the couch.

My neck feels tight and I bug my eyes back at them like, *what?* Some help they were.

Turning away from them, I shimmy back into my spot on the floor. My legs and arms feel shaky. I feel the solid floor under my body. My breathing is all chopped up, and I take a deep breath to try and make it stop. I'm glad he left. I wish he'd never come home.

As *Laverne & Shirley* ends, my chest feels heavy and my head aches. In the closing song, Laverne & Shirley sing about making their dreams come true. Someday I'm going to get away from here and never come back. That'd be my dream come true.

Chapter Seven

The evenings Dad stays home he likes to turn out the lights and spy on Misty's mother next door. He only does it when Mom is at nursing school.

Misty and her rotten younger brother Jake don't have a Dad. Their mom has big boobies and big blonde hair and she wears shorts so small her butt hangs out. Lots of different men come to see her. Dad laughs and says, "That's how she pays her rent." From what I see, she's mostly just doing dishes in her kitchen window when Dad watches with his binoculars.

Dad probably wishes Misty's mom were naked like the ladies on HBO. Mom says our HBO box is illegal. HBO scares me because Mom says Dad could get arrested for it. At night, I worry the police will bust into our house and take him away to jail.

Coming into the dark kitchen I ask, "Dad, can we get rid of the HBO? I don't want the police to come and get you." He glances over at me and laughs.

"Never mind," he says.

He just *loves* his HBO. He loves watching movies with naked ladies. Standing there at the kitchen sink in his white terry cloth bathrobe he puts the binoculars back up to his eyes, then he glances back over his shoulder at me and says, "Get the hell out of here, *now*."

One time, his binoculars disappeared and I had the feeling Mom got rid of them, so maybe she knows about his spying. It didn't matter though. He just went out and bought himself another pair.

One family that would never have HBO is the Johnsons. Mrs. Johnson is my Sunday school teacher this year. She has three kids and a nice house a couple of miles down the road from us. Her kids are so lucky. Mrs. Johnson is nice, and Mr. Johnson is a pilot. Mommy raises her right eyebrow when she mentions the "pilot" part. That's how I know pilots make good money. Mrs. Johnson has dark curly hair and she has that mom look about her. Not the tired look of *my* mom, but the kind of moms you see on TV. The ones who are home, making cookies and stuff.

We're meeting at the altar this week after church instead of in our usual classroom. "Today we're going to learn just how much God loved you when he gave his son for your sins," Mrs. Johnson says.

Us kids are sitting in a semi-circle facing Jesus. He's all skinny and hanging way up high above us on the cross, looking just like Father Duncan. Mrs. Johnson reaches under the altar and takes out some big silver nails. They're long and extra thick, kind of like the ones in the railroad tracks behind Gramma Bonner's house. She passes them around. Turning one over in my fingers a couple of times it's cold and heavy. I shrug and hand it to the next kid. "Death on a cross is one of the most horrid ways to die," Mrs. Johnson says.

Looking up at Jesus, at his sorrow-filled face, and half-naked skinny body I think, *Yep...that looks pretty awful.*

Next, she takes two thick wooden boards and lays them on the floor in front of us. She takes a nail in two fingers, twirls it around, and then presses the point into her palm. When she pulls away she holds up her hand for all to see like a magician showing his hat. There's a dent in her palm where the nail pressed in. Then, she takes the nail and with several hard blows, pounds it into the boards. The sound of the hammer echoes through the church and we all lurch back in our spots on the floor, imagining the nail going through our own hands. For *my* sins? What did I ever do that was so bad? It really gets me thinking.

Poor Jesus just hangs there while Mrs. Johnson talks about how much God loves us. But I'm wondering...if God didn't love his own kid enough to help *him*, why would he love me at all? Jesus was way better than me. He was always nice and didn't fight or think bad things like praying his dad Joseph would die in a car accident.

Mrs. Johnson talks and talks but my stomach starts to hurt and I try not to listen anymore. I wish I could just cover my ears but then she'd *know* I'm not listening. Then I start thinking. *Hey, I wasn't even born yet when all this happened,* and then I start to feel pretty mad about being blamed. Looking up at the statue of Jesus, the nails in his hands, the blood trickling down his side, I feel sorry for him, and I really do love him, but in my heart I whisper, *I didn't do this to you. It wasn't my fault.*

Tuning out Mrs. Johnson, I stare at the colors on the stained glass windows behind the altar. I focus really hard until I *feel* God. Not the mean God she's talking about, the one who couldn't be bothered to save his own son. What I mean isn't a person, it's a feeling. Like when I look at the leaves fluttering on the trees outside my bedroom window. When I *feel* God, I go floating somewhere else where it's warm, and calm and peaceful, and *nothing is wrong.*

Chapter Eight

LPN stands for Licensed Practical Nurse, which is what Mom will be today after her graduation. I've never been to a graduation but I can tell by the feel in the house it's a very special thing so I decide to wear my patchwork gypsy top, my jean skirt, and my brown cowboy boots. I stand in the full-length mirror and Sunshine purrs and does a figure eight around my legs. Stepping around her I don't like what I see. My skirt comes just above my knees, but my boots only come to my shins. My white socks come up higher than my boots, to my knees. This worries me. There is boot, then two inches of white sock, then an inch of knee skin, and then my skirt. I'm afraid it looks stupid to have my socks and my knees sticking out but Mom says, "Quit worrying about it. You look fine."

Hilary says, "It's not about *you,* anyway." Then she looks me up and down and smirks. Hilary is wearing a blue velour V-neck dress with a tiny little string belt around the waist, clear panty hose, and small heels. It's not fair because if *she* can't find something to wear, she just goes next door and borrows something from Misty. Misty has *tons* of clothes. I need to make do with what I have. Hilary always looks better then me. I pick up Sunshine and hold her on my lap 'til it's time to go. Her purring makes me feel better.

Mom makes Adam wear pants, not sweats, and he also has to wear a plain long sleeve shirt. Not one with cartoons on the front.

Mom is wearing a nursing dress that's so pale green it's almost white. A white nametag is pinned to her chest. "Diana Shea," it says. Her long hair is in a bun at the back of her head. She even put on pink lipstick! I've never seen Mom wear make-up before and it looks pretty, but weird. Me and Hilary and Adam pile into the car and drive to pick up Gramma Bonner at her apartment. She's wearing a black pantsuit and her long green quilted coat. She must have done her hair in rollers because it's curled all fancy.

We sit in the audience and the new nurses are standing in a line across the front of the stage. Mom looks like a pretty angel in the soft light with her pale green dress and her pink lips. Mom's teachers read a bunch of speeches about how hard the new nurses have worked and what it means to be a nurse. How it's a "privilege." Adam is fidgety and starts to kick the chair in front of him over and over. Gramma Bonner leans across me and pinches his arm. He pulls away, gives her a dirty look, crosses his arms, and slumps in his seat. Mom's teachers pin a white cap onto her head with bobby pins. Mom smiles all perfect big white teeth and pink lipstick, and she's every bit as pretty as Miss America, standing there on stage.

A box of candles is passed out. One of Mom's teachers lights the first one and each new nurse lights the candle next to hers, right on down the line. The lights go dim and a lady reads a poem. The new nurses wipe tears and I've never seen Mom so beautiful. *My mom*, up there on stage, holding her candle. I never knew she was so important. I'm proud and my throat gets tight and I blink really fast because I don't want to cry.

After the ceremony, we stand in the hall of the school and Gramma Bonner takes Mom's picture.

"Gramma, can you take one of me and Mom? *Please?*" I ask.

Gramma Bonner laughs as we stand in front of a red wall, just me and Mom. I put my arm around her waist and she gives my shoulder a big squeeze as the flash goes off. Then Adam says he wants his picture taken too so we all stand next to Mom and Gramma Bonner takes another one. Mom is all smiles in her dress and her new nurse's cap as we walk out of the building toward the car.

In the parking lot, Gramma Bonner says, "It would have been nice of your husband to show up."

Mom's smile goes away and she doesn't say anything. She looks down at the ground all the way back to the car. On the drive home I'm mad. Why did Gramma have to go and say that anyway? Why'd she have to ruin it? She knows Dad doesn't come to stuff.

Chapter Nine

Sunshine is missing. I've been hiking up in the woods looking for her. Maybe she's stuck someplace? Maybe she's hurt?

"Mom! I can't find her anywhere!" I say, flinging the back door shut on my way in.

"Mom! It's been two days!" I say, as I get ready for school in the morning.

At the supper table, Mom scoops a pile of canned peas onto my plate. Dad is home for supper tonight and while we're eating I say, "It's been a whole week. Where could she be?"

Mom and Dad look at each other a long time, and then Dad says, "She probably ran away."

He picks up his fork and knife and starts cutting his pork chop.

"Ran away? Why would she run away?" I say, pushing my food around on my plate.

I love her, why would she want to run away from me?
Mom says,

"Sometimes animals just do that. They don't like being cooped up and they run off."

She leans over and plops a blob of mashed potatoes onto Adam's plate.

"But she wouldn't do that. She *loves* me. Besides, she wasn't cooped up. She went out everyday," I say.

Mom and Dad look at each other again.

"Sometimes it just happens," Mom says and she gets up quickly and starts doing the dishes.

Sunshine doesn't come back the next day. She doesn't come back the next week either.

Every night I lie awake thinking about her. I loved her more than any toy I ever had. Must be she didn't think I was a good mommy. Must be she didn't love me. Did I not pet her enough? Did I forget to play with her? *I'm sorry I wasn't good enough Sunshine. I'm sorry I'm so bad. I'll do better. Please just come home. Please don't run away.* I pray really hard about it.

Every morning I look at the calendar hanging on the nail on the two-by-four where the wall should be between the kitchen and the dining room, counting how many days she's been gone. On the 20th day, on the bus ride home from school, Misty's rotten brother Jake says, "Too bad your cat got flattened."

My stomach braces itself.

"What are you talking about?"

"Your cat that got hit. We saw it on the side of the road."

"No you didn't."

"Whatever you say, but a couple weeks ago your cat was on the road, flat as a pancake, up by Mr. Brown's field. My mom's the one who told your mom."

All afternoon and evening I'm afraid to ask Mom because I don't want it to be true. Surely she would have told me? It must have been another cat Jake saw. If Sunshine *ran away* there is a chance she'll come home. If she's *dead,* she'll never be back. At bedtime, Mom calls Dad at the Rusty Nail to remind him to come home, and then she tucks us in and leaves for her night shift at the hospital.

Dad doesn't come home until after we've all gone to sleep. When he gets in, he stumbles up the stairs to our rooms, to tell us how much he loves us.

Dad kneels at the side of my bed. "Do you know how much I love you?" he asks. He stinks the usual. Stale beer and cigarette smoke.

I can't take it anymore.

"Dad, did Sunshine get hit by a car?" I pull my covers up to my neck and bite my lip.

He sits back on the heels of his work boots looking at me, his eyes all red and glassy.

"Who told you?" he asks.

My stomach lurches. It's true. Sunshine is dead. She's never coming home.

A moan starts way down inside me and then I'm crying hard. My whole body is shaking.

Dad climbs right into my bed with his boots on and wraps his arms around me. I put my face to his chest and he strokes my hair, and kisses the top of my head. His plaid wool shirt is itchy and stinky but I don't care. I let my nose run all over it.

"Daddy," I sob, "I loved her so much."

"You go ahead and cry, baby. I know it hurts," he says.

Burying my head further into his chest I cry and cry. Tears for Sunshine. Tears about Mom always being tired and gone at night. Tears about The Rusty Nail and Dad being mean. Tears because now he's here and being nice. My kitty is gone and she'll never come back and I hate that little pecker Jake.

From around the corner in her nook Hilary screams, "WILL YOU SHUT UP? I'M TRYING TO SLEEP!"

I've never heard Dad yell at Hilary before. Not *really* yell at her but he does now.

"*YOU* SHUT UP. DO YOU HEAR ME? *YOU SHUT UP HILARY!*" It's the first time anyone's ever stuck up for me and I love Dad. I really do.

He holds me until I can't cry anymore and I fall asleep in his arms with him saying, "Go ahead baby, I know it hurts. Let it all out."

***

Rascal is a big fluffy sheep dog and Mom says having him around for a while will help me feel better after losing Sunshine. That's how she talked Dad into letting him stay with us. Rascal belongs to Dad's brother, Uncle Tom. Uncle Tom is my favorite uncle. He's silly and fun and he always plays rough with me and Adam, twirling us around and tossing us on the couch. Sometimes he holds us by our ankles and calls Rascal over to lick our faces. We only have Rascal 'til Uncle Tom finds a new apartment.

Rascal is so sweet. He's gray and white and even though his hair hangs down in front of his eyes, Uncle Tom says he can see just fine. Rascal is almost as big as me and he knocks me over whenever he sees me because he gets excited. His jumping doesn't bother me though, because I love him.

Dad says Rascal isn't allowed in the house. He has to stay on the back porch. He was supposed to be here for just a couple of weeks but now it's dragged out all winter. Rascal's hair is matted and stinky and it hurts my heart to know he's out there in the freezing cold all by himself.

Mom is working full time nights and Dad is drinking more than ever. He's meaner than ever too.

"Hey Janie!" He yells up the stairs when I'm reading books in my room.

"Get your ass down here and clean up this kitchen for your mother."

I come downstairs to a huge stack of dishes in the sink. "You lazy kids don't give one damn about your mother," he barks. "You don't let her get any sleep and you don't even help around the house. She's going to wind up getting sick and when she does it will be *your fault*."

He paces the kitchen and points at me, "You hear?" he says, pushing his finger into my chest.

At the sink, Dad watches me like a hawk and yells at me again. "Jesus Christ! You aren't rinsing all the soap off. Do you think we want to taste soap when we eat?"

He stands there watching, picking at me until the last dish is done.

When I finish, he turns and marches into his bedroom and slams the door. Grabbing my coat, I sneak out on the back porch to wrap my arms around Rascal's neck. Even though the porch is enclosed, it's bitter cold out here. Wind whips right through and tiny icicles hang on the fur in front of Rascal's eyes. Digging my fingers deep into his fur, he feels wooly and thick. Sometimes he smells so bad, like poop and throw up combined. On those days, I can't stand to be around him very long, but then I feel guilty because he's such a good friend. He doesn't even jump when he knows I'm upset. I tell Rascal all my feelings and do my best to ignore his smell.

"I miss Mommy, Rascal."

Sometimes I ask him questions. "Rascal, why is Dad so mean?"

Sometimes I try to make *him* feel better. "Rascal, it isn't your fault you stink."

Sometimes I just hug him and cry. Rascal sits quietly, looking straight ahead through the mess of fur in his eyes. He licks the tears off my cheeks. Somehow Rascal pulls the yucky stuff all out of me and I feel better by the time I'm washing his stink off my hands back in the kitchen.

In the spring, when he finally comes to take him, Uncle Tom shakes his head in disgust at the way Rascal looks and smells. My neck is hot and my face goes red with shame.

"I'm sorry Rascal," I say quietly as I watch him hop into the car. As they drive away I whisper, *"I love you, boy."*

Chapter Ten

On summer mornings, when she gets home from work, Mom sits at the kitchen table in her nurse uniform, eating her Wheaties, and glancing through the newspaper. She dips her buttered toast into her cereal milk and lets it get real soggy. Then, she pulls it out of the milk quick and shoves it into her mouth before the soggy part falls off. Once in her mouth, she sucks all the milk out before chewing and swallowing. Dad hates it when she does this and if he's home he yells at her every time. I tried it once and it does nothing but turn your toast soggy and dilute the taste of it. It also makes your milk oily which is gross. Why she insists on dunking her toast, I don't know.

Mom, please look at me! Please talk to me!

Soon, she's gonna go upstairs to sleep in Adam's room and we won't see her again 'til 3:00PM. There's no one to play with. Mom says I'm not old enough to walk to Sophie's by myself.

Mom put tin foil on Adam's windows to block the sun. His curtain rod has a thick wool blanket hanging down to make it even darker. A window air conditioner goes full blast to cool it off up there and drown out the noise. It's the only cool room in the house.

"Don't wake me up 'til three," she says, standing up and stretching.

She doesn't even glance in my direction before she heads up the squeaky stairs. She's afraid I'll talk to her and hold her up. The sound of Adam's door shuts behind her, and she's gone.

Summer is so boring here. Mom never takes us anyplace. I wish we could go somewhere, just me and her. Sophie's mom sometimes takes her out to lunch and shopping for clothes. My mom is too tired all the time and we don't have money for things like that. I wish I were an only child like Sophie.

Last week I asked, "Mom. What if Hilary and Adam died?" She was doing the dishes and she stopped and turned to me real serious and said, "Oh honey, that's not going to happen. That's *one thing* you don't have to worry about."

Worrying? I was *wishing,* and I was very disappointed with her answer.

Dad tells us if we don't let Mom get her rest, she'll get sick and it will be our fault. I worry about Mom getting sick and I don't want to wake her up, but sometimes I'm just going to *explode* if I don't go in and see her. I think of a question and stand by the bed, watching her sleep in the light that filters in through the open door.

Mom's on her belly, arms straight at her sides, hands under her thighs like she's trying to get them warm. Her covers are off, her head is to the side. There's a wet spot on the pillow by where her mouth hangs open.

"Mom," I whisper. "Mom. I can't find the measuring cup. It's not in the drawer. I'm trying to make Kool-Aid," I say, nudging her shoulder.

She stirs, and says, "Look in the drainer, and if it isn't there, *do not* come in here again. Drink water and don't wake me up until three."

Even though she's mad now, somehow I feel a little better.

There is nothing to do. Hilary always gets to go over to her friend's house and me and Adam are stuck home. It's so boring.

But sometimes, if I lay on my stomach on my bed, with my face right up to the window, and if I squint my eyes just right, and make everything just a tiny bit blurry, I can get that God feeling. The leaves on the Aspen tree in Mr. Parson's yard shimmer like a million little sparkly angel friends waving hello. My breathing gets so relaxed, it's kind of like sleeping, but I'm awake. When I feel God, all the worry just drains right out of me and *nothing is wrong.* After, I'm not nearly as sad.

But some days, I just feel mad. I'll pick on Adam until he screams. Other times, we don't even *mean* to wake her up. Me and Adam just get silly and loud. Mom stomps out, her hair big and messy, a line from the blanket down the side of her face looking like a huge red scar. Her skin is ghost white and she's pointing to the back door, "GET OUTSIDE! NOW!"

Later, I worry. What if she *does* gets sick? Who will take care of us? If Mom dies it will be my fault.

Next time I get that lonely feeling, I stand outside the door and try to think of something important to ask her. Touching my fingers to the doorknob, I hold it a minute. Picturing her dead, in a casket, I let go of the knob, and head back downstairs.

Even though I just had lunch and I'm not even a little bit hungry, I make myself a huge bowl of chocolate ice cream. Sitting on the floor, I watch soap operas; watch the clock, 'til 3:00PM.

***

Mom had to work last night but she isn't going to
sleep today. Instead she's taking me and Adam
someplace fun! Our old car broke down but Gramma
Bonner scraped together enough money to buy a VW
Beetle so Mom could have something to get to work
with. She'd been begging other nurses for rides every
night and they weren't happy with her because we live
out in Centerville, *way* out of their way. We haven't been
anyplace all summer because we've had no car.

It's our first time in the Beetle and me and Adam
both want the front, so Mom says *no one* gets the front.
When I hop in the back seat, I see the gravel driveway
through a big hole in the floor. Mom says just be careful,
so I rest my feet lightly on either side of it. As we get
going, the Beetle rumbles and spits loudly and the
highway blurs underneath me. There's a ring of orange
rust around the hole and I'm scared my foot will slip
down and my leg will be snapped off. Pulling my knees
up to my chest, I rest both feet on the seat. Soon, fumes
are coming up from the hole and I feel like I'm gonna be
sick.

"Mom, it's so *fumy* back here. I'm feeling *sick,*" I
whine.

Nothing from Mom. She acts like she doesn't hear
me. Eyes on the road, hands on the wheel.

Pulling my knees in tighter, I look down at the hole,
which makes me dizzy and I feel worse. I try looking out
the window at the passing trees, and the bright blue sky
but as my head starts to pound and my stomach starts to
churn, a memory comes to me. When I was four we
moved to Florida. We packed up our four door Toyota

with all our stuff, and just before we left, Dad agreed to bring his friend's wife and their two children along. Three adults and five kids under seven years old, in a four door Toyota, all the way from upstate New York to Florida.

Dad screamed at me on that trip for crying when my legs fell asleep after sitting on the floor crisscross for hours.

My stomach lurches and as I stew on my memories, the fumes get worse and worse. Careful not to put my feet on the floor I sit on my knees on the back seat and stretch toward the front. Practically in Mom's ear I say, "Mom, I'm *really* getting sick. The smell is giving me a headache."

Again she ignores me and then I start getting mad.

A few more minutes go by and I'm *really* going to puke. "MOM! Stop the car! I need to get out, *now!*"

Mom slams the car to a stop and turns around in her seat. "You are so selfish!" She screams at me. "Do you think I *like* driving this car? What do you want me to do about it? Huh? *What* do you *want* me to do? Do *you* have any money to buy a new car? Here I am trying to take you someplace fun. I haven't slept in 48 hours, and all *you* do is complain. You need to stop thinking about *yourself.* Your brother isn't saying a word. Why do you have to act like a jerk? Just stop it, and we'll be there soon! I don't want to hear another word from you!"

Sinking way down into the back seat, knees to chest I pull my shirt up over my face and use it to wipe my tears and snot. This poison is killing me and the worst part is, no one even cares. Why doesn't anyone ever care about me?

When we arrive at the Carter's lake house I get out quick and gulp in the fresh country air. Soon I'm feeling better.

The Carter's have a daughter a year older than me named Hannah. Her father is a contractor and our Dad has done some work for him, but mostly they just go out drinking together. Hannah's mom is blonde and beautiful and it's not that she isn't nice, but somehow I get the feeling her husband *made* her invite us.

Hannah's mom tells us to go change into bathing suits. Hannah's room is very pink with lots of frilly decorations. She has a pretty face with just a few freckles across her nose and straight, shiny black/brown hair, down to her waist. Dad loves hair like hers. Next to Hannah, I feel plain and ugly with my light brown hair that isn't pretty or even all that long anymore since I got it cut to my shoulders. Hannah is quiet, but she's nice and she shows me some of her stuff. She's got lots of dolls and some trophies from riding horses. She's just being friendly, not braggy or anything, and I like her a lot. She seems pretty much perfect.

We change into our bathing suits and walk down the trail to the lake and it's Mom, Adam, Hannah, her mom, and me. Hannah's mom has loaned Mom a bikini, and it's weird to see her in such a sexy little bathing suit. It's too big on her skinny body but it looks pretty good and I'm feeling happy about being here. On the dock, Mom smiles at me and I can tell she's not mad at me anymore. I don't feel mad at her, either.

Me and Hannah and Adam jump off the dock and swim while the moms sit chatting under a big shade umbrella at the table. We stay in the water for a long time and when we're hungry we climb up the slimy dock ladder and sit wrapped in our towels at the table while Hannah's mom gets snacks out of a little cooler she brought. There is fruit and potato chips and bologna sandwiches and we each get a can of soda. Our lunch is so good after swimming all morning and this day is turning out to be terrific. I wish we could come here every day. After we eat, Hannah's idea is to get the floats out. Me and Adam walk to the shed and help Hannah drag two rafts and an inner tube back to the dock. I take the inner tube and jump in. Hannah and Adam take the rafts.

Once in the water, I dive under and come up in the middle of the tube. Resting my arms on it, my body is straight down in the deep cool dark water that smells like mud and fish. The sun hits the wet black rubber and I see my reflection on the tube. My hair is all wet and messy. Resting my head on my arms I close my eyes. My body is tired from swimming and it feels good just to float. The sun is hot on my shoulders and it's nice. Lifting my head I put my chin on my forearms. Opening my eyes to slits I stare at the water, and there are a million little sparkles bouncing on the lake. My eyes go slightly out of focus and the sparkles glint and I'm floating along with God. I'm part of God and God is part of me, and *nothing is wrong*. Resting my head on my arms, I close my eyes. Calm goes to the deepest part of me and I disappear into the lake, floating in the water, floating in the sky, a million little glints of me sparkling, twirling, beautiful, disappeared into all that is and all that will ever be.

When I look up, I'm way out in the middle of the lake and Mom is a tiny speck back on the dock. She's waving her arms, but I can barely see her. I dive under the tube, and then hold it in front of me, using it as a kickboard to get back to Hannah and Adam. Soon it's time to go.

In the driveway, I tell Hannah I hope I can come over again sometime. Carrying our wet towels, we walk behind Mom toward the Beetle. Over her shoulder she smiles, flashing her nice white teeth and says, "Adam, *Janie* gets the front." My heart swells with love for Mom. Summer is almost over, but at least we finally got to go someplace fun. We never did get invited back to Hannah's house though.

***

Today is Memorial Day and we're at Grandma and Clyde's for one of their clambakes. The grown-ups make a huge fire pit and they steam buckets and buckets of clams. One time, Dad convinced me to try one. It was salty and slimy but after you got past the slime it was just very chewy. It reminded me of those spit blobs you see on the sidewalks in the morning by school when it starts to get cold out.

Grandma Shea's parties are usually fun but not today. I'm hiding in her big bathroom closet with a washcloth between my legs because I got hurt. Me and Hilary were outside riding double on the bike down the hill toward the airstrip. I was sitting in front on the banana seat and Hilary was pedaling. My feet rested on the handlebars and we were going fast when we hit a rock. I flew off the seat, landing straddle on the bar. Pain shot up through my privates, into my belly and down through my arms and legs. I fell on the ground in a ball. At first I couldn't even cry. I had no breath.

"Are you alright? Are you okay?" Hilary kept asking, but I just lay there in the dirt, holding my crotch. "I'll get Dad."

"No!" I told her. I don't want Dad looking at my privates. How embarrassing.

"But you're hurt."

"I'm okay," I lied. "I'm okay."

Picking myself up I limped off to the house, leaving Hilary standing there by her bright green bike with the yellow banana seat.

I'm waiting for Mom and Grandma Shea to get back from the store. "We'll be right back," they said when they left, but it's been a really long time.

In the bathroom, I take down my pants and blood is everywhere. I'm all big and puffy *down there* with a cut down one side.

In the bathroom mirror, lines from my tears cut through the dusty dirt on my face. I want Mom. I'm not letting Dad anywhere near my privates. No way. I walk back into the closet and shut the accordion door behind me.

Slumped on the floor in the dark, I hope Gramma Shea won't be mad that I ruined her washcloth with my blood. Music is blaring outside and lots of people are here now. It's throbbing *down there.* People come in and pee, and they don't know I'm in the closet. I'm not coming out through. Not 'til Mom gets back.

Finally I hear their voices. Grandma Shea and Mom are home. They are laughing, paper bags are rustling. I get up and go to the bathroom door and poke my head out.

"Mom," I whisper. She doesn't hear me. A little louder, "Mom!"

She's standing in the dining room unpacking stuff from a grocery bag. She turns her head and looks at me confused, "What do you need?"

"Mom can you come in here *please*? I got hurt."

Gramma Shea stops unpacking the groceries and follows Mom into the bathroom.

Mom looks like she might faint when she sees the blood on the washcloth and my underpants. "What happened?" she asks, white as a ghost.

I tell her about the bike and I'm crying again. I'm so glad she's back.

Mom gets another washcloth and runs cold water over it. She dabs at my privates, real gentle. Grandma Shea leaves the bathroom quick.

"I'm trying to see how bad the cut is. You might need stitches."

"No!" I wail, grabbing the washcloth out of her hand.

"Its okay sweetie, you probably don't."

She takes the cloth back and runs it under cold water again. She wrings it out and then puts it *down there*. The pressure makes it not hurt so much. I can't seem to stop crying now that she's back.

"It's okay," she says. "You didn't have to hide."

All of a sudden, Dad comes barging in the bathroom with Grandma Shea right behind him. I put my hands over Mom's hand on the washcloth because I'm *not* going to let him see me *down there*.

"Let me see," he barks.

"No!" I cry, turning my body to face the wall.

He glares at me and grabs my arm, flipping me around. Then he snatches away my hand, "LET ME SEE," he demands, and just like that, Mom takes away the cloth and lets him get a good look. He puts his face right *down there* and I turn my head toward the wall, clenching my teeth together. Squeezing my fists, my face feels hot and more tears leak out.

They act like it isn't even MY body and I don't even have a say who gets to see my privates at all. He doesn't even care that I'm hurt, he just wants his chance to see my privates and prove I have to do what he says.

I hate him.

I hate her.

Mom never stands up for me. EVER!

They decide I don't need stitches. They make me sit in the recliner in the living room, with ice in between my legs, under my shorts. It's so embarrassing. Everyone knows. The clambake goes on all afternoon and into the night. It's the last party of summer.

Chapter Eleven

When school starts, me and Sophie aren't in the same class. The teachers separated us, saying we act too silly together, and our moms just let them. Sophie will always be *my best friend* but I do make friends with another girl this year. Her name is Siobhan Green and last weekend I spent the night at her house. She's real pretty with short blonde hair and bright blue eyes and she's funny too. She makes up all kinds of stories, about characters named Squirmy Wormy and Stinky Winky and my stomach hurts from laughing whenever I'm with her.

In Siobhan's rec room there are lots of little tables. They have newspaper clippings on their tops, sealed in something shiny called shellac.

They look just like the tables at Wendy's restaurants.

"My mom did these. It's called decoupage."

"Cool."

"Each clipping is from the days me and Malachy were born."

"Wow."

Malachy is her little brother. He has the same big blue eyes but his hair is brown and he has freckles.

We go outside and run around with Malachy and their dog Tally. Tally is a sheepdog but she's clean and not matted or stinky. Seeing her makes me miss Rascal something awful.

At Siobhan's there are leaves to jump in and we're running and yelling, "Tally Ho!" as we chase the big dog around their yard.

In her room, Siobhan shows me her Halloween costume. "It's almost finished. My mom just has to sew the buttons in the back."

It's a bright green dinosaur.

It's the coolest costume. There's a big head you put on, but your face sticks out so you can still see. There are silly googly eyes above the opening for the face. It has spikes all down the back, and a long thick tail. There are colorful patches here and there and the dinosaur has arms out in front. It isn't a scary dinosaur. It's friendly and cute, but not babyish.

Next, Siobhan shows me her costume from last year. She was a clown. The best clown ever. There is a huge wig made of red yarn, a suit with rainbow stripes, a red clown nose. It looks like something right out of the circus. Wondering where her mom learned how to make stuff like this, I wish my mom made *me* cool costumes. Ours are always so stupid. I think about asking to borrow Siobhan's clown suit for Halloween, but I don't. It's too nice and she probably wouldn't let me anyway. I have no idea what I'm going to be for trick-or-treating, but I know it will never be as good as Siobhan's dinosaur.

A week later it's Halloween. After school, Adam is excited but I'm worried. I don't have a costume and I don't know what to be. I wish I had a mom like Siobhan's that would make me something great. Since she started working nights it seems Mom never helps us with anything.

Hilary is over at Misty's and they are going to a Halloween party tonight. She thinks she's too big to go trick-or-treating, but I'll tell you what, she's not getting any of *my* candy.

Me and Mom and Adam sit around the table eating. Dad didn't come home for supper. He probably went straight to The Rusty Nail, like he usually does.

Adam says, "I want to be a pirate!"

Mom nods at him smiles, "We can do that."

When we get done eating, Mom puts Adam in a pair of black pants and a white and red striped button down shirt. She knots it at the waist. She ties a bandana over his head. She draws a little triangle beard on his chin with a make-up pencil and using black make-up, she paints on an eye-patch, and he's done.

I still can't think of anything to wear.

Clearing the supper plates, Mom says, "Maybe you could be a hobo? I could help with make-up and you could carry a sack on a stick?"

Thinking of Siobhan's dinosaur, I fold my arms and say, "I'm *not* going to be a hobo."

"Or a ghost?" she says, emptying three bags of candy into the white popcorn bowl.

"That is so lame," I say, rolling my eyes.

She runs her hands through the candy, mixing it up.

Adam and I stare at the lollipops, Reese's cups, and Hershey's kisses.

"Well, I don't know *what* you want to be, but you'd better figure it out soon," she says. "You're running out of time." She looks at the candy and then at us, "It's *not* for *you*. It's for the trick-or-treaters. *Stay out of it.*"

The second she turns her back, me and Adam each grab a Hershey's Kiss.

Chocolate melts in my mouth and as it glides down my throat I have an idea. I'll *be* a Hershey's kiss! I go to the old dresser in the dining room where Mom keeps all the paper and stuff and grab a piece of construction paper, a marker and some scissors. Up in my room, I cut out a long white strip and print KISSES on it, making it look just like the wrapper in my hand. There, that was easy!

I sneak another handful of candy, grab the tin foil out of the kitchen cabinet, and head outside through the back porch. My hands are full with my kisses flag and the foil and I have to use my shoulder to slide the barn-like garage doors open. White chalk rubs off on my shirt from the chipped paint. Once inside I leave the doors open, quickly eat the candy, and then start wrapping tin foil all around me.

It isn't working. My face is getting hot and this stupid foil is just getting all crinkled up. How can I get it to puff out at the bottom? No matter what I do it isn't right. I hear voices and when I glance outside, other kids have already started trick-or-treating. Ghosts. Hobos. Witches. More pirates, walking up and down the shoulder of Centerville Highway.

Tears start to come and my throat feels tight. *Why does nothing ever work out for me?*

Suddenly, Dad's black Chevy pick-up crunches onto driveway and he parks in front of the garage. He gets out and as he walks over to me I wipe my tears fast with the back of my hand. His jeans are brown from dirt. He's got on his red plaid wool shirt and his steel toed work boots. His beard is dark, his belly is bigger than ever, and he's scowling at me.

"What the hell are you doing with all that foil?" he barks.

"I was trying to make a costume. I wanted to be a Hershey's kiss, but I can't get it right." My shoulders slump. He says nothing. Hoping he'll feel sorry for me I say, "It's no use. I'll just have to be a ghost."

Dad puts his thumb and pointer on his scruffy beard and stands there stroking it, looking at me a while. Then he says,

"Wait here a minute."

He walks across the yard and into the house through the back porch. He didn't even seem that mad about me wasting the foil.

He comes out with some wire hangers, and a tiny shade from his bedside lamp. With thick fingers he unwraps the hangers from their tightly coiled necks like it's nothing. He bends them out into long straight lines.

"What are you doing?" I ask.

"You'll see," he says and he winks at me.

Jerking my head back, I smile big. Dad isn't usually a winker. In no time he's made a wire frame out of hangers. He puts it over me and it's kind of like a big birdcage. I stick my arms out and he wraps the foil around the frame, covering it in smooth shiny silver. It's the right shape, puffed out at the bottom!

I grin.

Dad's never helped me with *anything* before and I don't talk because I don't want to mess it up. Next, he covers the lampshade in foil, making it cone shaped on top. He presses my flag in and squishes the foil around it to make it stick. He puts it on my head, steps back, and shakes his head."That's not gonna stay," he grunts. He searches the dirty greasy shelves of the garage until he finds some duct tape and he tapes the flag onto the foil. He stands back, folds his arms, raises his eyebrows and smiles.

Stepping out of the garage I have to pull one of my arms inside my costume to hold the frame up off the ground. I don't care though, because I'm a *Hershey's kiss*, and not a *stupid* hobo or a *dumb* ghost.

Mom and Adam come outside and her mouth opens when she sees me, but no words come out. She looks at Dad, smiles, and shakes her head. She looks happy, but kind of sad too. I'm hoping they don't start fighting and ruin everything.

Dad leans against his truck and talks to Mom for a minute. He hands her some money. Me and Adam are dancing around the driveway. "Arrgggg!" he says, and I laugh because he isn't a very scary pirate at all. Dad gets in his truck, and heads down the road to The Rusty Nail, and we're off to trick-or-treat! My stomach drops and I feel guilty when I remember I forgot to tell Dad thanks.

At every door, people say, "*Will you look at this*?" or, "*How clever*!" or they call over their shoulder, "*Come here, you've gotta see this!*"

My arm is tired from holding up my costume and it's hard not to bump into people, but I'm smiling all night because this is the best Halloween ever. "My *Dad* helped me make it," I tell everyone, like it's no big thing.

Chapter Twelve

Most nights, before Mom leaves for work, she calls Dad at The Rusty Nail to remind him to come home. He always tells her he's on his way, but most of the time he isn't. It's more peaceful if he's not home, but it is kind of scary and takes me a long time to get to sleep if no grown-ups are here.

When Dad gets in, he clunks up the stairs to our rooms to tell us how much he loves us. Dropping to his knees beside my bed, he stares until I wake up. Sometimes he rests his head sideways on my stomach and starts to cry.

"Do you know how much I love you kids?" he'll ask. His shoulders shake and he sniffles.

Hilary just says, "I love you too Dad."

But I can't help but notice he stinks and his head is heavy. My arms and legs go rigid. "Dad, I'm trying to sleep," I say.

"I asked you a question," he barks, lifting his head up and glaring at me through his bloodshot glassy eyes.

"What?" I say, my body stiff as a board.

"Do you know how much I love you?"

I freeze.

I'm in kindergarten, and I'm looking, looking and I can't find Hilary. Everyone is running and kids are yelling and it's too, too bright. I go where everyone else is going. Out across the blacktop with the white lines painted on for basketball. Past the hopscotch. Going with everyone else past the chain fence and now I'm on the sidewalk but some kids are going that way, down the street by all the houses, and some are going the other way, back toward the busy road where they're waiting for the light to change, and which way am I supposed to go? It's hot and bright and loud and I don't know any of these faces and I can't remember what's right. Where is my sister?

I'm afraid to cross the busy road so I walk the other way down the sidewalk 'til the end of the fence and I'm looking, looking, but I can't remember and I can't find Hilary and I'm lost and no one is ever going to find me.

My heart is beating so scared and it's too hot. I hear something close to my head. Closer than the laughs and screams of kids walking on in front of me. It's a bee and it's trying to get me and I try to swat it but it just keeps on after me and I am crying, crying scared and the bee! I am so mad to be lost and hot and I don't remember how to get to this new apartment in the basement with Daddy walking on his knees from Hilary's cot to my cot.

"Good night head," he said and kissed my head quick.

"Good night shoulder," he said and he kissed my shoulder quick.

"Good night belly," he said and kissed my belly quick.

"Good night pee-pee," he said and he tried to kiss my pee-pee, but I said "no."

When I said "no" he yanked me hard and yelled loud in my face I can't tell him no, but pee-pees are private and I know it.

I hate new places that are hot and bright and loud and where Daddy says "Don't ever tell me no, you hear?" And where bees want to sting you and no one cares if you're crying and lost.

Walking, walking, I don't know what to do so I keep walking, and finally I see the apartment. When I come in Mommy holds me and says I shouldn't have walked home by myself. I need to wait for Hilary to get me and I tell her I couldn't find Hilary.

"Mommy, Daddy is mean," I cry.

"What are you talking about?" She asks, running her hand over my long hair. She rocks me side to side on her lap.

"He was mean when he tucked us in," I say nuzzling into her.

She stops rocking, "What did he do?"

"Did he hurt you?" She looks at my face.

I shake my head, no.

"Did he yell at you?"

"Yes, and he yanked me," I nod.

Mommy says, "Oh sweetie" and she holds me for a long time, rocking me and stroking my hair.

But Mom isn't here. Since she started working nights, we're on our own after 10:00PM. "Do you know how much I love you?" Dad barks in my face again.

"A lot," I whisper, arms frozen solid at my sides.

"You're damn right I do."

His head gets heavier and heavier and soon I hear snoring. When I'm sure he's asleep, I squirm out from under him, and his body crumples to the floor in a heap by my bed. Gathering up my blankets, I go downstairs to the living room couch so I don't have to smell him or hear his snoring all night.

Some nights, I wake to the sound of the heavy black cast iron pans crashing on the kitchen stove. Then I smell bacon. He slurs up the stairs, "You kiddsssss wan innie eggs?"

"Dad it's three o'clock in the morning!" I yell from my bed.

"And what's your *fuckin'* point?" he barks back.

I lay awake until the crashing stops and when it's real quiet, I go downstairs to make sure all the burners are off. Hilary and Adam never seem to worry about the house burning down, but unless I check the stove, I can't get back to sleep. Dad leaves the pans and plates in the sink, with scrambled eggs hardening on the surfaces. Mom will have to deal with his dishes in the morning. When sleep finally comes I dream I'm trapped in a house full of flames.

***

Dad says we don't care about Mom. He says we never let her sleep, and we never clean up after ourselves, and she's going to get sick and it will be our fault. We don't have school this week because it's spring break and Dad says we're going to Gramma Shea's so Mom can get some rest. In his truck on the way there I look out the window at the bright blue sky and move my leg away from Hilary's. Adam is next to Dad.

When Dad drops us off at Grandma Shea's, things don't feel right. She isn't happy to see us like normal on holidays. She's stomping around on her short stout legs and the angry way her heels hit the floor reminds me of Dad. No candy in the cupboard today. No soda.

Me, Hilary, and Adam go outside to play. Patrick comes with us and after a while his face is red from running around in the sun. He's having fun, but Grandma

Shea yells out the sliding glass doors off her kitchen, "Take it easy with him! You're getting him all riled up!" I don't know why it isn't okay for retarded kids to get excited and have fun too.

When we come in, Grandma is in the kitchen, making us lunch. Fried bologna sandwiches with ketchup. Patrick *loves* ketchup. He already has it on his sandwich, but still he dunks each bite into a big blob on his plate. He takes a bite. Looks at us and laughs. His food flies out of his mouth and we crack up.

Grandma Shea snaps, "Jesus Christ, don't laugh at him! You're encouraging him."

We can't help it though. Patrick is hilarious!

Grandma Shea raises her spatula over her head as she wipes her forehead with the back of her hand. She's always complaining about hot flashes and I guess she's having one now.

Suddenly, I wish it was time to go.

After lunch, in the bathroom, I lock the door. First, I pee. Then, I take off my clothes and weigh myself. Looking at my naked body, I wish it looked like the pretty ladies in Dad's magazines or on HBO. None of them have a bulge in their tummies like me. I hate my stomach and I give it a good quick punch. I shouldn't have eaten my whole sandwich. I'm 10 and already I'm over 80 pounds. What a cow. I put my clothes back on and wash my hands. The mirror above the sink is way up high and I can't see myself so I climb up onto it to get a good look at my face. Grandma Shea always tells Hilary how gorgeous she is, but she never says it about me. Looking in the mirror, I study my face to figure out what makes me not as pretty as Hilary. Our faces are shaped the same. Our eyes are almost the same color. Our chins match. We definitely don't have the same nose. It must be my nose that makes me ugly. It isn't huge, but it's long and straight, not cute like Hilary's. Hers turns up just a little on the end.

One second I'm running my pointer finger down the length of my nose and the next I'm slowly and evenly lowered to the floor. The metal pipe the sink rests on is completely bent over and the sink is on the ground. Hopping off quick, I pace the bathroom floor. *Oh God! What did I do?* Grandma Shea is going to kill me. Staring at the white sink just sitting there on the floor, I kneel down and try to shove it back up. That's when the pipe snaps. Water shoots straight up to the ceiling and back down to the floor.

For a second, I'm frozen, but then I run from the bathroom yelling, "GRANDMA!"

She drops her heavy pan in the sink and runs after me into the bathroom where it now looks like a park fountain. The whole floor is covered in water.

Grandma Shea takes my shoulders and shakes me. "God Damn it! What the hell were you doing in here?"

"Uh, I climbed up on the sink."

Her mad eyes drill into me with such hate I have to turn my head. It feels like she might even hit me. She lets go of me with a shove.

"God Damn it! Why would you climb on the sink? What's the *matter* with you?" In a frenzy, she opens the linen closet and hurls towels all over the floor.

"I wanted to see in the mirror," I mumble, embarrassed.

"What the hell do you need to look in the mirror for? God damn it! Clyde is going to be furious," she says, tossing more towels and now blankets onto the floor.

She runs into the kitchen and dials Clyde's work number.

"Janie broke the God damn sink in the bathroom! You have to come home quick! Jesus, Mary & Joseph! Water is everywhere!"

Hanging up the phone she runs back into the bathroom.

The thought of Clyde being mad at me is too much to bear. I stand in the doorway of the bathroom, hands over my mouth, shifting from foot to foot.

Within minutes, Clyde is home. Me and Hilary move out of the bathroom doorway so he can get past us and when he sees Grandma freaking out he calmly walks over and turns a knob at the bottom of the broken pipe. The water stops.

"Jesus Christ, you look like a drowned rat!" he says and he busts out laughing but Grandma doesn't think it's funny. She turns around and glares at me and that's when I run downstairs to hide.

The garage is under the house and the double doors to it are open wide. In a dark corner in back there are several rolls of carpet. I shimmy myself between two rolls and lay flat on my back on the concrete basement floor. Pulling a carpet scrap over the top, I make a little cave. Grandma is still stomping around up there, and I hear Clyde too.

I am so fat. I can't believe I broke the sink. I'm so ugly. I'm an awful, awful, girl. Grandma Shea hates me. I wish I were never born.

In my hiding spot, there's a tiny opening, just the size of my face, and if I turn my head sideways I can see the bluest sky outside the garage doors. It's kind of like watching TV because it's all dark and then just a square of color, but this screen has only blue sky and puffy white clouds hanging in the air, barely moving at all.

"Janie!" I hear Grandma Shea call down into the basement.

Nope. Nope. Nope. I won't come out.

Look at the sky.

"Janie!"

Adam and Hilary are sent to find me. Adam even steps on the carpet pile once, but I don't move a muscle and he goes back upstairs.

Look at the sky.

Squint.

Look for *God.*

They missed me in the basement a second time and they go outside to search. Later, they run right past me on their way in, and I hear them tell Grandma Shea, "We couldn't find her."

Grandma Shea comes down the steps and I hold my breath. She walks across the basement and sighs. Standing in the garage doorway, she lights a cigarette and stares out toward the airstrip behind her house. She stands with her left hand on her hip, and uses her other hand to hold her cigarette. Long lines of grey smoke rise up in front of her and drift off to the right with the breeze. Her black and gray hair is a mess and her face looks worried.

"Janie!" she yells a couple of times before tossing her butt. She has bare feet so she can't twist it out with her foot. She leaves it on the driveway and I smell it for a long time after she turns and goes back upstairs.

I don't care if Grandma Shea is worried. I don't care if there are spiders down here or if I'm cold. I don't care that I have to pee. I'm not coming out until Mom gets here. She's coming for us when she wakes up.

I look at the sky and it takes a long time, but finally I do feel God, a little. My body calms down. The clouds float slowly by.

When the puffy clouds have gone and the sky starts to turn gray I hear Mom's voice. Hilary and Adam's footsteps bounce around overhead and then the basement stairs are creaking and Mom is calling for me. All stiff, I climb out from the carpets and go to her. She sits on the bottom step and I cling to her crying.

"I didn't mean to break the sink."

"I know."

I'm so embarrassed with being so vain and so fat. "I was trying to see in the mirror."

"It's okay," she says.

Burying my face in her chest I cry, "Grandma Shea hates me."

"She isn't mad anymore. She thought Clyde would be really angry but he wasn't. In fact, he had a good laugh over it. Grandma's been worried about you. You shouldn't have hid like that."

"I don't want to go upstairs."

Mom sighs. "We have to go up. We've gotta go," she says.

Mom leads me by the hand up the steps and Grandma Shea is standing in the kitchen, wringing her hands on a dishtowel. Patrick is in front of the TV. Hilary and Adam are at the door, ready to go. Grandma Shea glances in my direction and I look at the floor. Neither one of us says anything.

She never baby-sits us again. The school year comes to an end, and it's another boring summer. Me and Adam watch TV all day, and wait for Mom to wake up. It's almost a relief when school starts again in September.

Chapter Thirteen

Today is the day! Dancing around the living room, I stop to pull back the plastic taped onto the front window. Peeking out, I think I'll *die* from all this waiting and then finally the girls start to arrive. First is Sophie. Next Amy, a girl who lives up on Pitcher Hill Road in Andover. I liked Amy instantly when I saw her play "Little Cat" in the production of Big Cat/Little Cat at school. She's short, with glasses and long curly hair. Next came Libby. Libby goes to my Sunday school. She's got big brown eyes and long golden brown hair that she wears in two braids. "Oh, you're remodeling," her mom said when she came in to drop Libby off.

At first I was confused but then I got it. She was talking about the wooden beams and the electrical cords dangling down between the kitchen and dining room. It's always been this way, but suddenly I start noticing how our house looks. I look at the walls in the kitchen lined with pink insulation like it's the first time I ever saw them. Hopefully, everybody else thinks we're remodeling too.

The only one not here yet is Jill Jones. Since she's late, we start bobbing for apples without her. Having my birthday in the fall means you always get to bob for apples. They float in a big metal tub that sits on one of the dining room chairs, just a few feet away from the wood stove in the corner. Some of the apples still have leaves on their stems.

Because it's my birthday I get the first turn. Sticking my face into the cold water a chill runs down my back, and I miss on my first try. Water drips down my front and onto the dark hardwood floors at my feet. Mom throws a white towel down in front of the chair and everyone laughs. Taking the towel, I mop up the floor and when I bring it up, it's dark brown with dirt. Hoping no one noticed, I throw it back down on the floor quick and try again. This time I sink my teeth into a Macintosh. Rising from the water triumphant, I see Jill Jones standing there grinning. Her mom is right behind her.

Jill is a tomboy. She is the fastest runner in our grade, and that includes the boys. She can also do back flips which is amazing. How can you just be standing there, and then all of a sudden flip all the way backwards and land on your feet? Jill lives in a nice house in Andover, right next door to her Grandpa's farm. Jill's mom has hair that's dyed red and she wears the latest styles. Today she has on dark jeans and a maroon fitted blazer jacket. She's tiny, always on a diet, and her mouth turns down on the corners even when she's smiling, though she hardly ever smiles. She should be pretty, but the pretty just can't seem to show with all the mean inside her. Jill's mom is not a tomboy. Her hair and nails are always perfect and she doesn't like the way Jill runs around getting dirty on the farm every chance she gets. She doesn't seem to like Jill much at all. It's easy to see why Jill likes hanging around the barn so much.

Jill's late because her mom just took her for a hair appointment. She got a Dorothy Hammill and it looks great. Her thick brown hair is cut like a bowl around her head and it curls under at the bottom perfectly. Jill has pale skin and her nose turns up just enough to be cute, but not enough to look like a pig.

On our birthdays we get to pick out whatever cake we want from Mom's cake decorating book. After studying the book for days, I narrowed it down to Raggedy Ann, or a Teddy Bear. Then I changed my mind and decided on a cat at the last minute.

After we finish our pizza, Mom brings out the cake. She's lined up the candles along the cat's tail and I blow out all 11, first try. "I want the eyes! " I say. They are made of Oreo cookies. "I want the whiskers!" Jill yells. They are made of licorice. "I want the tail!" says Amy. "The paw!" Libby says, "I want the paw!" Sophie says, "I want a paw too!" The paws have gumdrops.

Mom did a great job on my cake, and she does her best to get us the parts we ask for. She plops a scoop of ice cream on each plate. Hershey's Chocolate Marshmallow, my favorite! I don't even mind how Adam has been tagging along the whole time. It's a slumber party and we'll get rid of him later. Hilary is staying at Misty's, *thank God*. My friends think she's so cool and when *she's* around they hardly pay any attention to me. It makes me so mad! Why do they think she's so great?

Dad comes home while we're eating cake. His work boots clunk across the floor and he stumbles over to me, kissing me on the cheek. He says "Happy Birthday, Jaaaane-ie!" His red plaid shirt smells like stale beer and cigarettes. The girls giggle at the way he slurs my name, and my cheeks feel hot.

"Hello girrrlllls," he says, reaching over my friends to snatch a piece of pizza from the table. His eyes are red and shiny and his voice is slow. It's the first time I remember feeling embarrassed of Dad.

Dad takes his pizza and swaggers into the kitchen. He chokes down his slice, standing over the sink, and I'm relieved when he heads out the back door as soon as he finishes.

Later, we change into pajamas and go upstairs to listen to music in my room. Jill brought some of her Dad's favorite records. We dance to *At the Hop*. Then we watch the routine Jill made up to *Going Up, Up, Up, in a Puff of Smoke*. She starts all crouched down and with each "up" she gets a little higher. I play the Bee-Gees album and it's the five of us in footy pajamas, crisscrossing our bodies diagonally with our right arm, *"Ah-ah-ah-ah, Stayin' alive. Stayin' alive!"* Amy stands in the doorway to Adam's room and does a slow routine she made up to a song called *Hotel California*. She clings to the door frame like she just can't get out. When we're tired, Jill throws on a slow song, her Dad's favorite, *House of the Rising Sun*. She sings along, mellow and serious. Clearly she's very wise.

Mom comes halfway up the stairs and yells, "It's time to get in your sleeping bags and settle down."

"Okay," I yell. The stairs creak as she goes back down.

"Well, I guess we better say our prayers," Jill says.

"Why do we have to say prayers?" Sophie asks.

Jill's squatting down adjusting her sleeping bag, and she snaps her head around toward Sophie.

"You mean you don't say prayers before bed?" she asks.

Sophie shrugs and looks guilty.

"She's *Jewish*," I say, trying to explain.

"Jewish, huh?" Jill's in her sleeping bag now, lying on her side, propped up on one elbow with her hand under her ear. The front of her Dorothy Hammill is sticking straight up toward the ceiling, a result of the apple bobbing. The back is still curled under perfectly.

"Well, let me ask you this, Sophie Sheinmel, do you accept the lord Jesus Christ as your savior?"

"Um.....I don't know?" Sophie shoots me a worried look.

Jill drops her head, and shakes it slowly side to side. She hops up and marches across the row of sleeping bags, pointing her finger and asking us one by one, "Are you a Christian?"

I nod.

Libby nods.

Amy nods.

Jill goes back to Sophie and says, "I hate to tell you this Sophie, but unless you take Jesus Christ as your savoir, you're going *straight to hell* when you die."

Sophie's eyebrows crinkle together and she looks like she might cry.

She looks at me and then back at Jill.

"Why?" She asks, nervously putting her fingers to her mouth. She starts chewing on her thumbnail.

Jill shrugs, "I don't know. That's what it says in the Bible. Jesus is going to come again and all of us who have taken him into our hearts will be saved and the rest will burn in hell...," she leans into Sophie's face, "*forever.*"

Sophie cowers and starts crying, for real.

Jill jumps to her feet and says, "Sophie, don't cry. We can fix it. All you have to do is take Jesus into your heart. Are you willing to accept the lord Jesus Christ as your savior? Are you willing to take Jesus Christ into your heart?"

Amy, Libby and I are sitting up in our sleeping bags, watching.

Sophie nods through her tears.

"Well, get down on your knees," Jill commands.

Sophie kneels.

Jill grabs a Styrofoam cup of water that was sitting on the dresser, and stands in front of Sophie. She holds the cup in one hand and places her other hand on Sophie's head. Jill closes her eyes and says, "Sophie Sheinmel, do you accept the Lord Jesus Christ as your savior? Do you take Jesus Christ into your heart?"

"Yes," Sophie says.

Opening one eye, Jill looks down at Sophie and whispers, "Say, I do."

"I do," Sophie says.

Jill pours a little water on Sophie's head and says, "Sophie Sheinmel, YOU ARE SAVED!"

A big smile of relief is on Sophie's face as the water trickles over her right eyebrow. We're all happy for her. Mom yells up the stairs for us to be quiet and we settle down in our sleeping bags again. In the night, the sound of Sophie crying wakes me up. She's in her sleeping bag right next to me.

"Sophie, what's wrong?" I whisper. I can make out her face in the glow from the lights on the highway outside the window.

"What about my parents? Are *they* gonna burn in hell?" she asks.

Shooting a quick look toward Jill, I see she's sound asleep. I don't understand Jill's God. I wonder if there are different types of Christians? Father Duncan *never* talks about burning in hell, *or* being "saved" for that matter.

"No, Sophie. I think it only takes one person for the whole family to be saved," I tell her, trying to sound like I know. "Your mom and dad should be okay."

She searches my face with her big dark eyes and decides to believe me. "Thanks," she says. Then she adds, "Happy Birthday."

"Good-night Sophie."

***

The next Friday, I call Sophie and ask if she can spend the night. She says "hang on," and puts down the phone. When she gets back on the line she tells me her mom said no.

"But Sophie, why not?" I asked, disappointed.

"HBO," she says.

"My mom says letting us watch rated R movies on HBO was poor judgment."

"Oh," I say, and I feel my cheeks get hot.

I forgot we watched HBO the last time she stayed over. I don't know why she had to go and blab to her mom though. "Well, can I come over to *your* house?" I ask.

"She says not tonight, but maybe next weekend, okay?"

"Okay."

Dad's in a bad mood and I was really hoping I could go to Sophie's. After supper I go upstairs to my room and flop down on my bed. Sophie loaned me *Are You There God? It's Me Margaret,* by Judy Blume. The main character in the book is Margaret and she's in sixth grade, just like me.

Margaret is wanting to get her period so bad and I want to get my period too. My boobies are just starting to grow a teeny bit and Mom got me a training bra, and also deodorant, but she says my period probably won't be for another year or two. This is the third Judy Blume book I've borrowed. After reading almost 50 pages my eyes are tired so I decide to take my shower.

When I get done, I wrap my towel around my body and walk through the kitchen and up to my room, which sits right at the top of the kitchen stairs. My dresser is at the top of the steps, on the wall to the left. Standing in front of it, I search my top drawer for a pair of clean underwear. Dropping my towel, I pull my nightie over my head but then I see something out of the corner of my eye. Dad's there in the kitchen at the bottom of the steps. He's standing sideways, leaning way back, straining to see up the stairs. I wonder what he wants. He doesn't say anything so I smile at him and wave but he gives me the dirtiest look and walks away quick. My stomach clenches. Why is he mad at me? What did I do?

Later, I think to myself, *I sure hope he didn't see me naked.*

I try to think what I could have done to make him mad, but sometimes it is impossible to figure out.

***

School can be tough when you have a dad like mine. It's hard to concentrate on math, or get your homework done when you have no help and you're constantly worried about his moods. One place I can always forget about Dad and all my problems is music class though. I love to sing. Mrs. Shears is our teacher. She has thick glasses and tight brown curly hair. She's way older than Mom, but not as old as Gramma Bonner. She's not terribly fat but very round in the middle. She's nice and all, but Mrs. Shears is a *spaz*. When she's directing us, she moves her body around in quick jerky motions, all excited. Her thick glasses make her eyes huge and she looks like a bug asking "Huh? Huh?" If she wants us to sing softer she crouches down. For louder, she springs up tall, arms waving all crazy. She takes music very seriously. Even though Mrs. Shears is a little embarrassing, singing is easy and fun.

We line up on risers and I stand in front because I'm not tall. We've already sung a couple of songs when Mrs. Shears asks to see me out in the hall. Biting my lip as we walk toward the hall, I wonder what I did wrong. Am I off key? Did my voice crack? She shuts the door behind us and I lean against the wall, crossing my arms.

Looking at me with her big spazzy eyes, Mrs. Shears says,

"Janie....Rachel Peabody is having a bit of a hard time and I want you to...well, I'm going to stand you next to her and I want you to sing in her ear. *Subtly*."

Hmmmm. Slowly I get what's going on here. Rachel is a bad singer, and I'm supposed to drown her out! Nodding eagerly, I tell her, "Okay!"

Rachel is scrawny and plain. She rides my school bus but never talks to anyone. She's pale with some dark moles on her chin and cheek. Her face is blank. Her hair is short, dark and curly. There's no style to it at all. Even though I'm one of the shortest kids in our class, I'm way taller than her. What bugs me about Rachel is her wimpiness. Whenever anyone picks on her she doesn't do a thing about it but mutter under her breath. Mom mutters too, whenever Dad picks on her. I hate when people mutter.

Stepping up onto my new place on the risers, I wait for the piano to start and then sing loud in Rachel's ear. She starts inching away from me and when she does, meanness starts pumping through my body. We're singing about Mr. Dongato, a cat who has fallen off a roof. I lean in closer and sing even louder in her direction. I'm glad to be a better singer than Rachel Peabody. Stupid girl can't even carry a tune.

By the end of the song, there's a big space between me and the girl to my right. To my left, Rachel has the rest of the row all smushed together and she's giving me the evil eye. Raising my eyebrows I move my face toward her like, "*duh?*" Rachel shrinks back and starts to mutter. Mrs. Shears shakes her head and sends me back to my first spot on the other side of the risers.

At the next music class, Mrs. Shears has us sit on the floor. She calls us up to the piano one by one. She's testing every girl in our grade to see who will be in All County Chorus. When Rachel goes up she sings so soft I can barely hear her. That mean feeling courses through me again and I smirk.

Even though we're separated this year, me and Sophie still have music together. My friend Libby from church is sitting with us and we have the giggles. After the first few girls, no one is paying attention to the singing anymore. Everyone is gabbing and laughing; everyone but Sophie. She's wearing a dark purple turtleneck and it's her best color, but she looks like she's gonna be sick. Every now and then Mrs. Shears turns and says, "SHHHhhhhh," all *spaz-like*.

"I'm nervous," Sophie whispers. Her head is tipped sideways and she's biting the cuticle on her left pointer finger.

"Why?" I ask.

She moves her hands down into her lap and fidgets with them. "I can't sing," she says.

"What do you mean?" I say, pulling my head back, surprised.

"I can't carry a tune."

Her head is still lowered but she looks up at me with her dark eyes.

"Sure you can," Libby says.

Of course she can sing. It's the easiest thing.

Mrs. Shears calls my name and I walk up to the piano. She nods and begins hitting the keys, Do-Re-Me-Fa-So-La-Ti-Do. I love this song because it's from *The Sound of Music.* I've seen the movie and Gramma Bonner has the record. I listen to it every time I stay at her house. Mom's been dropping us off at Gramma's before she leaves for work at night if Dad happens to be home and in a bad mood.

I'm singing for Mrs. Shears, but in my mind, I'm the littlest Von Trapp girl, sitting in a meadow. My brothers and sisters adore me, unlike Hilary and Adam. Mrs. Shears is our beautiful nanny, Maria.

When my turn is over, I go back to Sophie and Libby. Before we can really get giggling again it's Sophie's turn, and when she starts singing, I can't believe it. She really *can't* sing. Her voice is all over the place, nowhere near the music. How could I not know this? She's worse than Rachel Peabody! Everyone stares at her but I shoot them a warning look and nobody says a word as she walks back toward us. Libby is next and she actually sings really well. Soon, all the girls have had a turn, and Mrs. Shears has an announcement to make.

"Janie Shea, Libby Carlson, and Christina Breckenridge have been chosen for All- County Chorus."

The other girls clap and it's neat to win something. Sophie doesn't clap and she won't even look at us.

Thanks a lot, Sophie.

Straight off the school bus I yell to Mom, "I made All County Chorus!"

"That's great!" she says.

Mom calls Gramma Bonner and then Grandma Shea. They've never made a big deal of me and I'm happy and proud but also a bit squirmy in my tummy about it.

Sophie calls while I'm doing homework.

"My mom says I have to call to say congratulations," she says. "I acted like a jerk because I was really upset I didn't make it."

"Sophie, it's okay," I say, chewing on the tip of my pencil.

"My mom says music isn't for everyone, and that I should congratulate you anyway," she says.

"Well, you're good at lots of other things. You're way better than me at math."

"Big deal," she says.

Later, at supper I say, "I can't believe some people can't even sing."

Mom ignores me. She butters a piece of bread for Adam.

"How could you *not* be able to sing?" I ask.

"Some people just don't have the ability. It doesn't make them a bad person," she says.

Mom plops a lump of potatoes on my plate.

Hilary says, "You're so full of yourself."

"Shut up," I say, glaring at her.

Mom says, "Not another word."

Later, in bed, I'm feeling a little sorry for Sophie, but I'm happy too, because for once, I've got something she can't have. No one, not her dad, not even her rich Nana in Florida can buy her a voice to sing with. Lying on my back in bed, my hands are folded behind my head. On my face is just a faint smirk, but inside, my head is cocked back, and I'm laughing like The Wicked Witch of the West.

Mrs. Shears has us practicing every day after school. Libby is a "lead." She sings the melody. Libby doesn't wear her hair in braids anymore, and she recently got a body wave perm. Her mom is always taking her shopping for Gloria Vanderbilt and Jordache jeans.

Christina is a soprano, which means she sings the very high notes. She's tall and very shy. She has curly blonde hair and doesn't talk much but she can sing really well. She has Jordache jeans too, and she carries a bright pink pic for her curly hair in her back pocket.

I'm an alto, which means I sing the low part. I don't have any designer clothes and my hair is flat and straight. Mom says a body wave is expensive and we don't have money for that kind of thing.

The first song is "Edelwiess" from *The Sound of Music*. Singing the alto part is kind of tricky and it bugs me that I'm not supposed to sing the good part, the melody.

Next, we sing a John Denver song called "Ei Calypso." My part is a total gyp because it barely even has any words. It's all, "Oooooo…Ooooooo... Ooooo…." until the chorus, when I get to sing "Ei calypso," but not regular. It has to be all low. There are a couple of other songs and again I don't get to sing hardly any words. I'm not sure this chorus is all it's cracked up to be, but Mom has both my grandmothers all riled up about it, so I guess I have to keep going.

At the end of the school year, it's finally time for the concert. I pick out a blue velour dress that used to be Hilary's. It has a thin silver belt that ties around the middle, which makes me feel fat because it's too clingy. I'm sure you can see the bulge in my belly just below my navel but I don't have anything else, so I suck in my gut and try not to think about it.

The actual night of the concert is the first time we sing with the girls from all the other schools. Before tonight, I didn't really know what "All County" even meant. Inside the big gym, my stomach braces itself when I see the huge set of risers. Looking around, I don't recognize anyone. A volunteer asks me what part I sing, then directs me to the alto section. There are tons of people milling about. So many girls stepping onto the risers. Families are filing into the building. Violins are getting tuned. This place is huge. I'll doubt I'll ever be able to find Mom and my Grammas in the crowd.

After a while, the audience is seated, and bright blinding lights come up on us. There is the hum of pitch pipes and my upper lip starts to twitch from nerves. There's another woman, not Mrs. Shears, at the front of the bleachers facing us. I wish it *were* Mrs. Shears. I don't know these girls next to me and now I don't even know the leader. How will I know what's going on? What if I mess up and blurt something out when I'm not supposed to?

The piano starts playing the beginning of "Ei Calypso" and just like we practiced with Mrs. Shears, the new leader points to my section and I come in with my "Oooossss" right on time, singing along with the rest of the altos. We sound *loud* and smooth and deep. Next, the leads come in with the melody and it all makes sense. Our oooooos are vibrating underneath the main music and it sounds good. Then, the sopranos come in and I can hear all three parts and somehow we're one big beautiful vibrating sound. The lady is directing us, waving her arms and the risers are shaking and I feel like a bee in a buzzing hive, important for doing my little part. The song is over quick, and all the people are clapping. During the next song, I see them. Mom, Gramma Bonner and Grandma Shea. They're half way back and to the left. I can't take my eyes off Gramma Bonner. She is smiling the proudest. We're not allowed to wave. We finish our song and there is more clapping.

Our last song is "Edelwiess." As the piano starts, a tingle begins in my heart, and spreads through my whole body. The feeling is just like watching the fluttery leaves on Mr. Parson's Aspen tree outside my bedroom window. It's like floating in the inner tube at Hannah's lake. *God* is here, softly blending these sweet voices together, and in this moment, *nothing is wrong*. Tears come to my eyes because I'm part of the song; part of all the love in the world. *Edelwiess* seems to go on forever, time doesn't exist, then suddenly it's over and the audience is clapping again.

After the show, my grammas hug me and tell me how proud they are. They're are all dressed up and I just really had no idea this was such a big deal. Then, Grandma Shea says, "I wish your father had come."

Seeing Dad at this concert would be like walking into math class on Monday morning to find him sitting at my desk. It just wouldn't make any sense. There are only three places for Dad. Home, up in a tree with a chain saw, or on a barstool at The Rusty Nail. Why does everyone always want him where he doesn't belong? Next thing you know, Grandma Shea will want him to come on vacation with us over the summer. I've never been on vacation before, but Grandma Shea and Clyde are taking us kids with them to the beach when school gets out. I hope they don't ask Dad to come. As far as I'm concerned, the whole point of going on vacation is to get away from him.

Chapter Fourteen

His breathing is heavy and dramatic. The vein in his forehead sticks out and so does the one on his neck. He says, "Don't make me angry. You wouldn't like me when I'm angry."

Patrick is doing his *Incredible Hulk* impression for the 100th time. He bulges his big blue eyes way out and holds his deranged stare until I laugh. When I finally do, he grabs my nose, "Gotchyer nose!" he says, then tips his head back laughing that almost silent whole body shake like Ernie on *Sesame St.*

I've been stuck in the middle seat of Clyde's Suburban with Patrick for hours. Hilary and Adam are in the *way* back. We're on our way to Assateague Island. No one came out and said it, but it's my job to keep Patrick happy. Clyde says I'm extra good with him.

We're pulling The Prowler behind us. It's a white camper with green stripes and a cat's face painted on the back. Grandma Shea has a cooler packed with cans of Country Time Lemonade *and* Reese's Cups and we can have as many as we want. Grandma and Clyde's best friends, Vincent and Olga are following us in their car.

Grandma and Clyde are listening to country music on the radio. Clyde's big hands are on the steering wheel and he glances at us in the rear view mirror, "So, are y'all excited to see the ocean?" he asks all slow and southern. It is strange for Clyde to just start talking to us and we answer back quickly.

Adam yells, "Yeah! I've never seen the ocean before." Turning around in my seat to face him I say, "Yes, you have. In Florida. remember?" Hilary rolls her eyes and says, "That wasn't the ocean, *stupid*, it was a little lake." She shifts in her seat and sticks her nose up in the air, like she's so smart. "But it had a beach," I say, trying to remember what it looked like. I was only four.

"Just because something has sand, doesn't make it the ocean," she says, rolling her eyes. "It was a stupid little park." Folding my arms over my chest I turn around and sit back in my seat. I'm so sick of her always trying to make me feel dumb.

"Never mind," Grandma Shea says. "We'll be there in just a couple more hours," says Clyde. He reaches forward and turns up the radio.

Kenny Rogers is on and Grandma sings along, "You Picked A Fine Time To Leave Me Loose Wheel!" She cracks herself up. It feels like we've been in the car forever.

Laying down on the back seat, I put my feet on Patrick's lap and after a while I fall asleep. The motion of the Suburban slowing down wakes me, and when I sit up we're at the camp grounds on Assateague Island. We drive around until we find our campsite among the rows of campers and tents. Vincent and Olga park in the spot right next to us. Way off in the distance, past all the campers, we see a pack of wild ponies standing in some tall grass. Grandma Shea is all excited because that's what this place is famous for. It's why she's always wanted to come here. She gets out her camera and snaps a picture.

We're gonna sleep in the camper, but Vincent and Olga brought a tent to stay in. Taking some bags out of the Suburban, Grandma Shea says, "Why don't you kids go get into your bathing suits and check out the water while we set everything up?"

"I don't know" Clyde says, taking a heavy bag out of her hands, "the tide's likely to be high right about now."

"Jesus Christ, Clyde. Hilary is almost 15. She'll watch them. They'll be fine," she says. It seems like she's already sick of us.

She gives us a nod and we run inside the camper to change.

When we come out she says, "You have a couple of hours until supper. Come back when it starts to get dark. Patrick, you're staying with us."

Patrick doesn't care about us leaving him behind. He's sitting cross-legged on the picnic table bench, fiddling with his little boom box. Patrick loves music more than anything in the world, and Grandma wouldn't let him have his radio 'til we got here.

Me, Hilary and Adam follow the trail to the sand dunes. The sun is still bright and as I run up the hill, a sprig of dried grass pricks my foot and I stop to rub my heel. Hilary and Adam keep going, and as I look up, I see them disappear over the top of the dune. To catch up, I start running; my towel flapping in the wind. I'm going fast but my eyes are on the ground, trying to avoid stepping on any more prickly things. Reaching the top of the dune I look up and suddenly the air is knocked hard out of my lungs. Shaking my head, I stumble back, my mouth wide open in awe and confusion.

It's as big as forever.

My throat gets tight and goose bumps go down my back.

It's impossible. The ocean is impossibly big.

97

The waves are as high as me, but far away it's calm and dark and it goes on and on and on. Little waves start way out and race to the shore getting bigger and bigger before crashing right in front of me on the sand. White birds skitter about, leaving tiny footprints as they go. Standing with my hands cupping the sun out of my eyes, I can't believe it. Steadying my feet in the hot sand I close my eyes and listen to the roar of the water and it feels like my body is being pushed back by the wind and the sound of the waves. It's so loud you can't hear anything. It's silence.

The smell is fishy and my hair blows across my face. Dropping my towel I run forward to Hilary and Adam who are skipping through the water now. It's freezing on my feet and I giggle as we jump and splash. Me and Hilary are smiling at each other, laughing. We're sisters. Adam dives in up to his waist and gets toppled by a giant wave. The water drags him to shore and he jumps up smiling, ready to do it again. After a while Hilary goes back to lay on a towel but me and Adam are in the water, out past where the waves crash. We ride wave after wave to the shore. The ocean scratches up our legs and leaves sand in our suits. We play until we're really, really hungry.

Back at the campsite, supper is ready. Hamburgers and hotdogs and Pringles and Coke. Food has never tasted so good. When Hilary gets up to throw away her plate, Grandma Shea looks up from her supper and says, "You sure are sexy in that little yellow bikini!" Hilary looks at Grandma Shea and shrugs, like she doesn't know what Grandma's even talking about. "What does *Jeffery* say about it?" Grandma Shea teases. Hilary's got her first boyfriend and Grandma Shea met him just before we left.

Hilary shrugs again and goes inside the camper without answering her.

Grandma Shea is always talking about Hilary's body, especially her boobs. I swear she's worse than Dad and his brothers combined.

"Don't you think so, Clyde?" she asks.

Clyde flips another burger, looks up from the grill. "What's that?"

Grandma says, "Hilary. Doesn't she have a sexy little figure? Not an ounce of fat on her and she's so curvy too." She looks toward the camper and shakes her head, "Umm, Ummm!"

"She's a beautiful girl, that's for sure," Clyde says. He looks back down at the grill and presses a burger with the spatula.

I'm glad my breasts aren't big and I hope they never do get as big as my sister's. How gross to always have everyone taking about your boobs like that. Reaching into the Pringles can, I pull out another stack.

After supper we get changed into pajamas and Clyde makes a campfire. We roast marshmallows and then, Hilary walks to the pay phone with a roll of quarters to call Jeffery. Grandma Shea leans over to Olga and asks, "Do you think Hilary is sexually active yet?"

Olga raises her eyebrows and in her thick German accent says, "Isn't she a vittle young for that?"

Grandma Shea smiles. "Well, I don't know. I *like* Jeffery and I think they're cute together. All I know is she might better go on the pill. Better safe than sorry!" she cackles.

Olga shakes her head, and rolls her eyes.

When she gets back, Hilary asks if I want to take a walk with her on the beach. I can't believe she invited me. The sky is pink and purple and it's as huge as the water. We sit on the sand and watch as the big orange ball slowly comes down. When it gets to be a semi-circle, two dolphins leap right in the middle of the sun. Never in my life did I think I'd see a dolphin for real. Then, just to prove it *was* real, the dolphins leap again. We don't say much but my heart feels warm and I'm glad to be here at the ocean, watching dolphins in the sunset with my sister.

Nighttime comes and I feel lonely lying on my bunk; my face just inches from the camper ceiling. Everyone's asleep. I miss Mom and thinking about Hilary having a boyfriend who loves her makes me wish I had someone who loved me too. I wonder if anyone ever will. Closing my eyes, it feels like my body is still floating on the waves. I don't know why, but I get the urge to touch myself *down there* and a tingly thing starts to happen. It's like I'm actually part of the ocean, part of the waves. If I don't stop, it feels like something big might happen. Maybe I'll even die. But it feels good and in a few seconds I start again and soon the waves are crashing right through the middle of me, but instead of dying, everything feels alive! Part of me is so embarrassed for touching myself like that, but part of me feels better; more relaxed, and I drift off to sleep to the rhythm of the sea.

Our last night at Assateague Island, I lay on my bunk, listening to Olga and Grandma Shea talking through the screen in the Prowler window. They are sitting at the picnic table just under my window. Grandma Shea said her husband (Dad's dad) was a mean drunk and used to beat her in front of her kids. She says he beat the kids too. I picture Dad as a little kid, getting beat up by his father. I never knew my real grandfather. No one's ever mentioned him. It never occurred to me Dad even had a dad. Dad can be really mean, but I'm glad he doesn't hit us. We've hardly ever gotten a spanking in our lives. I can't imagine what it would feel like to see your own mom get hit. I know he's a real jerk sometimes, but I feel kind of sorry for Dad.

When we get back from Assateague Island, our house is clean. I've never seen it like this before. Mom looks calm and pretty and well rested. Her long hair is combed nicely and she's baking in the kitchen. She hugs us. She says she missed us. But I can feel it in my bones. She didn't.

***

It isn't fair! While I was away, Libby slept over at Sophie's and tonight, Sophie is staying over at Libby's! She didn't even know Libby until I introduced them. *Thanks a lot.* Now they're getting together without me. It isn't my fault my stupid dad has HBO!

Moping around our crummy house I picture all the fun they're having and it makes me mad. I suffer through *The Love Boat* and *Fantasy Island* with a terrible worry, what if Sophie likes Libby better than me?

The next weekend, it's *me* who stays over at Sophie's. Saturday morning Mrs. Sheinmel is outside working in the garden and I have an idea. "Sophie, I don't think Libby is a very good friend to you," I lie.

"Why not?"

"Well...she talks about you behind your back."

Sophie looks at me, surprised.

Picking up the phone in Sophie's room, I say, "Watch this," and I dial Libby's number. Excitement and meanness runs through me as it starts to ring, and I tell Sophie to run down the hall and pick up the extension in the kitchen.

Libby answers and it's small talk. I hear Sophie's breath on the line. A few minutes into the conversation, I say, "Libby...don't you think Sophie is a little *stuck* up?"

Libby says, "Well, maybe *a little*."

I do a dance inside myself.

"Can you give me an example?" I ask.

I stretch the phone cord out of Sophie's room and into the hallway. Way down in the kitchen, I see Sophie sitting on a bar stool, phone to her ear. I wave at her. She stares back.

Libby says, "I really don't like it when she brags about going to Florida all the time."

"Uh-huh, uh-huh,.....what else?"

"Or when she goes on and on about her grades. I mean, come on, we all know she's smart. Like, she doesn't have to brag about it."

Slowly I say, *"Uh-huh. What else?"*

"She also thinks she's better than us because of all the clothes her Nana buys her. She's really spoiled."

Score!

In the kitchen, Sophie's hand is over the mouthpiece, her eyes big as saucers. Quickly I say, "Well, Libby, I gotta go now. Talk to you later."

"Uh, okay.

"Bye."

"Bye."

Sophie's face is squished up angry and before we can talk about what she heard, she dials Libby's number. This time it's me listening in. Libby says, "Hi Sophie, what are you doing?"

"Well, Janie is here and I just heard every word you said. *Thanks a lot!*"

CLICK!

Sophie and I badmouth Libby until my mom comes to get me in the afternoon and I feel powerful because Sophie is *my* best friend. Still, when I get home, my stomach hurts every time I think about Libby. I don't know how I'll ever face her at school.

Libby doesn't speak to me or Sophie for a whole week. I feel guilty about what I did. I try to ignore her when I see her in school. So what if she hates me? But when she and Sophie start talking again, I talk to her too, since she's not going away. Soon the three of us are doing everything together and I guess it feels okay to be three instead of two. In my heart I know I'm still Sophie's best friend. The one she calls first.

***

After school, I'm watching *Guiding Light* and the phone rings. It's Sophie and she's crying. "He's leaving," she says.

"Who's leaving? What are you talking about?"

"My Dad. They're separating and probably getting divorced."

"Oh Sophie, why would they do that?" I say, running my finger and thumb around the curls in the phone cord.

"They say they can't get along. They say they got married too young. For the wrong reasons. *I'm* the reason they married. Am *I* wrong?"

"Oh Sophie, of course not. I'm sure that's not what they meant. I'm so sorry."

Listening to Sophie's sobs I'm wondering why it can't be *my* parents getting separated. I'd give anything for Dad to go live somewhere else. I've been wishing for it practically my whole life.

"He says when they figure it all out I can come live with him, but we can't tell my Mom yet. He says he'll fight to get me."

"Of course he will. He's the greatest, Sophie."

Sophie's mom has been a real bitch lately. She keeps putting Sophie on weird diets and she's not even fat. Just a tiny bit chubby.

"Yeah," she says and she starts sobbing again.

"Sophie, not to be mean or anything, but whether he lives with you or not, you're lucky to have such a great dad. He really loves you. Believe me, it could be worse. You could have *my* dad."

Sophie laughs and says, "I know," and "Thanks," before hanging up the phone.

***

Sophie's dad moved out over three months ago and so far he hasn't told her mom he wants her to live with him. He says he needs more time. Even though her parents are officially separated, tonight they're together because it's her Bat Mitzvah. She's going from a child to a woman, but Sophie's not *really* a woman yet because she hasn't got her period. Neither have I, and we keep waiting and wondering which one of us will get it first.

Sophie's been going to Hebrew class for a long time but I never knew what she was up to there. Today she stands all dressed up at the podium, looking pretty, and talking in a whole other language! Even though it sounds all phlegmy and gross, it's still cool. I am so proud of her.

All Sophie's relatives are here. Her nana from Florida, her aunts, her uncles, her cousins. After the ceremony, everyone crowds around Sophie at the party in the basement of the synagogue. Sophie keeps coming over to us, and we're laughing and talking, but every few minutes someone grabs her and takes her away. Me and Libby head to the food table and there I see a real live pineapple. Mom always lets me pick the fruit and vegetable for supper and a can of pineapple is my first choice, but I've never seen a *real* one. A whole one, with tall leaves and ridges. Next to it, there is a platter with lots of cut up fruit.

I pick up a piece of pineapple, holding it by its brown jagged rind, and take a bite. It tastes like someone took the canned pineapple and added three times the flavor! It's so good, all sweet and sour on my tongue. When I pull at the rind, shreds of pineapple wedge between my front teeth. I fiddle at them with my tongue, but I can't get them out. Then I try with my fingernail. Sophie's nana comes by and, giving me a dirty look, hands me a napkin. I want to tell her the pineapple is stuck in my teeth. It isn't a matter of just wiping something off. Sophie's nana has dark black hair, lots of jewelry, tons of thick make-up and a Long Island voice like Mrs. Sheinmel, even though she lives in Flah'-rid-ah. She shakes her head at me all nasty and walks back to her table with her plate.

Sophie's dad heads our way. He's looking extra handsome in his suit and tie and he gives me and Libby big hugs. "Are you girls having a good time?" he asks.

He has a way of looking right at you when he talks. Like he's really listening.

Me and Libby nod our heads and giggle and say, "Yes."

"Are you getting enough to eat?" He gestures toward the buffet, raises his eyebrows. "Did you get some cake?"

"Yes, Mr. Sheinmel, and this pineapple is really good," I tell him.

"Are you girls excited to start junior high soon?"

"Yes," we chime. He smiles at us and then waves at someone across the room, and he's off to greet them. My eyes follow him. Mr. Sheinmel seems so happy today. He zips from person to person, smiling, chatting, adjusting his tie. Out of the corner of my eye I see him give Sophie the biggest hug. He kisses the top of her head and she beams. I hope Sophie gets to live with him. I really do.

Chapter Fifteen

Starting junior high is scary. There will be a whole bunch of new kids and what if I don't fit in? After I begged for weeks, Mom finally caved in and gave me fifty bucks to shop for clothes. She dropped me and Hilary off at the mall and we're heading straight to The Shed House to get me some Levi's. Hilary's going to help me pick out the perfect pair. The Shed House has boots, clogs, jeans and belts. The floor is shiny wood the color of caramel and there's an upstairs loft with fitting rooms.

"What size jeans are you?" Hilary asks, running her fingers over the high heel on a pair of leather clogs.

"I don't know," I shrug.

She eyes me up and down and searches through some stacks on the shelves. Hilary's dark hair falls at her shoulders and she's feathered it back with a curling iron, like Farrah Fawcett. She's got the perfect Farrah figure too and her boobs seem to get bigger every day. Not that *I'm* looking. It's just kind of hard not to notice when Dad, all my uncles, and Gramma Shea won't stop mentioning it. If I were Hilary I'd tell them to shut up, I mean, how gross is it to have your Dad and your uncles talking about your boobs? But she just ignores them. There's a show on TV called *One Day At a Time* and everyone says Hilary looks like the younger sister on the show. The truth is, my sister is way prettier than Valerie Bertinelli. She has huge, brown, wide set eyes with long lashes, high cheekbones, a cute little nose, and her jaw comes together at her chin to form the perfect bottom of a heart. She grabs a pair of jeans off a shelf and turns my way.

"I think maybe these will fit," she says, holding them out to me.

"Okay," I say, taking them in my hands and heading up the wooden stairs to the loft. Red barn-like doors mark the entrance to each dressing room.

Stepping into the fitting room, I glance at the tag on the back of the jeans. It reads, W28. Does that mean a 28 inch waist? The ladies in Dad's magazines always have waists of 24 inches or less. My head hangs down as I pull them on. I'm *such* a cow. This morning I was over 100 pounds.

There's a knock on the door and Hilary says, "Come out. I want to see how they look."

Peeking my head out, I see she's got a few more things for me to try on, but she was right. The 28's fit me. Stepping out of the fitting room, I say, "I can't believe I'm a 28. I'm so fat."

"No you're not," she says, taking a step back to check me out.

"You look great. I don't think *I* could even fit into those," she says.

"Really?" I say, letting out a big sigh. Soon we're at the cash register and I'm shocked that my new jeans cost over thirty bucks.

"They're worth it," Hilary nods knowingly as she takes my money out of her purse and pays the guy behind the counter.

Shopping with Hilary is weird. I'm not used to her being so nice and it seems like she actually might like me. We step out of the store and into the mall and we don't get too far before seeing a group of boys she knows from high school. Two of them are really cute.

They veer right over in our direction and each one gives Hilary a hug. "This is my sister," she tells them, nodding in my direction.

"Aw… a *Little Shea*. How cute! She looks just like you," they tease.

Hilary ignores their remarks and then ignores *me* completely. They're all joking around, and she is *totally* flirting with them and I'm left standing there feeling stupid. Then the boys make a big production of each hugging Hilary again before going on their way. When they're no longer in sight she turns to me, smiles and says, "Let's go get some ice cream."

We order cones at Friendly's and walk around the mall eating them, talking and laughing. Then, she helps me pick out a shirt at Barbara Moss. My new top is red and white striped with a thin red ribbon that you tie in a bow at the neck, just like the girls in the Love's Baby Soft commercials. I don't have enough, so Hilary gives me two dollars and says I don't even have to pay her back. That's all the money I've got, so that's it for school clothes.

It's exciting being here at the mall with all the cute guys checking out my sister as we pass by. She puts her nose in the air and pretends not to notice. We walk around for another hour, and then call home from a pay phone. Outside, we sit on a little brick wall by the theater entrance and wait for Mom to pick us up. Only four more days 'til school. I'll finally, officially, be in junior high.

***

At 5AM the first day of school I shoot up out of bed and hit the button on my alarm clock. The bus comes at 7:00AM and Hilary's already called the bathroom for 6 o'clock. I've never had to wake up this early before but I'm *not* going to junior high without a shower. I don't want people thinking I'm a scum. Whatever it takes, I will hide the fact we have no money and live in a dump.

Downstairs, I open the door to the back porch and a gust of cold air blasts up my nightgown. My whole body shudders and for a moment I stand with my back to the door, clutching the cold metal wrench in my hand tight to my chest. Running my hand along the wall I feel the click of the switch, but no light comes on. It's broken like everything else in this house. In the moonlight, my heart pounds and the rotting wooden steps creak beneath me as I start down toward the cellar.

The shower knob is also broken. It's been that way for months, and you have to turn on the hot water from the basement. I never had to do it in the dark before. At the bottom of the back porch steps, just outside the cellar door, I hold my breath, listening for Reagan who is sure to grab me, as soon as I step one foot into the cellar. After a few seconds, I don't hear anything, so I unhook the black metal latch and push the wooden door forward. Stepping inside I stand on my tiptoes, terrified, waving my hand back and forth in the pitch black. Finally, feeling the string, I grab it and give it yank. The basement lights up. Squinting, I quickly scan the room. No one is there. I let out my breath, and then suck in the dank air.

Shivering, and hoisting myself up on a concrete ridge about a foot off the floor on the basement wall, I grab onto a copper pipe under the ceiling with my left hand. My left foot balances on the ledge, and my right leg hangs in mid-air. Reaching across with my right hand, I use the wrench to turn the hot water on. Shutting the wooden door behind me on the way out, I fly up the stairs and through the back porch, just in case Reagan truly is hiding under the steps and missed me on the way down.

Back in the bathroom, I step into the shower and feel my body calming down. There's iron in our water and the shower stall is covered in orange streaks. Once or twice a year, Mom uses Iron Out to get it clean but the whole thing is orange again in a week or two. The shower curtain is clear plastic and that doesn't seem to pick up the rust.

Hot water falls on my back and the bathroom gets steamy. Dad comes in, and I cower in the corner of the shower. With my back to him, I'm hoping he can't see too much. He takes his time using the toilet and when he flushes, the scalding water nips at the back of my legs. Seems like every time I'm in the shower lately he suddenly has to be in here for something. The bathroom has two entrances, one from the kitchen and one from his bedroom. The bedroom entrance only has a knob from his side. We're not allowed to lock either door because, "It's the only bathroom, it's his *house,* and he can come in any time he *damn well pleases.*"

After Dad finally gets out of the bathroom, I finish my shower and get dressed. I'm wearing my new Levi's and the red and white pinstripe shirt I bought at the mall with Hilary. Buttoning it to the top, I tie the thin red ribbon around the neck in a bow. Next I put on my make-up. A little foundation, a little blue eye shadow, some mascara, and my bubblegum Bonnie Bell Lip Smacker. I dry my hair and try to feather it, but being pin straight, it immediately falls flat. I spray it anyway.

The high school and junior high are just a five-minute drive from our house but it takes almost an hour to get there on the school bus. Hilary *never* rides the bus. Her high school friends pick her up and of course she would never ask them to give me a ride too.

Our school district is called Andover-Baldwin and since I live in Centerville, I ride the bus with the Andover kids. Andover kids are mostly poor and live in the country. Baldwin kids are mostly rich and live in nice neighborhoods with rows of cute houses. Most Baldwin kids can walk to school in just ten minutes, and I bet not one of them has to use a wrench to turn on their shower before the crack of dawn. Centerville kids are just as poor as the Andover kids, but we don't live in either place. Centerville is just somewhere you pass through on your way to somewhere else. It's a bunch of crappy houses along the side of the highway, floating between Andover and Baldwin. In seventh grade, they throw all the Andover kids and all the Baldwin kids together into one big junior high school.

The bus comes to a loud hissing stop in front of our house. Stepping up onto it, I see a group of teenage boys in the back. They're high school boys; Andover boys. I know who they are, but don't know them well. One kid to a seat, they take up the last three rows.

Looking around, I take a seat toward the middle of the bus and as soon as I sit down they start giving me trouble.

"Aww," one says. "A *little* Shea. She looks just like her sister. Isn't she cute?"

"Aww...little Shea. Come sit with us!" another one says.

Pretending I don't hear them, I shift in my seat, rearranging my backpack.

"Awww......little Shea is shy! What's a matter little Shea? You *scared* of us?" they say, laughing.

Whipping around in my seat I look the loudest one in the eye.

"Fuck off!" I say, glaring at him.

His eyes go big as he jerks back in his seat before busting out laughing. The other boys crack up too and soon they're holding their bellies from laughing so hard, slapping each other on the back. They look at me like I'm just the cutest thing they've ever seen.

"Little Shea is a *brute*!" one says.

"Grrr. She feisty!" says another.

After that they nickname me "Brute," but mostly leave me alone to listen in on their conversations.

Riding the bus it's all, "No shit muther-fucker," and... "For real, man," and lots of... "You're muther-fuckin' crazy," and rowdy laughter.

Next to get on the bus are my friend Jenna and the twins Dean and Danny who live a couple of houses down from her. Rumor has it, the twins moved to our school district because Dean shot and killed a kid at his old school. Dean has white blond hair and he's wiry with crystal blue eyes. As the twins walk past, I sneak peaks of Dean out the corner of my eye. I've never seen an actual killer before. Dean's brother Danny looks exactly like him, same piercing blue eyes, but apparently, for variety's sake, God painted Danny's hair jet black.

113

Jenna squeezes past me in my seat to sit by the window because she's deaf in one ear and won't be able to hear me if she sits on the wrong side. The twins join the others in the back.

A boy named Craig gets on next. He's skinny with glasses, his voice is high pitched, and he doesn't really fit in with these tough guys but he's funny, so they keep him around. We stop at Kevin Wrangle's house next. He's blond with a round face and a thick body that lingers somewhere between chubby and muscular. I guess you'd call him husky. He laughs along with the others but seems kind of sad too.

John Crocket is the last to get on the bus and when he steps on, the boys in back all shout, "Hey Motherfucker!"

John Crocket is the only John on the bus, but for some reason everyone calls him by his full name, John Crocket. He has a puppy dog face with droopy eyes and a big droopy personality to match. He wears a flannel shirt and shit-kicker boots just like the rest of them, and he looks too old to be in high school.

Someone says, "Yo Motherfucker, did you see that fuckin' car?"

Kevin says, "You talkin' bout that fuckin' red one for sale in front of the sandwich shop?"

Dean says, "Yeah, man I'd give my left nut for a car like that!"

John Crocket says, "Sheeee-it, that car ain't nothin."

"And what do you know about cars, Shit-for-Brains?" Dean says, reaching forward to swat John Crocket on the back of the head.

John Crocket dodges the blow and says, "Well, I know when I get *my car* it ain't gonna be no candy-ass muther-fuckin red like that. Sheee-it. It's almost pink."

Dean says, "Like *you'll* be getting a car anytime soon." He shakes his head and adds his own, "Sheee-it."

John Crocket says, "I will be, and when I do, I won't be riding this mutherfuckin' bus no more, neither, and I sure as shit won't be giving *you* a ride."

Craig changes the subject by breaking into song and soon the whole back of the bus, to the tune of *She'll Be Coming Round the Mountain*, sings:

"There's a skeeter on my Peter and it hurts. (Whack it off)!

There's a skeeter on my Peter and it hurts. (Whack it off)!

There's a skeeter on my peter, there's a skeeter on my peter, there's a skeeter on my Peter and it hurts...(Whack it off)!"

And off we go on our mutherfuckin' way to school.

Stepping into Jr. High, there are so many unfamiliar faces. So many new boys. I'm feeling great, wearing the clothes Hilary helped pick out. No one from Baldwin has to know I live in a scummy house. They don't know my father's a drunk.

Jessica Samuelson sits to my left in history class. She has long straight blonde hair, down to her waist and just by the way she holds herself, head high, I can tell she's one of the popular girls in Baldwin. She smiles at me and I smile back. Halfway through class she passes me a note that reads:

I'm having a party this Friday. Do you want to come?

My stomach flips with excitement, but I try to act cool as I write back.

Sounds good, I'll ask my mom.

The bell rings and it's time for lunch. I'm sitting at a table, chatting with Jessica and a group of Baldwin girls. One of them is Lindsay and she says her older brother knows my sister. We're laughing and I'm munching on my Little Debbie nutty bars. You get to eat whatever you want for lunch in Jr. High. No lunch ladies inspect your tray like in elementary school.

A bunch of rowdy Baldwin boys are sitting behind us. They're dressed in Levi's, oxford shirts and wear Docksides on their feet. They are goofing off, trying to get our attention. Then, John Mahoney, one of the cutest ones, yells, "28! Oh My God! *Hers* are bigger than mine! He's talking about my jeans, I *know* he is. My stomach sinks and my face gets hot.

He's right. Boys are supposed to be bigger than girls. I can't believe my jeans are bigger than his. I'm such a big fat whale. Pretending I don't hear him, I nibble on my nutty bar, but it no longer tastes good. I bet I'm the fattest one at this whole table. Trying to change the subject, I ask who's going to Jessica's party. Everyone at our table is. Sophie and Libby are not invited, and they are going to be so jealous!

Jenna, my friend on the school bus, is a cheerleader, so she's popular. She was invited to Jessica's party too. On Friday Libby is spending the night at Sophie's, and for once, I couldn't care less.

Jenna's dad gives us a ride to the party and when we get there, we're early. Jessica and her sister Monica, who is a year older than us, are still getting ready. Both could totally be Love's Baby Soft models. Jessica with her long blonde hair. Her sister with reddish hair down to her shoulders. Both have perfect, pale complexions with no pimples. They have the sweetest faces, with big dark

116

brown eyes. Me and Jenna hang out in their bedroom while they put on make-up. We listen to Queen's "Another One Bites the Dust" and all four of us sing at the top of our lungs. The music has a strange new energy that shoots around the room in zigzags, tapping me on the shoulder and making my heart thump.

And another one gone, and another one gone, another one bites the dust.

It's fun hanging out here, just us girls. Jenna uses a curling iron on my hair and next it's the B52's *"Rock Lobster!"* We dance around the room going *down, down, down, down*! We apply our Bonnie Bell Lip Smackers to make our mouths extra shiny before heading downstairs to wait for the other kids.

The party is in the basement and Jessica and Monica's parents promise they won't come down. Soon, it gets crowded and beer is snuck in through the back door. A popular girl from Baldwin who I don't know yet, puts a can to her mouth, and tilts her head toward the ceiling. She guzzles the whole beer in one shot. I'm offered a can, but feeling scared I don't take it.

I'm an outsider here. I don't know anyone besides Jenna, and she's off flirting with some boys. I don't know how to flirt and act all goofy like these girls. Not one boy talks to me all night, and I wonder what is wrong with me. Why does everyone else know how to be cool?

All the boys have left by 12:30 and the girls finally fall asleep by 2:00AM, but I'm wide-awake. Laying there in my sleeping bag, I stare at the tiles on the ceiling. Led Zeppelin's *Stairway to Heaven* plays softly on the radio and I'm wondering why no boys talked to me, and if anyone will ever think I'm special. Even though I was lucky enough to be invited to the party, my chest hurts from the weight of being so lonely. Later, I lie and tell Libby and Sophie what an awesome time I had.

Libby and Sophie are jealous again because today I'm going over to another Baldwin girl's house after school. Becky Davis is a skinny tomboy who plays soccer, volleyball, and softball. She's really popular and so is her brother who's a year older than us. He's a champion hockey player and swimmer. We've raided her cupboards for snacks and scored big when she pulled out a whole package of Oreos her mom had hidden behind the cereal boxes.

"When you play sports," she says, leaning against the kitchen counter, pulling the plastic package apart, "you can eat whatever you want." She takes a stack of ten cookies.

"I *guess* so," I laugh as I take a stack, half the size of hers.

She twists an Oreo open and licks its creamy center. "I eat a lot," she says, "but if I ever got fat I would stop myself."

She eyes me up and down as I take my first bite.

My face turns red. Is she saying she'd never want to be as fat as *me?* I look away and try to pretend what she said didn't affect me. "I weigh 87,"she says.

With her mouth full she asks, "How much do *you* weigh?"

"About one hundred pounds," I say softly.

"And how tall are you?"

"I don't know, five foot…. I think?"

"Hmmm. I'm a lot taller than you," she shrugs as she twists another Oreo apart.

Suddenly, my stomach feels awful, like I might get the runs. Did she invite me over just to insult me? Or is she just that stupid, with no manners at all? I ask her where the bathroom is.

Inside, I stand sideways in the full-length mirror, sucking in my gut. Stepping closer to the mirror, I lift up my bangs with my hand and stare at the pimples on my forehead. Mom and Dad say there isn't a thing that can be done about this acne that's started on my face. Dad even said it was my fault; that I probably don't wash well enough. I *do* wash my face though. I stand in a scalding shower every day and scrub my oily skin 'til it's raw. It just doesn't help.

Sitting on the toilet, I notice a brownish smudge on my underwear.

Is it?

Oh my God. I think it is.

Opening the bathroom door a crack, I say, "Becky...I think I got my period, have you got anything I can use?" I'm so glad her brother isn't here.

She waltzes over to the door and peeks through the crack. "You got your period?" She asks.

"Yeah."

"Is it your first time?"

"No," I lie.

"Oh. I haven't got mine yet. Let me get you something from my mom's bathroom."

She comes back downstairs and hands me a pad and a tampon through the crack in the door. Taking the tampon out of its cardboard tube I hold it in the air. It dangles in front of my face.

No way.

After sticking the adhesive pad to my underpants, I wash my hands, come out of the bathroom and ask to call my mom.

"Mom," I whisper, cupping my hand over the receiver so Becky can't hear. "I think I got my period."

"Really?" she says.

"Am I allowed to use tampons?" I ask.

"Of course you're *allowed,*" she laughs. But I don't think it's funny. I never had my period before and I don't know what the rules are. I feel greasy and fat and I just want to go home.

Ever since me and Sophie read Judy Blume's *Are you There God? It's Me Margaret,* we've been waiting for our periods, but I thought it would be a bigger deal. Instead, it feels empty and sad and I'm stuck here with Becky who practically calls me fat to my face. I wish I were at Sophie's house.

"Mom?" I whisper into the phone.

"What?"

"Promise you won't tell Dad," I say, before hanging up. The thought of him knowing personal stuff about me feels creepy.

Later that night, when I get home from Becky's there's a curtain hanging at the bottom of the stairs leading up to my room from the kitchen. It's not really a curtain, but an old fuzzy pale green blanket, stapled to the top of the doorframe. We've never had any sort of door at the bottom of the stairs, but I guess it's a good idea, since anyone standing in the kitchen can see straight up to my room. Looking in the fridge for something to eat I glance back over my shoulder and ask Mom, "What's with the blanket?"

"Your father put it up. It's to keep all the heat from going upstairs this winter. It's already starting to get cold," she says, as she flips pork chops in a skillet on the stove. I hate pork chops.

Going to the cupboard, I take out a bag of chips.

"Now don't be filling up on junk," she snaps. "You can see I'm making supper."

"Fine," I crumple the chip bag shut, slam it back in the cupboard, and head upstairs.

As I push through the blanket I notice there is a little hole in it, about eye level if you're standing on the second step. The hole has brown edges, burnt in a perfect circle. Dad probably did it, smoking in bed when he was drunk. It's a wonder we all haven't been killed in a house fire. Walking upstairs I'm feeling pissed at Mom, but glad about the blanket/curtain. At least it gives me a little privacy, especially now that I'm growing up; becoming a woman, getting my period and everything.

Chapter Sixteen

Sophie and I have so much to talk about, what with me getting my period and her boy/girl birthday party coming up. It's going to be awesome. We only gave invites to the cutest guys; most of them from Baldwin.

The evening of her party, the girls have already arrived, and we take turns peeking out the windows, watching for the boys. *I Saw Her Standing There*, by the Beatles is playing on the stereo as we watch ourselves dance in the sliding glass doors of Sophie's rec room.

Sophie's mom comes downstairs in a flowy hippy skirt and says, "Pick up the phone, Soph."

Sophie grabs the phone off the wall. Mrs. Sheinmel turns and walks back up the steps.

"Hi Dad."

Sophie has one ear to the phone and is plugging the other ear with her finger.

Since he doesn't live here anymore, Sophie's dad doesn't get to come to her birthday party. Her mom has gone totally hippie flower child, and instead of it making her peaceful she's been extra mean lately. Just last week, I saw her hit Sophie for eating the last of the Haagen daz ice cream. Sophie dropped to the ground in their kitchen, and curled herself into a ball and her mom just kept wailing on her, slapping her back, screaming, "That wasn't for you!" It's like she's gone crazy or something.

Sophie's supposed to be on a diet, even though she's only just a little bit chubby.

"Yeah, Dad," Sophie says into the phone.

"Yeah," Sophie rolls her eyes.

"Thanks Dad."

"Sophie! They're here!" we squeal.

Jim Reynolds, John Mahoney, Mike Stinnet, Dave Tomsey, and Dave Smith all pile out of Mrs. Mahoney's white station wagon. The boys wear Izod shirts and baggy Levi's and they head toward the door like a pack of tumbling puppies. My stomach flips.

Sophie stretches the cord across the room to look out the window. "*Dad*, I have to *go!* Everyone is starting to get here!"

"Okay."

"*Okaaaaaay*. I love you too."

"Daaaaaaa-ud," she rolls her eyes again.

"Bye."

Even though her mom is dating a guy named Paul who looks like Grisly Adams, Sophie *still* hopes her parents will get back together. I know it's what she wishes for when she blows out her candles.

After cake, Mrs. Sheinmel promises to stay upstairs. We all go downstairs and it's Sophie's idea to play spin the bottle.

When John Mahoney takes his turn, the bottle lands on me. We walk around the corner, for privacy, and he kisses me with full, warm, lips. Wet, but not *too* wet. Our kiss is very slow, and gentle and our faces turn just right so it all works. It isn't gross at all. As we kiss, he sticks his hands in the tops of my back pockets. I hope he isn't thinking about how fat I am with my 28 inch waist. My whole body tingles, and when we stop he rests his forehead next to mine and smiles. His smile is slightly crooked and his teeth are perfect.

Last year, on the bus, I kissed Darrin Smallwood and it was awful, but *this* is different. With his hands still in my pockets I look into John Mahoney's big blue eyes and decide *this* is my first *real* kiss.

After our long kiss, John Mahoney gives me a quick peck on the lips to kind of finish things off and then we make our way back to the group. The bottle doesn't land on me again, and I'm glad. The rest of the time I just sit there in the circle, trying to look cool, but inside I'm giddy about kissing John Mahoney. Mom picks me up at the party, and in the car I just blurt it out.

"Mom, I kissed John Mahoney."

As she drives, Mom looks at me funny out of the corner of her eye, but she doesn't say much. I don't know what I expected, but her reaction is confusing. I'm 12 now and everyone is kissing boys, aren't they? I guess I wanted her to be happy for me.

The next morning, I'm still asleep when Mom touches my shoulder. My stomach lurches before my eyes even open. Something is very wrong. I don't know what, but it's thick in the air; something bad.

"A terrible thing happened," Mom says. She sits on my bed and a shiver runs through my body. The bed creaks as she shifts over closer to me and puts her hand on my shoulder.

"What?" I say, up on one arm. My heart is beating fast.

She pauses forever and now I sit up under my covers. My eyes dart to my alarm clock. It's only 7AM, and it's not a school day. Why is she waking me up?

"*Mom,* what?"

Mom starts sobbing and she just won't tell me what's going on. She's pissing me off and finally, she clears her throat, and whispers, "Sophie's dad was…," her voice chokes and then comes out in a faint gasp, "*killed*…in a car accident last night."

"What?" I hop out of bed. *"What?"* I say pacing across the room in my pajamas.

Mom falls onto me, pushing me down on the bed. She's hugging me hard and slobbering onto my neck. My arms stay at my sides. I'm confused and thinking, *"Get off me! You're smothering me!"*

Mom is *wrong*. She's such an idiot. Sophie's dad wasn't *killed*. That's crazy. She just talked to him on the phone, right before the party. Shrugging Mom off me, I sit on my bed; put my face in my hands. Moving my hands to my hair, I dig my fingernails into my scalp and try to think.

In the early afternoon, Libby's mom drops her off at my house and we walk the long mile up the highway and turn onto Sophie's road. We both feel we *must* go to her, but with each step I want to turn around and run back home.

"I'm scared," I say.

"Me too," Libby says.

Sophie knew we were coming and she stands at the top of her driveway, as we make our way toward her. Her weight is shifted onto her right leg and her elbows are crossed with one hand to her chin. When we get to her, it's the first time Sophie and I have ever felt like strangers. My hug is more like a stiff pat and I drop my arms to my sides and look at the ground.

"I'm so sorry," I say.

Libby says, "I'm sorry," too.

When I look up, Sophie meets my eyes and says,

"I blew him off on the phone. Everyone was just getting there and I didn't even talk to him. The last chance I'll ever have to talk to my dad and I blew him off."

Her face has no expression. Her eyes are red rims but she isn't crying. She's a stone.

Folding my arms across my chest, I don't know what to say. I don't know what to do.

"I woke up right when he died," she says. "I sat up in bed choking. I thought it was my retainer."

That gives me the creeps. She looks at me and I look at the ground. After a long silence, Sophie says, "You know, when my cat got hit by a car, I found her out in the road, dead. Her tongue was sticking out. I keep picturing my dad lying on the road like that." Her voice cracks and she starts wringing her hands. She bites her lip.

I've never seen someone in so much pain. Leaning forward, I try to pat Sophie's shoulder, but it feels like a stupid thing to do, and I draw back my hand. Patting her shoulder isn't going to help. Mom told me I should come see her but she didn't tell me what to say.

I don't know what to say!

I don't know what to do.

Sophie is my best friend in the whole world but I just want to run away from her right now. Run away from all this pain.

Libby shifts her weight from one foot to another.

I stand there squirming inside.

Then Sophie says abruptly, "Thank you for coming."

I try to hug her but she pulls away quick and scoots back down her driveway. She goes inside and the screen door slams shut behind her. For a minute we stand there watching the door. I picture her handsome dad, in his crisp white dress shirt and tie, on the road with his tongue hanging out, and I shudder.

Turning to start down the hill I feel like I can't breathe. I want to run fast, away from all of this hurt, but Libby is here and so we walk slow and silent, together. Not a thing we can do to help our friend.

At home, I try to be nicer to Dad, because after all, he could be dead at any moment. Joking around with him in the living room one Sunday afternoon, we start to horse around and when I tickle him on his side, he says, "Knock it off."

I tickle him again and he grabs my breast.

"Dad, cut it out. That's not funny," I say, crossing my arms over my chest.

"I told you not to tickle me. That's what you get," he says.

Stomping upstairs to my room I ask God the question for the first time, *Why couldn't it have been my dad instead of hers?*

***

We've hardly seen each other the last couple of months and when we do, we avoid talking about her dad. I think about him all the time though. Looking at Sophie, it's like she has a big red S on her forehead for "sadness" and she's labeled for life. I feel so helpless and just wish I could make her happy again. I do nothing because I don't know what to do. It's the weekend, but I haven't spent the night at Sophie's since before her birthday.

It's been snowing and Adam and I have been up on the hill, behind our house. There is a spot in the woods that has been cleared and it makes the perfect sledding trail. We're having a contest to see how far we can snow surf. The snow is icy and packed down hard. Standing sideways on my plastic sled, I can make it almost halfway down the hill. Adam can make it three quarters. It's freezing out but we snow surf until I can't feel my toes. When we come in I take an extra long, extra hot, shower.

In my room, at the top of the stairs, I unwrap my towel, bend over and start drying off my hair. With my head hanging upside down, I see something out the corner of my eye. There is a shadow on the curtain at the bottom of the steps. My stomach flips. My body knows before my brain catches on and a silent scream rips through me. It's Dad.

Standing straight up I wrap the towel back around my naked body. Oh my God! He's spying on me. Dad just saw me naked. I stand there frozen while my brain and my body have a quick chat. *"Don't let on you know,"* they decide.

But I've gotta do something. Looking around the room I gather up every piece of dirty laundry I can find. Next, I take the comforter off of my bed. I heave the whole pile down the stairs and hear Dad tumble down the last two steps. He thinks it was an accident. He thinks I was just throwing my laundry downstairs to take it to the basement. He doesn't know I saw him.

Taking clean clothes from my dresser, I shimmy in between my bed and the wall to get dressed. The rest of the afternoon I wait in my room for Mom to wake up. She worked last night and she's sleeping in Adam's room so she has to pass right through mine to get downstairs. The second Adam's door opens I pounce.

"*Mom*, he's spying on me! He's *spying* on me through the hole in the blanket at the bottom of the stairs. The cigarette burn hole."

She rubs her eyes. "Huh?"

"Dad was *watching me* after I got out of the shower," I plead.

She says nothing. She shakes her head and still looks half asleep.

"Mom, aren't you going to do anything?"

She glares at me and snaps, "*What* do you want me to do?"

"Tell him to *stop* it!" I hiss right back at her.

She shrugs and lets out another big sigh. "I guess *you* just need to start being more careful about where you get dressed."

She pivots and heads down the stairs. I stand there stunned as the wooden steps squeak beneath her feet.

***

Sophie's mom is almost as big of a jerk as my mom. She left Sophie and me home all day while she went for a hike with her hippie boyfriend to "celebrate the Spring Equinox." She's always saying weird shit like that now that she's with Paul. We're glad to be home without them.

It's only been a few months since her dad died, but Paul the hippie has already moved in and Sophie hates him. In her bedroom one night, Sophie heard her mother screaming and panting, "Oh God! Oh Paul!"

She got up and went to her mom's bedroom door.

"Oh God!" she heard again.

Sophie turned to go back to her own room. She thought she'd put a pillow over her head to drown out the sound, but then, "No one has EVER made me feel this way before!" she heard her mother cry.

That did it.

Sophie lunged at the door and pounded with her fists.

"I'm sorry if my father wasn't good enough for you, you fucking slut! I hate you! I hate you both!" she screamed.

As Sophie tells me this I can just picture it and I'm proud of her for standing up for her dad.

It's been a warm week and Sophie's mom says we can sleep outside tonight. Probably so her and Paul can fuck as loud as they want to inside. She had Paul set up the tent for us earlier today and I brought my sleeping bag.

We're lying on the floor in her living room, listening to The Doors. Me and Sophie think Jim Morrison was really cute. We've passed around the book *No One Here Gets Out Alive* all about Jim Morrison, and we've memorized every Doors song by heart.

Sophie stayed over at Libby's last weekend and Libby just couldn't wait to tell me they tried one of her brother's cigarettes together. I don't really *want* to try cigarettes, but still, I feel left out.

The floor vibrates under my back, *"C'mon Baby Light My Fire,"* and I ask, "Why didn't you ever try cigarettes with me?"

Sophie sits up and grins. "I can do better than that," she says.

"Huh?"

She looks me in the eye and says, "Pot."

"Huh?"

Sophie leads me to a secret door in the back of her mom's closet. She takes out a big popcorn bowl and snaps off the lid. It's full of dark green sticks and twiggy looking stuff. She takes a measuring cup that was on top of the popcorn bowl and fills up a plastic sandwich bag with the green stuff. She puts the bowl back and we take the plastic baggy into her room, along with a little book that looks like matches.

We lock her door and Sophie takes the booklet but it isn't matches, it's tissue paper. She tears out a piece and lays it on her dresser and puts a few pinches of the pot on it. Then, she rolls it with her thumbs and forefingers into a tiny little cigarette.

How does she know how to do this?

"We'll smoke it tonight in the tent," she says.

She looks up at my confused face and says, "They call this a joint." Sophie's mom must be smoking pot. And she must be doing it right in front of Sophie! I can't believe it.

It's dark now and Sophie's mom comes out to say goodnight. After she zips us into the tent, we wait a while and then Sophie takes the hand-made cigarette out of her sleeping bag.

She lights a match and touches it to the tip of the joint, then sucks hard on it and holds her breath. She passes it to me and says, "Hold it in as long as you can," through her clenched teeth.

I suck in the joint and start coughing all over the place. I can't stop. My eyes are watering and I feel like I'm gonna die.

"I need water," I croak.

131

Sophie takes another puff of the joint and hands me the thermos we brought out with us. Unscrewing the cap, I take a huge gulp. She passes the joint back and unconfidently I take another suck. This time I hold it in like Sophie. One more suck and it's the weirdest thing. I forget how to say my "s's". When I was little, I used to have a lisp, but Dad screamed at me and made me "talk right." Now, it's like the lisp has been in here, just waiting all this time.

"Thophie. My mouth ithin't working right. I can't thay my "eth'es,"

Thophie!"

I giggle and every time I try to stop, I call out "Thophie!" and end up screeching with laughter again.

Sophie says, "Shut up. You're going to get us in trouble. Knock it off!"

Trying to be good, I chuckle quietly in my sleeping bag. After a while I settle down and start to relax, but then....I hear something!

"Thophie! Oh my God ith's a monthster. Thomthing is out there! Thophie! Ith's going to get uth.Ahhhh!!!!!!"

Sophie reaches her arm from behind me and clamps her hand over my mouth.

"I don't hear anything," she says. "Knock it off and just go to sleep."

We lay there, like that. Her hand over my mouth, my eyes wide with fear. Finally I start to fall asleep. As she releases her grip, she whispers, "Good night."

"Night Thophie," I say and I'm taken over by another round of giggles.

Chapter Seventeen

Out at recess, Libby is trying to act like she doesn't care me and Sophie tried pot, but it's so obvious she's jealous. She's hardly said a word. We're standing on the edge of the basketball court watching some boys shoot hoops. There is nothing else to do during recess. The playground behind the Jr. High is just a big parking lot with a basketball hoop on one end.

One minute I'm giggling with Sophie and Libby, the next, a Baldwin boy is swaggering toward me. He wears a Neil Young concert shirt, and his blonde hair is short and feathered in the front, and longer in the back, with curls at his neck. He stops in front of me, puts his hands in his jeans pockets and smiles. "Are you a Shea?" He asks.

His teeth are big and perfect and white.

"Yeah," I say, wondering how he would know that.

"My brother knows your sister," he says. His dark eyes contrast against his blonde hair, and his long dark lashes remind me of Bambi.

"Oh really?" I say, shrugging. "Poor guy."

He laughs.

Sophie and Libby watch us and start whispering. He smiles, takes me by the elbow and leads me away from them.

We walk along the side of the school building and when we stop he moves in toward me and I back up against the bricks. He puts his hand on the wall behind my head. He's close. Too close. My stomach flips.

"Will you go out with me?" he asks, and a million thoughts go through my mind all at once. I like the idea of a boyfriend, but I'm not sure I want it to be him. In our school there are jocks and there are dirt-bags. He has kind of a dirt-bag feel to him and I think preppy boys like John Mahoney are cuter. Still, here he is looking at me and what am I supposed to say? I can't hurt his feelings, can I? If there's a way to say no, I have no clue how to do it. Plus he is very cute, so I smile a little and bow my head and whisper, "Okay," despite the little voice inside me saying "No."

Arm in arm we walk further away from my friends. Glancing over my shoulder I catch Sophie's eye. She tips her head to the side, smiles at me and watches us walk away.

Even though we're in the same grade, Eric is a year and a half older than me. He got held back a grade when he was little and I started kindergarten early, at four. It's not that he isn't smart. He is.

After just a week of being boyfriend and girlfriend, Eric is calling his mom from the payphone asking if I can come over after school. Next thing I know we're walking into Eric's house and when we see his mom in the kitchen he says, "Mom, this is my babe."

His mom laughs like this is just adorable, but I think it's the stupidest thing I ever heard. *My babe?* I don't say anything though. I never had a boyfriend before and I don't know what the rules are. I don't want to make him mad.

Soon, I can't see my friends without Eric tagging along. He pouts if I don't invite him. Shelly is one of my new Baldwin friends and she happens to be Eric's neighbor. We had plans for her to come over today after school. I'd invited her before I was even going out with Eric but once he found out she was coming over, he invited himself along. Shelly's mom drops them off and when they get inside, I can't help but notice Shelly look around warily at my house. I introduce them to Mom, and wince as Shelly looks at the electrical cords and beams hanging down and the exposed insulation on the walls in the kitchen. The filthy floors seem way more noticeable with her here. But Eric doesn't seem to notice these things. I guess boys don't care. Quickly, I lead them both upstairs to my room. At least up there we have real walls and it looks mostly normal.

So far, me and Eric have only kissed. We're sitting on my bed, and Shelly is sitting in the chair, when he pulls the covers up over our heads and starts trying to make out with me. I feel stupid. I mean, Shelly is *right there*, but what am I supposed to do? I pull the covers back down and see Shelly has wandered into Hilary's nook and is looking at all the pictures on her bulletin board. Eric pulls the covers back over our heads and starts unhooking my bra. He gets my shirt hiked up and his hands are all over my breasts and it does feel kind of good but it's embarrassing too because of Shelly and also because no boy has ever seen my naked boobs before. Certainly no one's ever touched them. Plus, Mom is right there in the kitchen, beyond the blanket at the bottom of the stairs.

Next thing I know, Eric is hiking down my pants. My body stiffens. I don't know what to do, but I don't want this. His head is down by my hips and he's got my pants almost down. Reaching to pull them back up he grabs my wrists and then he's got my pants down to my knees and he's plunging into me down there with his tongue. When

I try to move away, he grabs both my hips and sticks his face back down there. Peeking out I see Shelly is sitting in Hilary's rocker, facing the other way. I can see the side of her face and she looks a little worried and I don't know what to do. Every time I move away he pulls me back. I'm so confused and I don't know how this all happened so quickly. It goes on *forever*. He just won't stop, and then I get a feeling like I'm going to overflow and I try to hold it as long as I can but after a while I just can't. He laughs like he's done something great and I'm so embarrassed I could die. Next thing I know he's pulling himself up on his arms and when I look down his thingy is huge and it's right there hovering over my legs and I think he actually wants to *do it* and I'm not even a teenager yet and we haven't been together very long. Finally I whisper, "I don't think we should," and Eric says, "What?"

"Please Eric," I whisper. I don't think we should do it until we've been together a whole year. I'm not even 13 yet."

Eric hangs his head down but looks relieved.

"Sure…no problem," he says pulling his jeans back up.

Afterward, I can hardly look at Shelly and I feel so mad at Eric for embarrassing me like this. Shelly doesn't say much as we wait for her mom to come get them, but Eric looks just as happy as can be, real proud of himself as he gets in the car, waving and smiling as they pull out onto Centerville Highway.

***

136

Since I always get dressed squatting down between the bed and the wall now, Dad has to get his jollies by barging in on me in the bathroom. He's never bought anything for the house in his life, but he takes it as his personal responsibility to buy the shower curtains and he *always* gets a clear one.

He comes in from the entrance off his bedroom, pretending to get something; or suddenly he'll need to trim his beard. Sometimes he even sits down and takes a dump, polluting the bathroom with his stench. Huddled in the corner of the shower stall, my job is to act like he's not doing what he's doing. Like the whole point isn't for him to see me naked. Inside I scream, but my voice stays stuck in my throat. Hilary and I never talk about it. He must be doing the same thing to her, but she just acts like things don't bother her. Hilary and I never talk about anything. And talking to Mom about it just makes her mad.

"What do you want me to do?" she barks. "Take your showers when he isn't here." She stomps away from me like I'm the one doing something wrong. What am I supposed to do? What the fuck am I supposed to do?

Last week, I noticed the doorknob to my parents' bathroom entrance was gone. Normally it's a big one-sided diamond shaped knob from Mom and Dad's side, with just a metal post sticking out from the knob hole in the bathroom. They can get into the bathroom from their room, but we can't get into their room from the bathroom.

Later, my stomach braced itself when I went in their room and saw the knob lying on the dresser, right next to the bathroom door. Kneeling down, I looked through the doorknob hole and sure enough, he'd have a clear view.

For a week I've been shoving wads of toilet paper into the doorknob hole. The next time I go to use the bathroom, they're gone. Stuffing the hole becomes a silent dance. I stuff it, he pokes it out. It would be so much easier if Dad just beat the shit out of me. At least I could get him arrested for that. There's no one to tell. Nothing to be done. What he's doing is too awful to tell even Sophie. She already thinks my Dad is a creep because he watches slutty movies on HBO. She'd probably never come over again. What if she didn't want to be my friend because of it?

All this spying has my stomach in knots and I think maybe I'm getting an ulcer. I make the mistake of telling Mom about the pain in my side, and suddenly she gives a damn about me. Working herself into a tizzy she's convinced it's my appendix. After a couple of hours, we're in the car on the way to the hospital.

I know it's not my appendix. It's the same old pain I get every time I'm upset. A burning in my left side under my rib. I really should tell her it's nothing, but it's nice to lay here in peace on the stretcher. The concern in Mom's furrowed brow feels so good. She runs her fingers through my hair and I'm almost asleep when a guy in a white lab coat who looks like a teenager comes in. Mom stands by the stretcher, talking with him. I hear him say he's a resident and I wonder if that means he lives here, at the hospital. I hear him say something about tests. I'm so calm and relaxed now, my stomach isn't even hurting anymore, but I'm hoping I might get to stay the night.

My eyes pop open when I hear the word, "rectal."

Looking at her I say, "Mom, no! I don't want that."

She doesn't say anything.

"Don't let him do that Mom, ... please!" I whisper.

Mom looks blankly at the wall behind me, as the resident shoves his finger up my butt. My face burns with embarrassment, and my mother gets blurry like far away air on a steamy day. My hate for her is white hot. I can't count on her for anything. Lately it feels like Eric is the only one I can trust.

Eric doesn't have any friends. He thinks people are against him and seems to hate just about everyone but me. He's always accusing people of giving him dirty looks and he starts fights at school. Sometimes I'm embarrassed to even be going out with him. Even so, it's nice having someone who gives a damn about me. With his arm heavy around my shoulder, he walks me to all my classes. Most of my new Baldwin friends leave me alone now. He even gets jealous of Sophie and Libby.

Each day I save my lunch money to buy Doors Albums and other things I need, like make-up. After school I go to Eric's house. He drinks protein shakes and eats Little Debbie snacks from a drawer in the kitchen. He thinks he's too skinny and wants to get bigger for football. He never offers me anything to eat because he thinks *I'm* too fat. I don't want to be fat and I know he's just trying to help, but my stomach grumbles and I have a headache from not eating.

Sitting in front of the TV in his basement, he always wants to make out. His mom is right upstairs and I never let it get too far like it did that day at my house when Shelly was over. My stomach rumbles loud and *I know* he hears it. We keep kissing, but after a while it makes me mad he doesn't care if I'm hungry. So what if I get fat? Screw him.

Telling Eric I have to use the bathroom, I tiptoe into the kitchen, pull a Little Debbie snack out of the drawer, and shove it under my shirt. Locked in the bathroom, with the perfect tiles and the fancy peach colored towels, I sit on the rug and rip open the wrapper. I barely taste the first cupcake. The second one I'm slower with. *Fuck you*, I think as the white frosting slides down the back of my throat.

Stuffing the cupcake wrapper deep in my jeans pocket I look down at my stomach. I can't believe I have no will power at all. I am such a loser. Over and over I punch myself in the belly, hard. I promised myself I wouldn't be so weak. Why do I always fail?

Chapter Eighteen

Shrieks inside my head. I'm hopping over fallen trees, ducking under a barbed wire fence. Down a small slope, hopping over a stream. The mud sticks to my sneakers and cushions my pounding feet as I stomp up the wooded hill behind our house.

Fuck her! Fuck him! I HATE THEM. What the fuck am I supposed to do? I'm shaking and my face is wet with tears. What *exactly* am I supposed to do? This thing Dad's doing, this spying, is so dirty, so perverted, but there's nothing I can do about it and no one I can tell. Ever.

And yet, it's probably not even against the law. I mean, he's not hitting anyone. He's not raping anyone. He's not even touching anyone. *His* house. *His* everything. *He* can do whatever he wants. My stomach wretches and I stop to lean over, hands on my knees. It feels like I'm going to puke.

On top of the hill is a clearing and just beyond that is a pond. Sitting on the edge of the water I listen to a frog's low chants. A small turtle's head glides across the pond making slow steady ripples. Picking up a rock, I whip it in his direction and he disappears under the water. Yanking a golden stalk of tall grass out of the ground I roll it back and forth between my thumb and forefinger over and over. From here I can see the whole valley. Our house is just a rickety shack beside the highway. The sky is deep blue. The sun is shining. Everything is beautiful. The hate rises from my stomach and takes a seat in the back of my throat, "Fuck you!" I scream out loud, into the wind.

For the first time in a long time, I actually had a friend stay over. A girl from Baldwin. When she took a shower this morning I caught Dad spying on her. Somehow I never thought he would do it to anyone else. Somehow I thought he was *allowed* to do it to me, but not my friends. Not someone else's kid.

Last night, Mom went to work at 10:00PM, like always. Me and Cindy fell asleep in sleeping bags on the living room floor in front of the TV. Dad came in around three, stumbled over us and made a racket in the kitchen. It was embarrassing.

This morning, while Cindy took a shower, Mom was in the kitchen making sausage and eggs for Dad. Adam was on the floor in the living room, watching cartoons. Hilary wasn't home; she stayed over at a friend's house, as usual. When I walked by my parent's bedroom I couldn't believe it. There he was, on his knees, at the door to the bathroom, eye pressed up to the keyhole. His dingy white terry cloth robe, skimmed the floor. My stomach lurched hard. Could I *really be* seeing this? When it was clear I was, I ran into the kitchen, and in a whisper pleaded, "Mom! He's spying on Cindy! Right now, he's *spying!* Mom! Do something!" Mom dropped her spatula, turned, and gave me a very dirty look.

After a long pause, she casually walked into the bedroom, and I trailed behind her, fists clenched. *Finally* she was going to stand up to him, and I was ready. Dad hopped up from the door, like nothing was happening. He adjusted the belt on his robe and I stood behind Mom, glaring at him. Mom went to her dresser and started rearranging things in her top drawer. Dad got up and left the room. Not one word was spoken. When I walked out of the bedroom, Adam was there on the floor, still watching cartoons, oblivious. I stood there blinking, wondering, "Am I crazy?"

For a whole hour until Cindy's dad came to get her, I held it in. I walked her out to the car, acted like everything was *fine.* On my way back in, Dad was sitting there in the recliner, still in his bathrobe, reading one of those stupid horror books he likes. Adam must have gone upstairs.

Close enough behind Dad to smell his hangover stench, I stood and looked hard at the back of his head. I imagined a bullet entering his skull, thick blood dripping down his greasy black hair. If only we had a gun in the house he would be dead. No question. I would do it.

Mom came into the room and started making small talk and I just couldn't take it anymore. Shaking my head, I stumbled backwards from the chair, shoved past her, and ran out of the living room and through the kitchen. On my way out, I slammed the back door with such force, the big glass window in it shattered all over the kitchen. The sound of breaking glass was thrilling and scary and I ran toward the woods, not looking back.

Throwing another rock into the pond I watch the splash, then lay back on the hard dirt, looking up at the swaying tree branches. The Aspen leaves flutter and stop again. Closing my eyes, tears run down the sides of my face and into my ears and I vow never to have a friend over again.

Looking down at the field of tall grass, I notice how it moves in waves, kind of like the ocean. The sky is impossibly blue. How could the world be this beautiful when everything in it is wrong?

Squinting my eyes, I focus on the white puffy clouds. I stare and wait. I wait for God. There are glimpses in the pink sunset. Hints in the wind through my hair, but my God feeling can't get through all the way. It's all pinched off with so much hate inside me.

After the sun goes down, I walk back toward the house. When I get there, a piece of pressed board is nailed up to the empty window in the back door. I'm afraid to go inside, but when I do, everyone acts like nothing ever happened. No one says a word about it. In my mind, the fact my parents don't discipline me about breaking the window proves he was wrong. It makes me feel powerful and superior.

Chapter Nineteen

An inch of snow has come down in less than an hour this evening. Mom called our low-life father at The Rusty Nail before she left for work, reminding him he's supposed to give Hilary's boyfriend Jeffery a ride home soon. She dropped Adam off at Gramma Bonner's on her way to work, but I didn't go because Gramma won't let me watch "Fantasy Island." It's too scary for her. Every weekend, I watch *The Love Boat* and *Fantasy Island*.

When Dad gets home, Hilary and Jeffery are holding hands on the couch and I'm on the floor in front of the TV. Dad's all glassy eyed and he swaggers into the kitchen and picks up the phone.

"Jeff, what's your number?" he yells. Jeffery tells him, and Dad dials the phone.

He starts, "Hello, Mrs. Rallston? The snow is coming down pretty good. I don't know if we can get up over the hill in one piece. Do you mind if Jeffery stays the night? We'll get 'em home first thing in the mornin' if the roads are clear."

My stomach braces itself. Jeffery is all grins and Hilary's shoulders shoot to her ears. Her eyes look big and scared. Dad hangs up the phone and it's settled. Jeffery is spending the night.

The smell of bacon and eggs fills the air, cast iron pans clank in the kitchen. Dad sits at the dining room table to eat, then throws his dishes in the sink. He leaves the dirty pans on the stove for Mom to clean in the morning. Dad walks into the living room for a minute, looks at the TV, then walks toward his bedroom. Stopping to steady himself on the doorframe, he looks back at Hilary and Jeffery and says, with a smirk, "I'm going to bed. You kids have fun."

The sick feeling in my stomach matches the expression on Hilary's face.

During a commercial I get up, fix myself a big bowl of chocolate ice cream, then plop down again in front of the TV. Halfway through *Fantasy Island*, Jeffery is leading Hilary by the hand upstairs to our room.

When *Fantasy Island* is over, I walk into the kitchen to put my bowl in the sink. I'm not hungry, but I open the fridge, lean in and look. Shutting it again, I turn and glance at the stairs. Through the spy curtain, I make my way up the steps, careful to avoid the squeaky spots. Sitting on the top step I peek my head around the corner so I can see into Hilary's nook. She and Jeffery are lying on the bed, on top of the covers, in a kissing frenzy. His hands are all over her. He's feeling her boobs, and her butt. He's so hyper, it looks as if he like he might swallow her whole.

Having seen enough, I head back downstairs and wonder if my sister is going to experience "the ultimate." Will they actually *do it?* Dad practically encouraged it. Sophie loaned me this Judy Blume book called *Forever*, and in it, a girl named Katherine does "the ultimate" for the first time with her boyfriend Michael. Katherine and Michael call his penis "Ralph" and I wonder if Jeffery's penis has a name.

Back in the living room, I turn off the TV and lay on the couch. It's not like I can go upstairs to my bed or anything. Staring at the light blue ceiling tiles, I think about how on the news, they say we might have a nuclear war. The whole world will just get blown up. Sometimes I'm so worried about it I can't sleep. Then I have a thought. What if it the world ends before *I* experience "the ultimate?"

I don't really want to "do it" yet. I'm gonna wait 'til me and Eric have been together at least a year. A whole year is really something. I mean, otherwise it would just be kind of slutty. After a whole year it's practically expected.

The next weekend, Eric is over for the evening. Dad calls from The Rusty Nail and tells Mom to get ready, because he's taking her out to a restaurant with some friends. Mom is all giddy as she gets dressed up and I don't remember Dad *ever* taking her out before. Not once. Adam is at Gramma's again and Hilary is out with her friends so Eric and I will be alone when they leave. When Dad stops home to pick up mom, his eyes are red and glassy. As they head out the door he stops, looks at Eric, and says, "Just don't get her pregnant."

Eric shrinks back, embarrassed.

Glaring at Dad I say through clenched teeth, "Don't *worry*."

I'm so pissed. Dad acts like me and Hilary are nothing more than a couple of sluts. It's like he gets off picturing us with our boyfriends. As soon as they leave, Eric is eager to make out with me, and heck, Dad gave him the green light, but I don't feel like it. I fake an upset stomach and Eric pouts 'til his mom comes to pick him up at 9:30pm. Sometimes I wish I never met Eric, but I guess I'm stuck with him.

***

147

After a long winter it's finally spring, and Becky Davis is having a slumber party to celebrate her 13th birthday. There are eight of us girls here and when it's dark, we sneak outside and run around the golf course behind Becky's house. Her brother Brandon is one year older than us and he's brought a bunch of his friends. Eric thinks the party was just girls and I feel so *free* without him here, draping his arm around me, marking his territory. I don't know where they got it, but the boys brought beer and when I'm offered one, I take it. As the bitter, cold, fuzzy liquid goes down my throat I shudder.

This is Dad. This is his thing.

Soon we're feeling silly and me and Sophie and the other girls are running around laughing, shrieking and flapping our arms like birds as we tear down the hills. The boys watch us and drink their beers, shaking their heads. Someone hands me another bottle and I've never had so much fun.

On our way back to Becky's I make it as far as her yard, before tumbling into the landscaping on the side of her house. Lying in the bushes, I look up at the clear black sky, full of white stars, and contemplate just how comfortable shrubs can be.

Soon, Brandon is here and he's grabbing my freezing cold hand with his warm strong one and he pulls me up out of the bush. He herds all us girls back into the basement. Brandon says I'm definitely not allowed to go upstairs to the bathroom. His parents are home now and I'm too drunk.

"But I'm feeling really woozy!" I tell him, stumbling forward, bracing myself on his shoulder. "What if I throw up?"

Brandon sits me in a corner of the room, and hands me an almost empty popcorn bowl in case I get sick. Sitting crisscross, facing the wall, *I do get sick.* Over and over I wretch into the big white Tupperware bowl on my lap, thinking,

This is Dad. This is his thing.

My long hair is dangling almost into the puke and now Sophie is behind me, pinning it back with barrettes. Turning to look at her, she smiles at me and she's so beautiful with her dark eyes and her dark skin and her dad's little cleft in her chin. Just like that, all the words I've wanted to say for months come tumbling out.

"Sophie," I cry. "I am so sorry about your dad. It's not fair! He was so good! He loved you so much!"

Sophie hugs me and then she's wailing and soon every girl in the room is crying. Brandon is freaking out, shushhh-ing us.

"My parents are going to hear you!" he whisper yells, marching back and forth across the room like a soldier.

"You guys! SHHHHHH! You're going to get us in trouble!" he pleads.

We ignore Brandon and hover over Sophie. Hugging her, holding her, running our fingers through her chestnut hair, a bunch of little girls crying with her, for her. For her dead daddy. We tell her, "We love you Sophie."

We say, "We are so sorry."

I tell her, "He *knew* you loved him. It doesn't matter that you didn't talk to him at your birthday party."

Our eyes lock and there is so much gratitude in hers. We both start sobbing again. We cry until there are no more tears and all the girls slip into their sleeping bags on the floor. Sophie, and I have our bags right next to each other. My head spins and I hold her hand 'til we fall asleep.

Chapter Twenty

Sophie had to help her mom train show dogs, and Libby joined a swim team this summer so I've mostly been hanging out with Jenna, my friend up the road who sits with me on the school bus.

Jenna has been *so good* this summer, really starving herself. She looks great in her bikini and all the Centerville boys at the swimming hole are checking her out. Wearing my black one piece, I try to cover up my belly by putting my left hand on my right elbow and holding my right forearm at an angle over my stomach. Jenna says I'm not fat, but I know she's just being nice. I do the same thing with Sophie. I weigh *at least* 105. If I could get below a 100 pounds, I might be okay. Adam is with us today. He's not allowed to go to the creek by himself yet.

The swimming hole is just up the road. From Jenna's back yard, you follow a dirt trail, which gets you to the water. The creek bank rises about ten feet above the deep end. If you stay on the trail a little further, you can walk across shallow water to get to the flat rocky shore on the other side. That's where me and Jenna set up our towels and start working on our tans. We rub baby oil on our skin, and bake in the noonday sun, watching the Centerville gang take turns swinging from a rope tied to a thick tree branch up on the creek bank.

"Oh Shit!" says John Crockett, just before he lets go.

Danny takes a running start with the rope, and swings way out over the water. He lets go, sticks up his two middle fingers and screams, "Muther-fucker!" to no one in particular before disappearing into a huge splash.

The boys are all ropey muscled and tanned. When they jump, they have to swing out far enough to clear a big old log that's fallen parallel to the bank. When we swim to the deep end, we use the log as a bench. Looking from the shore, it's common to see seven or eight kids sitting chest level on the fallen tree. After sitting in the hot sun for a while I decide to go in the water. It's cool, but not too cold. Swimming out to the log, I climb up and sit, straddling it. It's so big it reminds me of the time we rode an elephant at the circus. I rub my feet back and forth along the slimy green algae growing on its sides. Adam swims out to me and sits on the log too. Then, he dives down to the creek bottom to look for clay. He comes up with a big clump of the gray slimy stuff in his hands. I nod my approval and he smiles. I used to dig for clay too but now I'm more careful about my fingernails.

After a while I join Jenna back on the towels and we watch a teenage girl named Helen who sits on a blanket in front of us just a few yards away. Helen is petite with big breasts and long dark hair. She's in a tiny black bikini and her body is slick with baby oil. She's way darker than me or Jenna. Helen is reading *Seventeen* and her hair is perfect, so you can tell she hasn't even been in the water once. She's Kevin's girlfriend.

Kevin comes dripping out of the water, sits on her blanket, and rolls his wet body on top of hers. She screams but she's laughing and they start to kiss. The way he rests his hand on her tanned belly shows he's very comfortable with her body and I can tell they've totally done *the ultimate*. After a minute, he swims across the creek and climbs up the bank, joining his friends. She picks up her magazine and starts to read. In my mind I picture her and Kevin *doing it,* and I wonder what it's like to feel someone's weight on top of you like that.

I'm thinking about going back in the water when I hear Craig yell.

"Sheee-it!" he says all angry.

It seems instead of swinging out on the rope, John Crockett and Dean decided to *dive* right over the log, skimming the heads of Craig and Danny who were sitting on it.

As John Crockett and Dean swim to the shore, Craig yells to them, "That's not cool, mother-fuckers! You almost landed on us."

"Lighten up there, pussy," says Dean, and my stomach lurches, because after all *he is* a murderer and do we really need to get him upset?

Kevin and Mark are the only two left on the muddy creek bank. Mark dives in, clears the log and Craig shakes his head, and yells, "Assholes." He and Danny push off the log and swim toward shore.

Kevin stands alone on the bank. He lets out a big whoop, but as he starts to dive his foot slips on the mud. At the sound of his voice Helen looks up from her magazine just in time to see him smack head first into the giant log before disappearing into the deep end of the swimming hole.

Everyone stops. Everyone waits, but Kevin doesn't come up. Helen stands up and tries to walk but her knees buckle under her. Strange low animal noises come from her throat. She's kneeling, holding her belly, and her whole body starts to shake. Craig climbs up the creek bank and he's gone in a flash. He's running to the fire station across from Jenna's house. We all know he is.

Without speaking, the boys from Centerville take turns, diving under the dark, murky water. One dives down; the others wait and watch in silence. The first comes up and another dives down, and they wait. The third boy comes up carrying Kevin. He's unconscious and blood is pouring from his head. John Crockett's arms are wrapped around Helen from behind, holding her back from going in the water. She's moaning, and struggling and I wonder what it must be like to love someone that much? Eight strong hands keep Kevin floating on his back on top of the water. Dean the murderer, softly cradles Kevin's bloody head, with its face toward the bright blue sky. Someone yells, "He's breathing! He's fucking breathing!" and now Craig is back with the paramedics and they're stumbling down the creek bank with a cage-like stretcher. Kevin, still unconscious, is carried up onto the bank and then they're gone.

"C'mon," I say to Adam. We gather our towels and walk home in silence.

"He's probably paralyzed from the neck down!" Mom frets when she hears the story. Lately, when she frets she runs her tongue over her front tooth, which has been getting grayer and grayer.

"They shouldn't be diving over that log! Don't you two EVER dive off that creek bank! In fact, I don't even want you swinging off the rope! Do you hear me?" We nod but Adam and I are too chicken to ever dive in from the creek bank, *or* swing off the rope. Still, it feels good to have Mom tell us not to. She stands there at the kitchen sink, staring into space, working her tongue over that tooth, again and again.

For the next two days I sit in chairs and try not to move, imagining what it would be like to be paralyzed. I can't think of anything worse and I wonder, will Helen still love him?

Finally, Jenna calls me with the scoop. Kevin needed brain surgery. He's not paralyzed. He's going to be okay. Shaking my head I let out a sigh of relief. Those Centerville boys are fucking invincible.

***

Over the last year, Mom's front tooth gradually turned darker shades of gray and a month ago it finally broke off and fell out. She's not even making an appointment for the dentist. It's like she's just given up. She sleeps and goes to work and that's it. I'm so embarrassed to be seen with her in public, looking like such a hillbilly.

On top of that, something is wrong with our plumbing, and we haven't had any running water for two weeks. Our bathroom has turned into an indoor outhouse. We lug our dishes in laundry baskets to Gramma Bonner's apartment. We bring a dozen plastic milk jugs, fill them with tap water and then lug them home. Only one jug a day is allowed for flushing the toilet. The sight and smell of my family's shit makes me gag, so sometimes, I just go to the bathroom in the woods up on the hill.

If we still have no water when school starts, Mom's going to have to drive me to Gramma Bonner's every day for a bath. I'm *not* going to school looking scummy.

On payday, Dad comes home and counts his money at the dining room table as I sit and watch. Three-hundred-and-seventy-five dollars. Three-hundred-and-seventy- five *whole* dollars and they say we have no money? No money for school clothes. No money to get the water pipes fixed. No money for Mom's tooth.

There he sits with *all that money* and what's he do with it? He takes it to The Rusty Nail. None of it is for us.

Any time I ask for anything, it's always the same.

"You don't understand, we have bills to pay," Mom says, defending him.

Plenty of money for beer.

I'm sick of it.

Mom is folding laundry in her bedroom. I walk in and ask, "Mom, can I have fifty cents for a candy bar?"

She glares at me and snaps the jeans she's holding out in front of her, "We don't have any money," she says.

"But Dad just cashed his check. He's got tons of money. I just watched him count it."

Under my breath, I add, "He's got plenty of money to spend at The Rusty Nail."

"Well then, why don't *you* go talk to your father about that," she says sarcastically.

Fine.

Back in the kitchen, "Dad, can I have fifty cents for a candy bar?"

"No."

"But Dad, you *have* three hundred and seventy-five dollars."

Looking up at me he says, "What *I have* is none of your God damned business." He folds his arms across his chest.

Again, I mutter under my breath, "But you have plenty to spend at The Rusty Nail."

Dad jumps up from the table and gets in my face. "What did you say?"

I glare at him.

"I work hard and I deserve to have a beer or two. Not that it's any of your business how I spend *my* money. You're lucky I let you live here in *my* house. Use *my* television. *My* heat. *My* phone. Barely a dime left because of you kids."

He sputters in my face, "Once you have kids, life…is…over."

Standing with my fists clenched, I stare at the pores in his greasy face. The whiskers in his beard are thick and wiry, gray and black. He makes me want to puke.

Three hundred and seventy-five dollars and I can't have fifty cents?

I snap.

"Well, I never asked to be born! If you never wanted kids you shouldn't have had us! Haven't you ever heard of something called *BIRTH CONTROL*?"

Dad raises his hand to swat me, but then he just drops it and laughs.

Mom had a talk with me about birth control last week.

"If you ever need it I want you to come to me. I don't want you to end up *like us,*" she'd said.

I'd looked at that big old hole in her mouth where her front tooth should be and thought to myself, *Believe me, I'm never going to end up like you.*

Dad fans out his wad of money like a hand of cards and waves it in my face as he walks past, smirking. He folds it up, sticks it in his wallet, and shoves it in his back pocket. He flashes me a nasty smile as he walks out the front door and the next sound I hear is tires as he peels out of the gravel driveway and down the road toward The Rusty Nail.

Mom stomps out of the bedroom, angry at me. "Now he's gone, and I didn't get any money to pay the bills," she hisses.

"You *told* me to talk to him," I scream as I stomp upstairs to my room.

I'm so sick of this crap. Everyone else has everything they need. Libby's mom takes her shopping and buys her Jordache jeans. Jill's mom buys her nice clothes from the L.L. Bean catalog and pays for her perfect haircuts. Sophie's nana in Florida takes good care of her. During school I have to starve all day if I want any money at all, and in the summer I get nothing. My parents won't part with fifty cents for a candy bar. I'm not even allowed to flush the fucking toilet.

***

Jenna and I have been lying out in the sun at the creek all day and it's Hunger that taps me on the shoulder and whispers the plan. I'm dreaming of a pizza sub. At the sub shop down the road, half-way between Jenna's house and mine, they start out by putting some really soft, juicy meatballs on a long fresh roll. Next, they drown the meatballs in a sweet tomato sauce. After that, they load heaps of mozzarella on top. Then, they wrap it in foil and stick it in the oven to melt the cheese. Biting into a pizza sub, the sauce is salty and sweet and the cheese is so thick you have to pinch it off in long strings with your fingers. The bread is doughy on the inside, with just a slight crunch on the outside. Pizza subs are best if you wash them down with a cold Coke.

How to get money for a pizza sub, from Dad:

1). Bring Jenna.

2). Walk ¼ mile down the highway, stop at The Rusty Nail, and go inside.

3). After your eyes become adjusted to the darkness, find Dad on his bar stool.

4). Tell him you were going for a walk and you just stopped by to say, "Hi."

5). Act sweet to the bartender, Dad, and his friends.

6). Wait 'til he starts to order another beer and then ask for money. Tell him you and your friend are *hungry*. Make sure his friends hear you ask. Make sure they hear the part about you being hungry.

7). Take the money and thank him.

8). Enjoy the meatballs, the mozzarella, the sauce, the bread, as it slides down your throat. Go all out. Buy yourselves a Coke.

Note: This only works twice. After that, you are forbidden from setting foot in The Rusty Nail, *ever* again.

Chapter Twenty-One

Eric has been gone every day this summer, working for his Dad, but he gets a ride over to my house every chance he gets late afternoons and stays most of the evening. We go for walks up on the hill and it's always the same thing. He wants to make out. I know he wants to *do it.* We've been going out practically a year and it's not like I'm a little kid. I'm almost 13. Besides, Hilary and Jeffery do it. I know, because she's on the pill. And there's always the threat of nuclear war. It may be now or never.

Thinking about the talk Mom had with me about birth control, I wonder if it means she thinks I'm ready? She wouldn't have mentioned it if she didn't expect me to *do it*, would she?

One month before my 13th birthday, Mom's hanging clothes on the line that stretches from our back porch to the huge weeping willow tree in the yard. I make Eric come with me to ask her.

We stand, facing her back and I say, "Mom, me and Eric are thinking about having sex and I want to get some birth control."

Eric's hands fly up to cover his face when I say the word "sex" even though Mom isn't looking in our direction.

She says nothing and just keeps hanging out the clothes. It's dark inside the porch, but as she leans out the window her face is lit up in the sunshine. She's white as the sheet she's fastening to the line. There is a squeaking sound as she reels the sheet further out to dangle over the yard. She reaches into the laundry basket and grabs a towel.

"*Mom*, did you hear me?" I ask.

She pauses, but still doesn't turn to look at me.

"Mom?" I ask softly.

She flips in my direction but stares up toward the ceiling.

"Fine! I guess I better get you to Planned Parenthood," she says before stomping into the house in a huff. She left the laundry basket on the porch, half full with wet clothes.

Why is she mad when she told me to come to her? Isn't sex what everyone thinks I should do? Geez! I already told Eric I would. Does Mom think I'm some sort of slut now? Eric and I have been going out almost a whole year! *Hilary* is having sex. Why is Mom mad at *me*? That night, in bed, I decide if Mom tells me not to, I won't do it. I won't go on the pill and I won't have sex with Eric.

A week before my 13th birthday I lay naked on my back with my legs up in stirrups and I'm so embarrassed. A tear trails down the side of my face and lands in my ear. Picking a spot on the ceiling I stare while the woman in the white lab coat pushes things into me. She asks me if I've ever had sex before and I tell her no. She tells me I'm very responsible to get birth control before becoming sexually active. She sends me on my way with a three-month supply of pills. Eric counts the 14 days 'til it's effective and then we're up on the hill behind my house. It hurts too much. Eric tries to be gentle, but it takes a month of trying before I'm able to stand the pain and let

161

him get all the way inside me. After that it's not so bad. Usually, I just stare up at the leaves in the trees and fade out.

***

Sophie is so jealous because Eric and I are "doing it." Laying on her brand new waterbed in her room, she looks at me and sighs. Flipping through a *Seventeen* magazine I stop and say, "You have nothing to be jealous about Sophie. It's not all it's cracked up to be."

"Still, she says. Your lucky to have gotten rid of it."

"Rid of it?" I ask.

"Your virginity. No one is ever going to want mine, because I'm so fat."

"Sophie," I say, rolling my eyes. "You are *not* fat."

She sits up and gets serious. "I have something to tell you."

"What?" I ask.

She pauses, then blurts out, "We're moving to Maine."

"What?" I ask. Shocked, I get up and turn off the TV. "Why?" I whisper, my voice cracking.

My mom wants to make a fresh start. We have no family here, just bad memories because of my Dad. *I can't believe it.*

"Do you have family in Maine?"

"No, but my mom has always wanted to live there."

"Can't you talk her out of it Sophie?" I say, flinging myself back on the bed. I grab a pillow and hold it to my chest.

"I kind of *want* to go," she says softly.

I suck in my breath. She *wants* to go?

"To get a new start," she adds.

"But what about *me*?" I ask.

Even as I say it I realize, Sophie is already gone.

"We can still talk on the phone and maybe I can visit? Or maybe you could come up to Maine for visits!" she says all cheery.

I'm furious at Sophie for being so damn happy about it. The rest of the night is ruined. I feel like an idiot for spending so much time with stupid Eric and leaving her out. It will never be okay that she's moving. Never.

After Sophie leaves it's just Libby and I. Libby lives halfway to Baldwin from my house, so I stay at her house on the weekends and we sneak out at night, meeting Eric and some other boys down by the high school. Libby has started going out with one of Eric's friends and they are already having sex. Libby is so jealous my mom took me to Planned Parenthood. She and Greg have to use condoms.

From Maine, Sophie calls and tells me she's tried Ecstasy with her new friends.

"Sophie, that's a bit hard core, isn't it? I don't think you should be doing drugs like that. *Pot* is one thing, but Ecstasy seems totally different."

"Don't knock it 'til you try it!" she says and I can hear the smile in her voice over the phone. I wonder if she's stoned right now?

Sophie calls me two weeks later. "What did you do over the weekend?" she asks.

Before the words are out of my mouth I regret them. "I went to the mall and bought an album."

Please don't ask.

"Which one?" she says.

"Culture Club," I mumble into the phone.

Sophie and I only listen to classic rock, but now that she's gone, I've been listening to a lot more stuff, even top 40.

"You mean, like, *Boy George*?" she says. Disgust drips through the phone line.

"Well, yeah. There's one song that's pretty good."

There's a long pause and then she snickers, "I can't *believe* you would buy that crap."

"It's not *that* bad," I tell her.

"Well," she changes the subject, "I might as well tell you. I got it over with."

"Got *what* over with?" I ask.

"Duh. My virginity. I got rid of it."

"Sophie, you didn't tell me you had a boyfriend?"

"Oh, he's not my boyfriend. He's known around school as The Virgin Killer.

There is a long pause and then I say, "That makes me sad." Then I'm angry and I tell her, "You shouldn't be having sex unless you're in love with someone, like me and Eric, it isn't right to just *sleep around.*"

I'm mad at her for doing Ecstasy. Mad at her for throwing her virginity down the toilet. Most of all I'm mad at her for moving away from me.

"You've gotten to be really judgmental, you know," she says.

"Well Sophie, you're out of control. You're doing stupid things. Ecstasy? *Fucking* someone who calls himself, The Virgin Killer? *Please!*"

Click.

I never heard from Sophie again. Maybe I *was* judgmental, but in my heart of hearts, I believe Boy George had something to do with it.

***

Libby's parents said I couldn't sleep over tonight, but she snuck me in anyway, through the back door. I'm hiding in her room until they go to bed and it makes me feel like a criminal. We have plans to slip out and meet the boys and Eric will be such a whiney pain in the ass if I don't show. When her mom and dad *finally* go to bed, we tiptoe downstairs and out the sliding glass doors of her rec room.

Walking down the hill toward Baldwin the air is cool, and I shiver in my hooded sweat jacket. Soon the walking warms me up. Sometimes it's spooky, out late at night like this, but it's also thrilling to be so free. From far away we see the dark shadows of the boys in the McDonald's parking lot. Eric, Greg, and a two other boys are with them. When we get close I see they're taking swigs from bottles in brown paper bags. Eric offers me a sip and when I take it, it's piss warm. I spit it out.

"I'm not drinking warm beer," I tell him.

Sophie gave us a stash before she moved and we smoke some of her mom's pot and then walk around Baldwin for a couple of hours, and then the boys walk us up the hill toward Libby's house. Eric insists on walking arm in arm and I hate the feel of his weight on me, slowing me down.

Lately I just can't stand Eric. He isn't *that* bad. Physically, he's gorgeous. He has sweet dark eyes, blonde feathered hair and perfect teeth. He works out all the time so he's got lots of muscles. His body is like the Solo Flex guy in the commercials. Plus, he practically worships the ground I walk on, but he's so jealous and needy and he always wants to have sex, and sometimes the whole thing is just too much.

The boys walk us almost to Libby's house before turning back toward Baldwin. We sneak in and head up the stairs to her room where we try to sleep all squished together in her twin bed. I'm so scared Libby's parents will find me in the morning and be mad. By 3AM the thought of being anywhere I'm not welcome is unbearable.

Nudging Libby's shoulder I tell her, "I'm going to take off."

"Huh?" she asks.

"I'm going to walk home."

"Why? What time is it?" she squints, trying to read her alarm clock across the room on her dresser.

"I'm afraid your parents are going to be pissed in the morning. I can't sleep."

Libby yawns as we tiptoe downstairs to the rec room. She opens the sliding glass doors and then shuts them again, trying to stop me.

"It's too far," she whispers. Her big eyes look tired. She's still half asleep.

"It's not that far," I say.

I *have to* get out of here. I feel like an animal trapped in a cage.

Slipping past her, I open the doors and step outside. I take a big gulp of fresh air, hear the click of the lock as I slide the glass door shut, and I'm off into the night.

It's bright out for nighttime. There are tons of stars and a full moon, which I didn't even notice earlier. It's also colder than it was before. Walking down the big hill toward Twist Run Road, I hear dogs barking in the distance and I shudder. I hadn't thought about dogs. Glancing back toward Libby's, I pick up a big rock on the shoulder of the road and keep walking. No turning back now.

As I approach the curvy part of Twist Run Road my heart starts beating fast. This twisty part is narrow, with just enough space for two cars to drive through. The path was made a long time ago by blasting dynamite into the hill. There's a guardrail on one side, to keep cars from sliding off into a creek. The other side is a steep rock wall. There's no room for give. Cars will either slam into the guardrail or slam into the rocks if they go off the road by even 12 inches.

My school bus takes Twist Run Road every day, to get to Baldwin, and Mom drives on it all the time, but I've never actually seen it up close, out of a car. Now, lit up by the moon, I see the blasted rock is grey with black flecks and it's sparkly. There are black streaks running through it and lots of places where water trickles down in drops and tiny streams. Running my hand over the rocks, it's cold and gritty and wet.

Out of nowhere I hear a sound, *cht..cht..cht..cht.* Oh shit! Was that a bat? Oh my God, I have to get through this curvy part quick. Once I get through the curvy part I've got just one more mile 'til home. The curvy part winds and winds and suddenly I hear a car.

Practically flying across the road, I hop the guardrail, hang onto it, and squat down on the other side. The creek is right behind me. The sound of the water and my nerves from hiding make me feel like I have to pee. The car passes, and then slows down.

Did they see me? Oh God, what if it's a psycho killer. I won't live to start high school next month.

167

I hold my breath. The car moves on.

Maybe it just slowed for the curve.

Hopping back over the guardrail I start running down the road. My sneakers slap loud on the pavement. I'm afraid of making noise, but I'm too scared not to run.

When the curvy part is over I'm on Lincoln Road with one mile left to go. Walking in the moonlight, I watch the blue shadows of the trees and it occurs to me that my parents have no idea where I am. Mom thought I was staying at Libby's. If that *was* a kidnapper in the car, and if he *had* gotten me, they'd never know what happened. I try to convince myself my parents would be devastated.

Making it to Centerville Highway, I have a half a mile to go. Once I pass the sandwich shop, just five more houses.

Three more houses to go, and suddenly I hear a car. It's coming slow from behind and its lights are on me now. I run.

Please, don't let the door be locked. Please don't let tonight be the night they lock it.

Tearing across Mr. Parson's lawn, across our gravel driveway, and up the front steps, my hand is on the knob when I hear the car stop in front of our house. It's a deep, man's voice yelling, "You okay?"

Flinging the door open, I step inside, shut it quick, and lock it. Too afraid to even peek out the window, I slide to the floor and lean against the front door, whispering,

"Please God. Don't let him come up to the house. Please."

After a minute, I hear the car drive away and I lay on the floor whimpering, whispering over and over, "Thank you, God."

The next morning, no one asks why I'm here or how I got home. The only question is, "Who locked the front door?"

Chapter Twenty-Two

When high school starts, Eric waits for me every morning by my locker. It's so annoying how I don't ever get to talk to anyone else. In ninth grade we get to choose electives and since I don't know what else to pick I take art. Mr. Peters is the teacher, and even though I suck at drawing, I'm pretty good at painting, which surprises him.

"Most people have to be able to draw something before they can paint it, and you can't draw for squat," he says, laughing.

It's true. If I try to draw with a pencil, my work is really bad. Without color, I can't seem to see what I'm doing. I like to paint with big thick brushstrokes, leaving the mark of the brush on the canvas. Mr. Peters says my style is "painterly" and I like the sound of that.

Today Mr. Peters has us all painting pictures of a big houseplant. Once we get cracking on our projects, he puts on classical music. Everyone gets quiet as we work at our easels. Mr. Peters walks around, asking questions and offering suggestions. He stops behind me for a long time and doesn't say anything. My stomach braces itself and I imagine he thinks my painting sucks. Beating him to the pass, I turn and say, "My painting doesn't look like everyone else's." I shrug. "It doesn't look real."

He rushes over to a shelf, pulls out a thick book and ruffles through the pages. He shoves the open book in my face and asks, "Does Van Gogh look real?"

He flips through some more and shows me the work of a painter called Matisse. "Real or no?"

He snaps the book shut, pulls it to his chest and says, "The point isn't to look *real*, the point is to find your own expression of what's real. You've got some real talent kiddo. What you did there with the yellow is brilliant."

I look back at my painting. I don't remember adding yellow, but there it is. All along the tip of one of the many green leaves. Looking at the actual plant, I see there is no yellow. I don't know why I put it there. Class is almost over so I grab my jar of brushes, and I walk across the room toward the sink, thinking about it.

On the school bus home I stare at my hands stained with blue and green and yellow splotches. No matter how hard I scrubbed, it wouldn't come off. I like the paint on my hands though. It makes me feel like a real artist. No one ever called me brilliant before. No one ever called me talented.

***

The energy seems to drain right out of me as fall turns to winter. I'm about to flunk math but instead of doing homework I'm lying on the floor in front of the TV. Adam watches a lot of TV too, and Hilary just never comes home. If she's not working at the mall, she's at her boyfriend's house in Baldwin. When I hear Dad's truck pull into the driveway my stomach braces itself. *Fuck.* I wish Mom would just leave him. The evening is shot to hell if *he's* gonna be home.

171

There's a rattling in the basement, and then the sound of metal being dragged across the concrete floor. I hear Dad's heavy boots clunking around down there.

Shit. Shit. Shit. This sucks.

"JANIE! Get down here!" He yells to me from the basement.

Here we go.

Standing by the landing at the front door I yell down, "What?"

He's there on the bottom step, with that sickening smile. The one he wears when he comes into our rooms at night, to tell us how much he loves us.

Tell me this Dad? Why don't you ever love us when you're not drunk? I think to myself.

"C'mon," he slurs. "I wanna show you something."

The last time he wanted to show me something, he brought home a huge dead fish that one of his friends had caught. He plopped it in the kitchen sink and told me I was to "gut" it. I'd never touched a dead fish before in my life and there was no way I was coming near that one.

Glaring at me he said, "Yes *you will* gut this fish, because I am telling you to. When I get back I want it done."

"*Fuck you, and your goddamn fish,*" I thought at the time. That fish lay stinking in the kitchen sink all day. Mom finally took care of it when she woke up.

Stepping cautiously down the stairs, I follow Dad into the basement. Adam is curious now and he's right behind me. There's a sweet smell in the air and a long empty wire cage sits on the floor. A small bale of hay is next to it. Dad's stupid grin is ear to ear as he points to a cardboard box. The box moves and he nods for me to open it.

172

Inside are two jet-black rabbits.

Dad always knew I loved rabbits.

We're living in Florida and Daddy is taking me to see our neighbor's bunnies! We step out of the trailer and he holds my hand as we cross the road. All the way through the big field tall scratchy grass tickles my legs. Daddy didn't invite Hilary or Adam. Only me! I'm the one that likes bunnies best and I've begged to go see them. I give his big hand my strongest squeeze.

There are chicken coops in a big circle with a fence around it. Bunny cages are in the middle, stacked up, like blocks. Black bunnies, black and white bunnies, brown bunnies and gray bunnies. The hay smells sweet. I pull a piece of grass out of the ground and stick it into a cage and laugh when a black bunny wiggles his nose and then slurps it straight in, like spaghetti! The black bunnies are my favorite.

In the chicken coops there are big chickens and roosters and also little baby chicks that are cute and fluffy. I'm going to ask if I can hold a bunny. I'm going to ask if I can hold a black one.

Daddy is talking to the man. The man has a grumpy face, all crinkly and tanned. He doesn't even look at me and I'm glad because he doesn't seem nice. Him and Daddy are talking and I'm so happy to be here. Wandering around, I'm looking in every cage.

The man goes over and opens a black bunny's cage and I suck in my breath. Is he going to let me pet him? I can't believe it. It's my lucky day!

He sits on a stool, holding the rabbit kind of upside down in his elbow with one arm. My tummy braces itself, as he starts tying Black Bunny's feet with a rope. The bunny is squirming, kicking its legs fast. Hey, what's

*happening? Black Bunny is scared! I don't get it? I don't
need to hold him. I'll just pet him on your lap. You don't
need to tie him up. But the man isn't looking at me at all.
He takes Black Bunny and hangs him by his tied together
feet on a big nail sticking out of a tall pole in the ground.
Before I can get my words out, he takes a bat, like in
baseball, and clubs Black Bunny on the head, hard.
Black Bunny's eyes pop right out of his head and he isn't
squirming anymore. Covering my face in my hands I
scream real loud. Inside me, I'm asking "Why would you
do that to him? Why would you hurt him? I wanna go
home! I want New York! I want Gramma! iiiii-eeeeee----
ahhhhhh!"*

*Back in the trailer, Daddy is yelling, "For Christ's
sake, Diana. I didn't know what he was doing. Besides,
kids who grow up on farms see that shit all the time. It
ain't that big a deal!"*

*Mommy is yelling too, "Well she hasn't grown up on
a farm. She loves animals. She loves bunnies. How could
you do that to her?"*

*"I know she loves the God damned rabbits! That's
why I fuckin' took her over there. I had to talk to the guy.
He wanted some trees cut down. How was I supposed to
know he was in the middle of a slaughter? Jesus Christ,
she's been wanting to see those damn rabbits for months.
I was trying to do somethin' good."*

*Mommy is slamming dishes in the kitchen. Hiding
under my covers, I hear Daddy stomp out and then I hear
his truck squeal as he drives away. Every time I close my
eyes I see Black Bunny's eyes popping out of his head. I
couldn't help him and now Mommy and Daddy are mad
because of me.*

"For you," Dad smiles at me, bowing his head.

174

These little rabbits are so shiny black their fur looks wet.

I look at him, in disbelief.

"Me?"

"Yep. I got 'em from a guy who lives across the road from The Rusty Nail."

Before I realize what I'm doing, I fling myself into Dad's body, burying my head in his chest, hugging him hard. It's been a long time since I hugged Dad but maybe I do still love him, a little.

"Thank you," I choke out, surprised at the lump in my throat.

Adam stands there with his hands in his Wrangler pockets, smiling. His face is round and his straight hair hangs over the frames of his new glasses. He is such a good person. He doesn't even seem jealous the rabbits aren't for him. He's just happy for me.

One rabbit climbs out of the box and lands on the basement floor. She hops around a bit, sniffing everything. Her sister stays in the box, huddled in a corner, not so adventurous.

"You can keep them in the basement for the winter, but the cage goes outside just as soon as the weather warms up," Dad grunts.

"Okay," I say, not taking my eyes of my new pets. Reaching into the box, I pull out the second rabbit. Her nose twitches and she kicks her back legs all spazzy as I lift her out, but once I hold her close she settles into letting me pet her. She is so soft. Putting my nose to her fur I breathe her in and she smells sweet like hay. Sitting on the floor I pet her and then let her down to explore the basement with her sister. Adam and I are so focused on the bunnies hopping around, we don't even notice Dad leave. We put the cage up on cinder blocks and line it with hay. Then, we lay newspaper underneath to catch the droppings. Adam runs upstairs to fill up the water bottle for me. When he comes back down I tell him I've named them Molly and Maxine.

Everyday I let Molly and Maxine run around the basement. Every third day I clean their cage. Rabbits poop a lot. It's a lot of work but they're worth it. It doesn't take long for them to know me and they run to the side of the cage and stand up waiting for me to get them out.

In the spring, we move the cage outside. It's better because their poop goes right on the ground and I don't have to clean up so much. Molly and Maxine get lots of fresh air and they're getting big. I pet them, but I'm afraid they'll get away if I let them out so mostly they just sit there, huddled together, eating and getting fat.

I'm getting fat too. Mom and Dad are fighting all the time now. Well, *he's* fighting and she retreats. It's like she's left her body. I don't know where she went but she's no longer here.

"Mom. Mom........MOM!" I call and she looks right through me.

"You never listen!" I say.

She mutters to herself as she washes the dishes, folds the laundry, makes the beds. Work, sleep, work, sleep, church, church, church. That's her life. No room for me in it.

The worse Dad gets, the more she's at church, and not just *our* church. She's trying out every church in town. She and her friend Mindy are going to a different church every night, which is *fine,* but what about us? It's like I don't have a mom anymore. One night, I asked if I could go with her. She left Adam at Gramma Bonner's and brought me along but it was a mistake. The people there were waving their hands in the air and talking jibberish. It scared me. Dad has no idea about all this church hopping because he's never home. Sometimes I think about telling on her, but I don't.

"You're big enough to take care of yourselves," she says on her way out. I know we're big enough but I still need a mom. I still *want* a mom. From the time I get home from school 'til the time I go to bed I do nothing but lie in front of the TV. My middle is getting a fleshy roll and I hate myself for being fat. Eric doesn't like it when I gain weight either, but I can't seem to help it. The only time I get up off the floor is to fill up my ice cream bowl or grab a bag of chips. In homeroom, I panic and beg to copy homework assignments from other kids. Usually they let me, but I don't know how I'll ever make it through tenth grade.

***

On school days, I find out what the afternoon has in store for me on the bus ride home. If Dad's truck is in the parking lot when we roll by The Rusty Nail, I let out a sigh of relief. He's probably not coming home. If he isn't at The Rusty Nail, he might still be at work, but if his truck is in our driveway as the bus pulls up, my stomach knots up. It means he's home, hung over, and *we're screwed.*

Today, the truck is in our driveway. Dad's been home all day, sick. He's greasy and smelly in his white terry cloth robe. Black wiry hair covers his stout pasty legs. He's naked under the robe and not at all careful about what hangs out where. The bathroom smells like shit and puke.

We all tiptoe around until supper, staying clear of him. Mom makes hamburgers and we eat in silence. Adam drops his spoon and Dad glares at him. I ask for more lemonade and he sighs, even though I wasn't asking *him* to pass the pitcher. After supper, Mom goes upstairs to Adam's room to take a nap before work.

Dad gets going on how none of us care about our mother. How we need to be quiet and considerate and let her sleep.

"You kids will be the death of her," he says as he makes a big production of taking the phone off the hook.

This might have fooled me when we were little but not now. He's taking the phone off the hook because he's hiding from bill collectors. They call all the time and he's too chicken to talk to them. Nothing he says can convince me he gives a shit about Mom, up there with that big hole where her front tooth should be.

Adam is in the living room watching TV and I lay down on the floor to join him but then Dad comes in and lies on the couch with one of his girlie magazines. He's got a blue and red plaid throw blanket over him, and he's touching himself under it. He's such a fucking pig, as if we can't tell what he's doing? More likely he doesn't even care. He lets out a huge fart because obviously rules of politeness don't even apply to us. Disgusted, I get up and go to my room. Lying on my bed, I glance at my alarm clock and, *Oh shit! It's almost 7:00PM.*

Eric told me he'd call right at *7PM*, on his break from work. He's helping out at his dad's business. If I don't answer the phone when he calls, he'll be sure to whine about it.

Mom has the fan from the air conditioner blasting in Adam's room. She won't hear the phone ring. In the living room, the TV is blaring. At exactly 6:58, I tiptoe down the steps and stand in the dark by the phone on the wall in the kitchen. Holding the button down with my finger, ear to the receiver, I wait.

At exactly 7:00, there is a "rrinng,"and I snag it fast. Sneaking as far up the stairs as the cord will go, I whisper, "Hello?"

"Hi Babe. How's it going? Why are you whispering?"

"My dad wanted the phone off the hook. If he hears me..."

Suddenly, Dad whips the spying curtain open. In his hand is the hunting knife he uses to cut thick ropes with at work. He switches it open and stands there for a second, glaring at me, blade straight up in the air, inches from my face. He's breathing hard. His face is greasy. Maybe I should be scared, but he looks like an idiot in his stupid bathrobe, holding that knife. What's he gonna do, stab me? Fuck him.

He brings the blade down, slashes the phone cord, and Eric is gone.

"How DARE you defy me?" he thunders, not giving a damn about waking up Mom now.

"When I tell you to leave the phone off the hook, you do it! You hear? Now we just won't have a phone for a while. See how you like that! You're mother is going to get sick, and it will be all on you. You inconsiderate little brat!"

Staring him down I tell him "Fuck you," with my eyes.

After a few seconds he breaks eye contact, turns and stomps back into the living room. Walking up to my room I look at the receiver still in my hand, little colored wires hanging out of the cut cord.

***

The next day, Dad is home again after school. I go outside, to feed the rabbits, and halfway across the back yard I see the cage tipped over, lying sideways on the ground. Did the wind blow it off the cinder blocks? Poor Molly and Maxine must be scared to death. I break into a run and when I reach the cage, the first thing I see is a big chunk of black fur stuck to the wire by the door. Inside, there's only one rabbit. She sits panting in the rear of the cage. One of her legs is just a white bone, peppered with flecks of blood. She's using her whole body to breathe, short and fast. Stumbling backward I hold my stomach.

Oh my God. What happened?

Running back toward the house thoughts criss-cross my mind. Where's the other one? Can a rabbit with a leg ripped off be saved? She must be in so much pain! Oh God! Please help me! Crashing through the back door, I scream, "Mom! My rabbits!"

Mom goes outside and Dad stands on the back porch in his bathrobe, looking out the clothesline window. Running upstairs to my room, I lay on my bed with my arms wrapped around myself and cry. I don't go back outside. I don't clean up the cage. I don't know until later that Dad took the remaining rabbit to Big Harvey's house across the street to be shot. Much as I hate Dad, I keep picturing her leg, with that bone, and I know it was the right thing to do.

The next day there's a knock on the door. It's Mr. Brown from a few houses down the highway. He's the nice old man who lets us play ball in the field by his house. Mr. Brown is wearing a pair of dirty overalls. Opening the door I say,

"Hello."

He takes off his hat and holds it at his chest. It's strange for him to be here. He's never come to our door before.

He starts, "My grandson comes to visit every month and we got 'em a dog to play with when he's here." I don't know Mr. Brown's grandson, but I've seen him around. He's little. Maybe five or six?

I nod, waiting.

"A beautiful dog. A husky," he nods again.

He pauses; looks at me. I smile, wondering if maybe he's gone senile.

"I just want you to know," he says. "I shot him."

I shake my head, confused.

Did Dad take my rabbit to Mr. Brown's to be shot…instead of Big Harvey's?

He gives a polite nod, puts his hat back on his head and starts to shuffle away down the front steps. From the shoulder of the road he turns to me and yells, "Can't get a pet for one child and have it go killin' another child's pets."

He tips his hat and walks back down the shoulder of the highway toward his house as I shut the door.

With my back against the front door I slide to the floor. His dog killed my rabbit? And he killed his dog? And Harvey killed my other rabbit to put her out of her misery? I've already had two cats die on this highway, and one puppy. Now my rabbits were eaten alive by Mr.

Brown's dog. Dad broke my heart with Rascal. Pets are nothing but heartache.

It sneaks up on me at school, or on the bus, or before I go to sleep. Visions of my rabbits. The meat of her leg torn off and that bloody bone sticking out. I imagine the other one being thrashed around in the mouth of a furry white dog with one blue eye. Shuddering, I remember the black rabbit in Florida. I don't want another animal. Not ever.

Two weeks later, "You don't seem very *enthused*," Dad barks after calling me down to the basement and presenting me with another box.

This set of rabbits has black and white spots and they are much bigger than Molly and Maxine.

I hate him.

I shrug out a "Thanks," as I take the box out back toward the cage.

Dad shrugs before walking out the door and heading back down the road to The Rusty Nail.

This time I secure the cage with rope and weigh it down with cinderblocks on top. Not so easy to tip over, but still a smart fox, or dog could figure out how to get at them. These new rabbits, I don't even bother to name.

* * *

We do need to start thinking about names though, and not for the new rabbits. After being so worried about Hilary or me turning up pregnant, mom's the one who got knocked up. She even got mad at me for having the nerve to be happy about it when she told me. I love babies though. I can't help it.

Dad's been drinking more than ever and the worse he gets, the less Mom seems to care about anything. The rule is: *don't need anything* and I agree to her terms rather than facing her hate for me if I refuse them. Everyday after school, I gorge myself with whatever junk food I can find. Chocolate ice cream. Soda. Chips. Violently I shove them into my mouth until my stomach throbs with pain. Afterward, I fall asleep on the floor in front of the TV. Hilary isn't around. Adam watches TV too, but we don't talk to each other much.

Those damn rabbits. I keep forgetting to feed them.

Lifting my head from the carpet, my belly is too full to get up. I'll go out later, after supper. The thing is, *later*, I'm even more tired.

Each time I notice their bowls are empty a guilty shock runs through me and I tell myself they must have just finished their food. When did I feed them last? Yesterday? The day before? I can't remember.

You awful, awful girl.

From now on I'll feed them every single day. I promise to do better.

The next day, I'm on the living room floor with the theme to *The Guiding Light* lulling me to sleep and once again, I forget.

The fleshy roll around my middle has Eric thinking I should go on a strict diet. He's always mad at me for not wanting to have sex, and accuses me of being frigid, because I don't seem to enjoy it. *He* wants to do it all the time. Thank God football practice has started. I'm relieved not to see him so much. I hate myself for being fat, but my body is like lead. I can't get up off the floor. Homework hasn't been done for weeks. I'm about to fail math. I miss Sophie. All I've got is Libby and Eric and I'm so tired of his always wanting to bang away at me.

Mom and I pass in the house like two ghosts. If only I were little again. She'd take me in the swimming pool for my lessons and I'd feel the warmth of her body on my cold skin. The motion of the water would rock us and we'd cling tight to each other. She'd take me for walks in the woods and pick Black-eyed Susans, and place them in my hair. She'd smile big and pretty with a mouth full of healthy white teeth. She was so beautiful. She used to care for me. I know she did.

Day after day, it's *The Guiding Light, The Brady Bunch, Little House, Bosom Buddies, Three's Company,* and I'm way down underneath it all. When Libby tells me her family is moving to Pittsburgh, I guess I'm sad, but it's down in me, so deep, I hardly feel it.

Chapter Twenty-Three

Eric has always gotten good grades, but lately he's taken it a step further and become chummy with Mr. Morris, head of the math club. Mr. Morris even took Eric aside and told him he was "going places" and his relationship with me seemed risky. I was furious when I found out Eric told him I was on the pill. With that little piece of information, Mr. Morris isn't concerned anymore for Eric. Evidently, he never had any concern *for me*. Eric has a future. I'm just the daughter of the drunk at the bar.

Mr. Morris has Eric all psyched up about applying to Purdue, his alma mater, so Eric has traded his Rolling Stones concert shirts for Khakis and Izod shirts and we don't smoke pot anymore. Eric, because of his plans for college. Me, because my mom's having a baby. How am I supposed to tell the baby not to do bad stuff if I'm doing it?

I'm taking two art classes and spending my study periods in the art room so I'm actually there almost half the day. I have a new friend named Kasey who is an artist too. She's a shy, brainy girl. Her dark hair is cut in a short, asymmetrical bob. She's got pale skin and green eyes. She's quiet with a very dry, sarcastic sense of humor. We make each other laugh, a lot.

Some days, the art room is a great place to forget about home. Mr. Peters encourages me, and compliments my work. Other days the art room might as well *be* home. If Mr. Peters is in one of his moods, he'll stomp around, telling us we don't appreciate how lucky we are to have all the art supplies we need. He calls us "spoiled" and goes around belittling us.

Kasey and I have been having a giggly day, and apparently this bugs Mr. Peters. He stops at my station and looks at my painting. He steps back, looks me up and down and says, "I suppose you think you look so cool today?"

I stare at the floor, not knowing what to say or where he's going with this.

He adds, "Too bad your pants are covered with orange stains."

This morning I'd searched for something to wear and I had nothing. This was the least stained pair of pants I could find, and I wore a long buttoned down shirt *untucked* in an effort to cover some of the orange spots caused by the iron in our water. I can't help it we have well water. I'd been having so much fun with Kasey I'd almost forgotten about the stains.

Biting my lip, I turn to my easel, and continue painting, acting as if what he said didn't bother me at all. I'm working on a portrait of a hard, modern 80s woman. She wears a big red hat with an attached scarf that ties around her square jaw. Her features are harsh. She's solid and strong. She doesn't take any shit.

When Mr. Peters walks away, Kasey comes over and whispers in my ear, "He's just bitter because he thinks he's some great artist, but he's stuck here teaching high school. Don't pay any attention to him. He's an asshole."

If I look at her I might cry, so I just stare ahead at my canvass, and let out my breath. I hadn't even realized I'd been holding it.

That weekend I set up a table in front of the house, just a few yards away from the highway. I hold a yard sale to earn money for more clothes. I do it all the time, selling things I scavenge from the house and the garage. You'd be surprised the junk people will buy.

***

Mom still works the graveyard shift at the hospital. Dad spends most of his time and all of his money at The Rusty Nail. He only comes home in the middle of the night. At the sound of a man's voice I shoot up in bed, pulling the covers to my neck. Craning my ear toward the stairs, I struggle to make out who it is. Two men's voices, then a woman's float up to my room. My heart pounds. Damn my stupid parents for never locking the door. Finally, I hear Dad's voice and I let out a breath. It's just Dad. There's loud, slurred conversation at the bottom of the steps, then the popping of cans being opened. With my blankets still gripped in my hands I look at the clock. 2:10AM. In three hours I have to get up for school and today is a math test. Letting go of the blanket I get out of bed. In my nightgown, arms tight to my chest to cover my chest, I tiptoe down the stairs, through the spying curtain, and sit on the bottom step in the kitchen.

"Hey, Jane!" Dad smiles, glassy eyed, as he glances over his shoulder at me. He's taking things out of the fridge, putting them on the counter, making room for a case of Budweiser on the second shelf.

"Dad, we have school tomorrow. I have to get up in three hours."

He looks at me confused, as if I'd spoken in Spanish.

"Will you look at her!" Dad's friend Dennis yells, shaking his head.

"How old is she now?" he asks Dad.

"I have school in the morning," I reply.

"She's really growing up," he beams at me like I'm an adorable toddler. Apparently, Dennis doesn't speak Spanish either. He shakes his head and pops the tab off his can of Bud.

Fuck you, I think to myself, glaring at them.

Scanning the dining room I recognize most of the faces of Dad's loser drinking buddies. Like a deer in a gun's scope, my eyes rest on Sally Reynolds. She's the only woman among them and she's the target of my disgust. She sits there in her skin-tight Jordasche jeans, beer gut zipped inside, fat roll hanging over her waistband. She's Mom's age. She has blue eyes and long straight blonde hair and I'm sure she could be pretty but right now she's just a bloated, drunken mess like the rest of them. Sally feels the heat of my stare, looks up at me, and quickly averts her eyes.

That's right bitch. How does it feel to be keeping three kids up all night when they have school in the morning? Fuck you. Go home.

The drunks talk over each other loudly as Dad passes out beers. The smell of cigarette smoke gives me a headache. Hilary and Adam don't bother to get up but there's no way they're actually sleeping. *No way.* It's so convenient Mom works nights and gets to miss all Dad's little parties. Just as well. If she were here, she'd probably wait on all of them and I'd hate her even more.

Sally's husband Chuck staggers to the piano and starts a raggedy attempt at honky-tonk. He misses every other note with the drunks starting and stopping their singing each time he flubs.

"Wait a minute. Wait a sec," Chuck slurs, before trying again.

Chuck gives up on the piano and takes the guitar he brought with him out of its case on the floor. The one guy I don't recognize takes a seat at the piano and starts pounding the keys, hard. He's better than Chuck, but not by much.

They massacre several Beatles songs.

How am I gonna pass my math test?

Watching them sing, they lean together like a drunken gospel choir grinning at each other laughing, *"AH-HA-HA-HA-HA-HA!"*

The wood floors under my feet are shaking from all the noise. The light fixture above the dining room table sways.

Sighing loudly, I stomp my foot on the bottom step. My attempts to bore a hole into Sally's skull are no use. My evil eye can't register if she won't even look at me. Turning around, I march back up the stairs.

I'm back in bed, and the Shea Suck Band has switched to the Everley Brothers. Dad and Sally are attempting harmonies. Dad's drunken falsetto almost matches Sally's regular high drunk voice, so it really isn't harmony at all. They sound like that cooking lady on TV, Julia Childs, and I lie there imagining her at the piano, with a can of Bud in her hand.

Closing my eyes tight, I pray they all go home tonight. Seeing random losers passed out on our couch in the morning startles me, no matter how many times it happens.

At 5:00 AM my alarm goes off. Dragging myself out of bed I tiptoe down the steps, skipping the squeakiest ones.

The smell of stale beer wafts through the spy curtain as I enter the kitchen. Budweiser cans on the dining room table; Budweiser cans lay crushed on the floor. An ashtray filled with cigarette butts reeks on the kitchen counter.

Taking the wrench off its nail by the back door, I go down into the cellar to turn on the hot water for my shower. On my way back up, in the kitchen, I round the corner toward the bathroom and hear something which stops me quick. Dad is in there. Over the sound of the shower I just turned on, I hear loud, violent gushes spraying the toilet bowl, followed by trickles, then spitting noises, and moaning.

Dad is sick, but there's no compassion in my heart. He's holding up my shower and that's all I care about. I'd like to go in and kick him in the ass, sending his face smashing into the toilet bowl. Imagining him looking back at me with blood on his nose from hitting the rim, I swear I'd kick him again. All I know is there's *no way* I'm going to school without a shower today, and I'm *not* taking it in front of him, the perv.

After a few minutes Dad stumbles into the kitchen where I wait. He takes a glass out of the cupboard and fills it with tap water. Standing there in his white underwear, with his bloated beer belly hanging out, he drinks the whole thing then fills it up again. He walks past me, through the bathroom and back to his bedroom, shutting the door behind him. He didn't even bother to flush the toilet and the bathroom reeks of shit and puke, stale beer and cigarettes. His jeans are on the floor next to the toilet. Using my foot I hit the flush handle and try to avert my eyes as his orange puke disappears. Kicking his pants out into the kitchen I leave them there on the floor in a heap. Then, I stuff the doorknob hole with toilet paper, just in case.

Later, Adam is up, dressed and ready for school. He's eating a bowl of cereal in front of the TV. Mom doesn't get home from work 'til after the bus comes for us. Hilary's in the bathroom and I'm pouring some cereal for myself when Dad yells out, "Hey Janie! I need you to call the tree service."

My body contracts. I put the cereal bowl down.

"Jane!"

I pour my milk.

"Janie, get the hell in here!"

Walking through the living room to his bedroom, I stand in the doorway. He's sitting up in bed. "I need you to call the tree service and tell them I won't be able to make it today. I'm sick," he orders.

My stomach lurches. I tighten my fists and I say, "I don't want to call."

Dad glares at me.

"I didn't ask what you *wanted* to do," he barks. "I'm telling you what you're *gonna* do. Get on the God damn phone."

He lies back down.

My fists clench tighter. I set my jaw. "You shouldn't be up all night drinking if you can't go to work in the morning! If you can't *handle* it!" I scream, my throat tight, my voice two octaves higher than normal.

He sits up in bed but I turn quickly and march back into the kitchen.

Adam is on the couch, watching the scene unfold, his brows furrowed. He sets his bowl of cereal on the floor. Hilary comes out of the bathroom and gives me a dirty look. Me? *How is this my fault?*

Dad bellows from the bedroom, "HEY JANIE YOU *MOUTHY LITTLE BITCH*! HOW WOULD YOU LIKE TO FIND ANOTHER PLACE TO LIVE? YOU GET ON THAT PHONE OR DON'T BOTHER COMING HOME AFTER SCHOOL, YOU HEAR? *DO YOU HEAR ME?*"

The words hang in the air for a second and then, like doors on a jail cell, my heart slams shut. I am *done* with him.

With shaky hands I grab my backpack and my coat and stand outside. It's 20 degrees and there is still a half hour 'til the bus, but I don't care. When Hilary's ride pulls up she hops in without a glance in my direction. She probably made the call for Dad. Someone always does.

Adam comes out early to wait for the bus with me. He doesn't say anything, and doesn't look at me, but he stands closer than usual and somehow I know he's with me. Quiet, tough, gentle Adam. Love for him fills my heart as we wait in silence on the shoulder of the road.

On the bus I sit in my usual spot. Jenna gets on and she's chattering away for a good five minutes before she turns to look at me and stops mid-sentence.

"Oh my God. Are you okay? You're white as a ghost!" she says.

I shake my head, no.

Tears stream down my face and my whole body shakes.

"Do you want to talk?"

I shake my head.

I can't. My voice is stuck in my throat.

The bus is loud and the kids are hyper. No one notices the bubble of silence over our seat. Jenna doesn't prod and I'm grateful. I'm like a row of dominoes and it would take just about nothing to topple me over.

At school, I'm floating down a long corridor of lockers when I see Eric. He's smiling his big white teeth smile, his back flat against my locker. His arms are folded, and his legs are crossed all casual at the ankles. He's wearing a pink oxford shirt, khaki pants, and shiny new Docksides on his feet. His expression changes from the suave practiced pose of a model to one of confusion as I close in on him. Mascara is probably bleeding down my face. I don't even care. The jig is up. I'm not normal.

"What's wrong?" he asks, taking hold of my shoulders.

I shake my head. I can't talk to him any more than I could talk to Jenna. What would I say? He ushers me back down the hall and we go out the side door of the high school. Soon we're off school grounds and we're walking, walking, until we get to Eric's house. He holds my hand the whole way and talks softly about nothing and tells me "I love you, Babe," and "It's okay," over and over. My tears just won't stop. I'm so lucky to have him.

Eric's mother is sitting in a housecoat at the kitchen table. She looks up from her newspaper, surprised, as he leads me past her, to the door of their basement. In the rec room he tells me to lie down on the couch and I do. He covers me with a blanket and goes upstairs. Turning on my side toward the wall, I pull a throw pillow between my knees and start to shake. I don't know what's wrong with me. I just can't get it together.

Eric comes back down and kneels at my side. He whispers, "My mom is cool with you being here. Just rest and I'll see you after school," he kisses my cheek, says, "I love you Babe," and then quickly retreats back up the steps.

A few minutes later, Eric's mom is here. She smells like perfume, and she's adjusting my blanket and talking softly. She sits beside me on the couch and I can feel the warmth of her body. Too close for comfort, but I just don't care anymore. Tucking the blanket up over my shoulders she says,

"You know, when I was your age, my father was *very* abusive. He used to whip me with a belt, right up until I left his house as a teenager."

My eyes are closed and it takes a few seconds for this information to sink in.

Mrs. Nowak? Perfect Mrs. Nowak with all her preppy little tennis outfits? Astonished, I picture her at my age, trembling, frightened and humiliated in front of a faceless monster. I think of Dad's spying. Of his stupid drunken parties. His threat to kick me out. Where would I go? What would I do? Her Dad sounds even worse than mine. At least my Dad doesn't *beat* us. And here she is. Somehow she's okay. Maybe I'll be okay too.

Being mothered by Mrs. Nowak snaps at an ache inside me and the tears come out in wrenching sobs. She pats my shoulder and hands me tissues, never asking any questions. When jagged sighs replace my shrieks, she stands up and says gently,

"You rest."

The stairs creak as she climbs them and at the top she flicks the light switch off. The basement is dark and I flip onto my other side, facing out. The only light comes from a neon sign over the Nowak's wet bar. *Budweiser*, it reads.

***

No one ever mentions the big fight with Dad or his threat to kick me out. No one ever mentions how I didn't go to school that day. It all just blows over and everything is the same. School. Binging on junk food, day after day I'm groggy on the floor in front of the TV, when suddenly my eyes snap open and I jump up.

The rabbits.

Walking out into the back yard, I approach the cage and see one rabbit is lying on its side. As I get closer, I realize, it's dead. Sucking in my breath I step back. What should I do? The other rabbit sits toward the back of the cage. Its breathing is shallow. I'm afraid to touch the dead one, but I'll at least take the live one out. She shouldn't have to sit there with her dead sister. When I wrap my hands around her, I lift her and feel the sickening sensation of fur on bone. She's nothing more than a skeleton.

Dropping her, I step back from the cage, and wipe my hands on the thighs of my pants.

Oh my God. They starved. I starved the rabbits and one is dead.

My throat closes in on itself and a moan starts in my chest. My hands start to shake.

With the food and water bowls, I run to the back porch and fill them. Setting them in front of the remaining rabbit I beg her, *"Please, eat. Drink!"*

She won't come forward. "Fuck you," she says to me.

In two days she's dead too.

There is nowhere to go to with this. I'm the most evil, lazy person on the face of the planet.

You awful, awful girl.

Recently, Mom converted to Catholicism so I go to church with her every chance I get and pray for forgiveness. I think about confessing, but they won't let you if you're not Catholic. Besides, I'm sure what I did is unforgivable.

You awful, awful girl.

But I have to confess to someone. I *need* to take my punishment. I decide on my old friend Jill James. Her family still goes to the fire and brimstone church in Centerville. She's the one who had Sophie Sheinmel take Jesus into her heart at my 11th birthday party. She knows all about God's wrath. She grew up beside her grampa's barn and loves animals more than anyone I know. She'll know the right punishment.

Jill has long since left her Dorothy Hamill behind, and she wouldn't be caught dead bobbing for apples. She wears her hair bleached blonde and sprayed high. Dark make-up lines her eyes and she has the best figure in high school. The boys are wild for her. On weekends, Jill answers phones at her dad's used car business down the road from my house. I walk the mile to her dad's office and pay her a visit. She'll despise me, but at least it will be off my chest. Whatever hate she sends my way, I deserve it.

Sitting there in Mr. James's office, I tell her what happened. How I starved the poor rabbits. My eyes find a stain on the carpet and I focus on it as I speak. I can't look at her.

Jill sits across from me at her dad's big desk, pen in her hand, tapping lightly. To me it's a judge's gavel and I wait for my sentence. After a long pause she says, "Janie, you don't know for sure how they died. They could have had a disease or something. They could have been sick."

I stare at the carpet stain as she continues, "Besides, animals starve all the time in the wild. My grandpa says it's part of nature."

Looking up at her through my bangs, the compassion in her eyes makes me weep. I can't believe she doesn't hate me.

"Are you sure?" I ask, my voice choking on the words.

She nods, compassion in her voice and on her face.

And just like that, Jill James "saves" me.

Chapter Twenty-Four

Mom's belly is getting huge. The stretch marks are enough to convince me, but I'd already decided if I can't even keep a couple of rabbits alive, there is no way I'm ever having kids. The doctor sends Mom for a sonogram because her belly is too big for how far along she is and there might be something wrong with the baby. Greeting us in a white lab coat, the technician says, "Your husband couldn't make it so you brought your daughter. How sweet."

As if Dad would ever come.

The lady squirts blue gel on Mom's belly. Next, she wiggles a white wand all over the gel. After a few seconds, she looks at the screen, then stops, like something is wrong. She gets up and goes to the door.

"I'll be right back," she says on her way out.

She comes back with the doctor who is all smiles. What a jerk. How can he be smiling when something is obviously, terribly wrong? He points to the TV screen and says, "Here we have a baby."

Mom smiles her closed mouth smile, where she tries to wrap her top lip down over her missing front tooth. Squinting, I try to make out the little figure on the screen. It's nothing more than a black little blob with a white blob in it. The doctor keeps rolling the wand over mom's belly, and then he says, "And here we have *another* baby."

Mom shifts up on her elbows, looking closer at the screen. Then, she flops her body down, the back of her head hitting the exam table hard as she closes her eyes.

I don't get it.

The doctor looks at me, broadens his smile and says, "Twins!"

***

It's hard to concentrate in school when all I can think about is Mom carrying two babies in her belly. Mr. Carter is my English teacher this year. He's a sarcastic little guy, scrawny, like a runner. He's got wire framed glasses and curly brown hair. His mustache is kind of smallish, like Hitler's. The boys in this class are wild. They throw paper airplanes and spit wads. They interrupt and don't listen.

Mr. Carter seems to have given up on the whole bunch. Day after day, he stands, leaning back on the front of his desk, looking at the ceiling as if asking God, "Why?"

Today he gives us an essay assignment, to be completed by the end of the period. The boys moan and protest, but he tells them they're wasting valuable writing time.

"Here's the assignment," he says. "Look around the room. Choose an object. Any object. Write about it. Let it take you someplace."

The first thing my eyes rest on is the door. I can't *wait* to get out of here.

"Oh man…this is stupid," one boy groans.

"What the…," another boy starts to say.

Mr. Carter interrupts, "Gentlemen, you may certainly exercise your option of failing this class. I'd be glad to do it all again with you next year."

Putting my pen to my lined yellow paper, I look up and start describing the door. It's just a plain brown door, with a small square window at the top. It's propped open with a little wooden triangle door stop. There is a pattern in the grain of the wood. Little black lines one over the other, all curving in the same direction. The grain goes up and around like a ghost. It reminds me of the painting, "The Scream," which I saw in a book in the art room, so I write that. Next, I find myself writing about doors in general. The varieties; wood, glass, screened. Then, I move on to what doors might symbolize. How you can walk through doors into other places and different opportunities. What the hell am I even talking about?

My pen is moving fast but I feel like I'm floating above the whole thing, watching some stupid Centerville girl write about doors and wondering just what the hell does she think she's up to. This probably isn't what Mr. Carter wanted at all.

I'm about to cross out the whole thing and switch to another topic when he says, "Time's up. Pass your papers forward."

Turning red, I pass my paper up, face down, so no one will be able to see it. My stomach squirms at the thought of Mr. Carter actually reading the nonsense I wrote.

On Monday, I slump in my chair when he passes the essays back. There's a big 99 written in red ink on top of mine.

A ninety-nine?

After a few more essay assignments, and a few more papers with bright red marks in the 90s, Mr. Carter calls me aside as I'm leaving class.

"You don't belong here," he says.

"What? But I'm doing really well. I'm getting 95s."

"Exactly. You're not being challenged. I'm requesting you be moved to accelerated English."

"*Honors*? I can't do honors." I say softly.

"You can," he says, all business. He hands me a slip telling me where to report for English next week. Walking to my next class, I'm wondering what exactly Mr. Carter's been smoking.

On Monday, when I walk into honors English, my stomach knots up when I see all the smart kids, and I'm sure Mr. Carter has made an awful mistake. Students are filing in, and no one is talking to me. Sitting down at a desk I pretend not to care. Feeling a little tap on my shoulder I turn and it's Kasey, from art. My body lets out a huge relieved sigh. Smiling big, she sits down right behind me. I smile back.

The bell rings and the teacher comes in. She's a fat woman with an enormous round ass. Her posture is a bit crooked, with her left side higher than her right. As she walks down the row by my desk her body goes up and down with each alternating step, as if someone is turning a handle, like a jack-in-the-box. Thick panty lines show through her tight beige polyester stretch pants, framing her gigantic behind. As she passes my desk I smell stale cigarette smoke and something else rancid, perhaps her crotch. She drags her chair out from her desk and forcefully throws herself backward onto it. Her breathing is labored. Her yellowish gray hair is extremely short , and it sticks all greasy to her head. She sits there, taking attendance and at the end she looks up at me and says, "Miss Shea?"

I nod and when she smiles at me, her teeth are pointed and gray.

"Welcome," she says.

Smiling faintly, I sink lower in my seat.

Halfway through the period, Ms. Buss is in the middle of a big speech about the book they've been reading, *Ethan Frome*, and I feel an eyelash in my eye. I start dabbing at it with my pinky. I can't interrupt her to ask to use the mirror in the girl's bathroom. Not on my first day in honors English.

After a while, my eye is really watering so I lean down and grab my purse from under my chair. Placing it all the way forward on my desk, I hope the body of the kid in front of me will block Ms. Buss' view. Ever so slowly, I reach into my purse, and feel around for my pressed powder.

Pulling it out, I open it silently. Leaning, way, way down on the desk, I hold the compact level to my eye. Looking in the mirror I dab at the eyelash and snag it easily.

"Miss Shea!"

I sit up quick in my seat.

"I don't know what you were doing in your last class but we most definitely aren't playing *beauty parlor* in here. Keep the make-up in your purse or I'll have to confiscate it."

Snapping my compact shut I glare at her and say, "I had something in my eye."

She gives me a dirty look, then continues droning on about Edith Wharton. She doesn't think I belong here. Therefore, I find it my duty to get all As in her class.

***

As the school year goes on, and her stomach grows, Mom looks more and more like the walking dead. Her skin is so white you can see her blue veins through it. Her hair, long, dry and bushy, is down past her shoulders. Then, there is the missing tooth. From behind she looks like a spider. Huge belly poking out the sides, skinny arms and skinny legs.

Once again the plumbing is broken and we're taking plastic jugs to Gramma Bonner's and lugging laundry back and forth. Dad is home less than ever, and it's just as well. It's not like he'd ever help carry a bag of laundry down the front steps, or help bring water jugs into the house.

Our bathroom is again an outhouse. It's not just the smell, but the sound of my pee splattering on piles of shit that makes me gag. We're not allowed to put paper in the toilet, so the nasty toilet paper we use to wipe ourselves sits in the little garbage can next to the sink. Only at the end of the day are we allowed to use one jug of water to flush the whole fucking thing. Mom takes us to Grammas to bathe at night but I still feel oily and dirty at school without a morning shower. After her friends pick her up in the mornings, I raid Hilary's dresser for something decent to wear and hope no one can tell how scummy I feel.

This goes on for a couple of weeks and then, in November, the babies are born. It happened while I was at school and it's like finding out about a party after the fact. I'm mad I wasn't invited. Dad says Mom had an

203

emergency c-section and one of the twins is in the baby ICU. They don't have names yet. No little sisters for me. Two boys.

Dad says he'll take us to the hospital after we eat supper and I hurry through my meal and run upstairs to curl my hair and put on make-up. I don't want the babies to think I'm ugly the first time they see me.

We arrive at the hospital where Mom works. She spends so much time here but I've hardly ever been inside. The hospital smells like acne astringent and the floors are shiny white. We take an elevator to the fifth floor and follow the signs to the nursery.

Looking through the glass window I search the ten or so cribs until my eyes fall on one right in the middle. The one with the card that says "Shea B." My throat tightens and my whole body feels warm. Shea B wriggles a little in his crib and his pink and blue hat slides off his head, falling on the tiny mattress. His face is chubby and red and perfectly round. His eyes are closed. He is definitely the cutest baby in the nursery. Staring at him I can't believe how lucky we are. Hilary and Adam are talking but I don't hear a word they say because Shea B is *ours* and he just let out a little yawn. I am completely in love. *Nothing is wrong.*

It's hard to leave Shea B but there's someone else I have to meet. As we walk down the hall, toward the baby ICU, Dad takes a piece of paper out of his dirty jeans pocket and reading the scribbles on it says, "That one weighed 7lbs 11 oz. He came out second. The first one weighed 6lbs. 10 oz."

The nurses are a little snotty and you have to wash your hands with special soap before you can even look through the window in the baby ICU. We can only go back one at a time and Dad lets me go first. One of the nurses is sitting at her station, flipping through a magazine.

"You can take a peek at him through the window, right there, just ahead," she nods, without getting up.

Stepping up to the window, I freeze. My breath gets stuck in my chest and my knees feel wobbly. The baby in the window looks half-human, half bird. Its eyes are open and looking at me and there are tubes up his nose and one sticking into the top of his head. He's a skeleton. His arms are the width of a nickel and monitors blink all around him. Bracing myself on the windowsill I start to cry.

"Oh my God! What's wrong with him?" I ask the nurse.

It doesn't make sense. If the other baby was 7 pounds, this one *can't* be six pounds.

The nurse looks up from her magazine, rolls her eyes and points beyond the creature in window to a crib against the back wall, straight ahead.

The baby in *that* crib is Shea A, and he's perfect. He's on his belly, naked, except for a little diaper sticking up in the air like a duck's bottom. He has a tiny black mask over his eyes, like the one Felix Unger on *The Odd Couple* uses to sleep. He's got lots of dark hair on his head, unlike Shea B, and he has a pointy little chin. He's really cute and looks just like all the babies on the Shea side, dark hair, small sharp features. My shoulders drop and I let out a sigh of relief.

Mom's too tired from surgery to see any of us today. We walk out of the hospital into the cold evening air, and I float through the parking lot on pure love. That warm

God feeling pulses through me and never, in my wildest dreams, did I think I would be so lucky.

The next day while we're at school Dad gets the water fixed and when we get home, it's boot camp. "You kids need to mop the floors," he orders. "Clean the toilet," he barks. "Clean the shower," he yells. "Vacuum," he stomps.

"You kids are so lazy. You are going to make your mother sick. Do you want your mother to get sick and die? If she does it will be *your* fault. You don't do a God damn thing around here to help her."

How do we even begin? We've never had to clean before. I wish he'd just go to The Rusty Nail, but he'd rather stay here and yell at us. I feel like an animal trapped in a cage.

On the way to see Mom at the hospital, Dad tells us he's named the babies after his brothers. Charles and Bobby. I hate these names and I'm pissed at Mom for not even considering the names I liked. She's such a doormat. She doesn't even get a say on what to name her own babies! Dad walks us to Mom's hospital room and then leaves to go have a cigarette.

Mom is paler than ever and she's groggy. Still, I'm so stressed. I *need* her. Leaning into the side of the bed, I take her cold hand in mine. Tubes are running into her veins.

"Mom?" I whimper. "He's being just awful."

She stares at the ceiling.

"Mom," I plead.

"He's making us clean the whole house. Can you please just say something to him? Will you tell him it doesn't matter? Tell him the place doesn't have to be spotless. *Please*?" I whisper.

Mom slowly rolls her head toward me. Her body is weak but I've never seen such strong hatred shoot out of anyone's eyes.

"*What* do you want me to do?" She seethes, sarcastically through clenched teeth. I drop her hand and shrink back from her disgust for me.

She closes her eyes and turns her head. My own hate fans up through every cell in my body. I hate Dad. I hate Mom for never coming though. Most of all I hate myself, for needing her so much.

The next day, Mom gets a blood transfusion and her color comes back. She looks like a whole different person when we come to visit. She tries to talk to me but I can hardly bring myself to look at her.

I walk to the nursery and stare through the window at baby Charlie. His crib is right there in the front. His eyes are open and he's looking right at me, though the nurses say he can't really see yet. He lets out a big yawn, and I smile. Silently, I tell him, "I love you," and "I'll take care of you."

***

A couple days later I come home from school to find two bassinets in the living room. Both babies are asleep and I go back and forth, peeking at each one. I know I shouldn't wake them, but I can't help it I'm so excited. Scooping Bobby up, I rest him on my shoulder. He hunkers right in and a surge of love shoots through me. This feeling is stronger than anything I've ever known. I pull him down from my shoulder and study his face. How is he possible? His little tiny lips. His ears? Eyes that open and shut. Mom walks into the living room and I look at her expecting to be in trouble for waking the baby, but she just smiles at me.

Then, Charlie starts to fuss, so I hand Bobby to Mom. I pick Charlie up. He stops crying the second I lift him from the bassinet. Holding him out in front of me, I memorize his face. Touching my nose to the top of his head he smells sweet, like Pampers. Staring into his little eyes, he looks right back at me, and I have to turn away because these love feelings are too much.

At school, all I can think about are the twins. When I get off the bus I run inside to hold them and in just a couple of months they recognize me and break into big grins whenever they see me. Bobby has some problems from when he was born and he chokes a lot on his formula. It scares me, so I usually give him to Mom and I take care of Charlie.

When the boys are a few months old, I start taking them to the mall and to the high school basketball games and sometimes people who don't know us give me dirty looks, thinking they're mine. They look at me like I'm some kind of teenage slut and I want to tell them, "They're my *brothers,* you jerk."

All the girls in my class flock around the stroller and squeal over how cute the babies are. The adults tell me how lucky Mom is to have me as a "second mother" helping her. The twins give me something to do and something to talk about rather than just standing there feeling stupid. Bobby and Charlie are the best things that ever happened to me. I'm so proud to be their sister.

Chapter Twenty-Five

Eric is working at his dad's business again this summer. I won't be sixteen 'til fall so I can't work yet. It's July and the babies are eight months old already. It's late afternoon and Dad is hung over and miserable so I decide to get out of the house and go for a run.

At first, running was a punishment. I only did it because I felt fat. I also tried standing out behind the shed after dinner and making myself throw up, but it didn't take. No matter how hard I tried, my fingers wouldn't stay down my throat long enough to throw up very much. For me, running is a much better way to keep my weight down around 112.

Once I got past the initial hard part, and got my breathing right, I started to love running. Sometimes if I go long enough, I can even get that God feeling, where it's just me and my breath; one strong leg in front of the other and *nothing is wrong.* I've worked up to a six-mile loop around Centerville. Three miles down Lincoln Road, then back onto the highway and another three miles 'til home.

After my run, back in our yard, I bend over, elbows to knees, catching my breath. Out of the corner of my eye I see Bobby and Charlie's little plastic kiddie pool under the weeping willow tree. Mom got it for them at a garage sale and they love to splash in it.

There are only about three inches of water in it but I'm hot, and I think, "Why not?"

I go over and plop in.

My legs muscles twitch from the run and the water feels cool on my sizzling body. Looking up I watch the willow branches sway in the slow breeze. The sky is bright blue with white puffy clouds. The back of my head rests on the edge of the pool. It smells like grass and honeysuckle and I look out at the wooded hill at the back of our yard. Breathing in, I close my eyes and rest.

Suddenly, I hear yelling.

The noise comes from inside the house.

Hopping out of the pool, dripping, I walk toward the back porch and go inside.

Mom stands at the kitchen sink muttering. Dad is pacing back and forth behind her in his dingy terry cloth bathrobe barking, "You got somethin' to say Diana, go ahead and say it. Don't stand there muttering like an imbecile."

Mom stops washing the dishes and dries her hands. Eyes to the floor, she walks evenly out of the kitchen, past the babies in their walkers in the living room, and into their bedroom, shutting the door behind her.

As she passes, Bobby holds up his arms to her. He wants out of his walker. When she shut the door, he started to cry.

Dad follows Mom and stands outside the bedroom yelling, "That's right, Diana! Run away."

Dad's loud voice scares Bobby and his cries become shrieks. Charlie's bottom lip goes out too but before I can get across the room to pick them up, Dad stomps over to Bobby, gets right in his face and bellows, "SHUT *UP!*"

Bobby's whole body straightens. His shoulders come up to his ears and his toes point to the floor under his walker. His eyes shut and his face puckers. His chin gets all wrinkled and he's silent for a few seconds before he lets out his air and starts shrieking again.

Shoving past Dad, I glare at him and he shrinks back, just a hair. Bobby reaches his arms up to me and I scoop him out. Soothing him on my shoulder, I lean over and snatch Charlie out of his walker with my other arm. Down the stairs we go, right out the front door.

Setting the babies on the front walkway, I open the back of Mom's latest beater car, a rusty white station wagon, and pull out the double stroller. I flick it open with one great shake. Grabbing the diaper bag from the front seat I shove it under the stroller, buckle the babies in and take off walking down the highway, duplicating the 6-mile loop I just ran.

The stroller seats face each other and Bobby is riding backwards, looking toward me. Charlie faces his brother. My heels hit the road hard as I push the stroller. I look at Bobby's precious face. His pointy little chin, his tiny nose, his chubby cheeks, covered in red blotches from crying. How can anyone scream at a little baby like that?

I've never hated my father more. Chewing nervously on the inside of my cheek as I walk, I wonder what to do. What can I possibly do? As much as I love these babies, if I came across a happy family that wanted them, I swear to God I would give them away on the spot. I would do *anything* to give them a chance to grow up without Dad in their lives.

After a while, Bobby seems okay, like he forgot Dad yelling at him, but every now and again he lets out a jagged little sigh and I know at least his body remembers. The babies are barefoot, wearing just diapers and t-shirts. I didn't even think about getting them dressed. I've no idea when they ate last. My thighs are chafing together in my wet shorts but I don't care. The walking and the pushing calms my nerves.

For the first time, I understand why Mom wasn't happy to be pregnant. I'd rather not have these beautiful babies at all, than subject them to a lifetime of Dad.

On Lincoln Road the shoulder is practically non-existent. Cars swerve way over into the opposite lane to give us space and I appreciate that. Once we pass the bottom of Twist Run Road it's all country and there's no traffic. We can walk right down the middle of the road, no problem. The houses are old and falling apart with an exception here or there. Stopping for a second, I yank giant maple leaves off a tree and give them to the boys to play with. They twirl the leaves and shake them in their hands. Soon Charlie is smacking Bobby in the face with his leaf and then Bobby tries to eat his, so I take them away.

They start to cry but I point out an old truck in someone's driveway, and then a barn. "See the barn? The barn is red."

They forget their leaves and look at the barn and they're happy to just be pushed along in the stroller. They babble and drool and I stop to wipe their runny noses on my T-shirt.

Lincoln Road ends and we're back on the highway, still three miles from home. I'm not ready to take these babies home though. We pass a little plaza with a CVS, and a grocery store. We go in and wander around for an hour but I don't have any money to buy anything. After that, we approach an elementary school. It has a playground, but the babies are too little to really use it. I stop anyway. Maybe I'll be in trouble for taking off with them. Or maybe Dad won't even be home when we get back. He loves to find a reason to stomp out of the house, angry, justifying going to The Rusty Nail. Thinking about him, my stomach lurches and my hands form into fists. If he ever screams at my babies again, I swear I will kill him. Taking Charlie out of the stroller, I set him on the long dry grass beside the playground. He draws his feet up off the ground like it's contaminated. Bobby does the same thing and I laugh. Patting the ground I tell them, "Grass. It's just dry. It does feel a little prickly though, doesn't it?"

After a minute they get used to it and start to crawl around. I have to keep taking rocks and walnut shells away from them before they put them in their mouths.

Rummaging through the diaper bag I find a plastic zip-lock bag full of Cheerios. The boys sit there, begging like little dogs, and I feed them Cheerios slowly, one by one. They gobble up every last one. Next, I change their wet diapers and throw the old ones into the dumpster behind the school.

After the sun goes down, I put them back in the stroller and head down the highway toward home. Walking slowly, it feels like we're going to the death chamber. The boys aren't crying so they must not be too hungry. It gets very dark quick and soon I'm pushing two babies down the highway in the black of night, lit up only by the street lights along the road. I'm gonna be in big trouble but at least the babies are happy. At least no one is screaming at them. Each time a car comes toward us the lights shine too bright and the babies stare mesmerized. During long stretches between cars we listen to the crickets.

Stopping the stroller I point out the stars to them and sing,

"Twinkle, Twinkle."

Finally, I see our house up ahead. Mom is standing out front, leaning against the station wagon. I walk the stroller into the driveway, pick up Bobby and hand him to her.

"I was worried," she says, walking toward the house.

"He screamed right at him Mom. Got right in Bobby's face and *screamed* at him. Who does that to a little baby?" I ask.

Mom says nothing. Lifting Charlie out, I put him on my right hip and carry him into the house behind Mom. Dad is in the recliner, still in his bathrobe, watching TV. He doesn't look up. Doesn't say a word.

That's right motherfucker. Don't you even dare.

The rest of the summer if Dad is home, we pretty much avoid each other. I don't have one ounce of respect left for him.

Chapter Twenty-Six

Even though I got all As in honor's English, my guidance counselor says I should go to cosmetology school this year. Mom and Gramma Bonner think it's good to have a trade, and I like the idea of doing make-up and stuff, so I agree. My regular classes are in the morning and after that I take the bus to GOED for beauty school. GOED is a technical school, which has cosmetology and auto mechanics. It also houses the school for retarded kids, like Patrick. In our town, calling someone a "GOED" is the same as calling them a *retard.*

As the bus pulls into GOED the first day, I look out my window and see a girl standing at the entrance. She's petite, and wears stonewashed jeans with red pumps. She's got a red shirt and a necklace with big bulky white beads. Her hair is permed and sprayed high on her head. She looks *perfect.*

I watch her as my bus crawls along in front of the school. The girl seems to be waiting for someone and soon a boy is there, kissing her on the cheek. Off the bus, I find myself following them on the way to the cosmetology room. Her name is Julie and she's from Sherburne High School. There are kids from all the high schools around here, together at GOED.

At beauty school, every girl gets a station and a big leather bag full of supplies. We learn how to do old lady roller sets on each other and we're sent on break with hairnets on our heads. It's embarrassing to go to the snack bar with our hair in curlers, but we're all in the same boat so we just laugh and have fun with it. I usually buy a Pop Tart for 25 cents and if it's good weather we take our snacks outside and eat at the picnic tables. We talk about boys. Everyone in the group I hang out with at cosmetology school is 15, has a boyfriend, and every single one of us is having sex. I always thought Eric and I were the only ones who were doing it, and that's why I kept it top secret besides telling Sophie and Libby.

Julie is really good at hair, but she's always skipping class and doesn't take it very seriously at all. Even though I never miss a day, I'm not great at doing hair. It makes me nervous. We take clients from the community and cut their hair for free and I'm always afraid they won't like it.

Today, I rolled a whole head of long hair for a perm and Mrs. Tanner, the big fat teacher with the blond bouffant came over and told me I'd done it wrong.

"Start over," she said.

I'm getting my period and I have cramps. My back hurts and I'm not in the mood for this shit, but I re-roll it, just how she told me to. It takes an hour and a half, and my arms are so tired. Next thing I know, Mrs. Buttons, the skinny spazzy teacher comes over, and tells me to take it out and do it exactly the way I'd done it the first place.

"That's how I did it the first time, but Mrs. Tanner told me to do it this way!" I snap.

Mrs. Buttons draws back, shocked. I've never been rude to a teacher before in my life, and I don't know what's wrong with me. For some reason it's all just *too much.* I throw the rollers on the floor and run into the bathroom, slamming and locking the door behind me. The fat teacher bangs on the door.

"Leave me alone!" I yell at her, my voice sounding fiercer than I meant. I hear her footsteps walk away on the tile floor outside the bathroom door.

Sitting on the floor I sob. I hate GOED. I suck at doing hair. These teachers are imbeciles. They don't know what the fuck they want. Dad had another party last night. My cramps hurt. I'm so tired.

After a while there is a little tap at the door.

"What?" I bark.

There's a giggle and then, "Janie...let me in. It's Julie."

I blow my nose quick and unlock the deadbolt.

Julie scoots in and locks the door behind her. She takes one look at me and busts out laughing. She thinks my yelling at Mrs. Tanner was the funniest thing she ever heard.

She grins and says, "I brought you some cookies."

We sit Indian style on the bathroom floor, eating chocolate chip cookies she bought at the snack bar. I tell her about having to roll the whole head of hair twice and the teachers not making up their minds on how to do it. I tell her about my cramps. I don't tell her about Dad keeping me up 'til 3 AM, banging around in the kitchen, or his spying, or my mom and her tooth.

She laughs and gets me laughing and when the cookies are gone I splash cold water on my face and walk back out with her. Both teachers leave me alone the rest of the day.

The next day, Julie takes me into her chair. She gives me a perm, then cuts and highlights my hair. When I look in the mirror, I can't believe it. My hair is almost as perfect as hers.

"Look at you," she stands behind me and reaches her hands around from behind to cup my jaw.

"You have such a pretty face. Now we need to do your make-up!" she says.

Julie gets to work on my make-up and when she's done she steps out of the way for me to see in the mirror.

I almost don't recognize myself. My hair. My make-up. I look...pretty.

Another girl walks by and Julie grabs her by the arm.

"Look at this!" she smiles.

"Doesn't she have the cutest face?"

The girl nods her head, agreeing and I look back to the mirror and stare.

"We just needed to be able to *see* you," Julie says.

Moving my head forward, in the direction of the mirror, I study myself. I can't believe this is me.

Back at school I'm instantly cool. Boys who never knew I was alive start noticing me. I'm wearing pumps like Julie and I'm walking taller. With my lunch money I get myself a nice collection of bulky beads and colorful pumps. No one would ever guess I'm from Centerville just by looking at me.

Eric may look all snazzy in his chinos and preppy shirts, but I look good now too. Along with a lot of kids at school he's cramming for his SAT's, studying hard. I'm not taking the SATs. I'm all about hair, make-up, oil painting, and of course, my baby brothers. I'm too busy to even think about college and it's not like anyone's ever mentioned it to me. I'm probably not smart enough to get in anyway.

***

Hilary is the smart one in the family and after one year of community college, she's transferring to Alfred University, where she will study to become an executive secretary. Dad pitched the biggest fit when she decided to go away.

"So, you think you're *too good* to go to the community college?" he'd said.

Anyone can see Dad's just jealous because he didn't even graduate high school. He was 17 when they got married and that was because Mom was pregnant. My sister has the right idea to get the hell out of here.

Senior year for me is more of the same. Classes in the morning, GOED in the afternoon. Julie skips all the time but she has some sort of spell over the teachers and never gets in trouble. I know if I skipped once, they'd fail me.

I got a job at the CVS drugstore up the road and it's great to finally be making some real money. Every paycheck is spent on hair products and clothes and it feels good to finally have things. Most of the kids who work at CVS go to Irving Central High School in the next town over. The Irving boys flirt with me, and it's fun to be around guys who don't know Eric and aren't afraid to approach me. The kids at CVS are really funny and nice and we have a great time stocking shelves and ringing the cash register. It's good not to be home in the evenings, but I do worry about Bobby and Charlie something awful.

One Friday, halfway through our senior year Julie from GOED invites me to stay over. In her room, I tell her how unhappy I am with Eric. How he's basically driven all my friends away. How he never leaves me alone about sex. How much I'm enjoying the attention from the guys at CVS.

"Break up with him," she says.

"Break up with him? *Really?*" I ask.

The thought never occurred to me. Break up with him? I honestly didn't know I was allowed.

She gives me a big smile and raises her eyebrows.

"Really," she says, handing me the phone.

"But it will *hurt* him," I say.

Rolling her big brown eyes she assures me, "He'll get over it."

She hands me the phone and I dial.

Eric answers and I tell him what I need to say.

After four years, it was that easy. I broke up with him in two minutes.

The next afternoon, Eric drives over to my house. We go into my bedroom to talk. He says he wants to *do it,* one last time, for "closure." He promises after this, he'll leave me alone for good. With one foot out the door of this relationship, I don't want to get him mad, so with Mom 20 feet away in the kitchen, and the boys in the living room, I slip my clothes off. He has his *closure* as I count the cracks in my bedroom ceiling, waiting for him to finally be done with me for good.

Within a week Eric is dating Veronica, a girl I've been casual friends with for years. She slinks by me all guilty faced in the halls at school. Seems I should be jealous, or mad, but the only thing I feel is relieved. It guarantees he's not going to come begging, talking me into another chance. Let someone else experience "the ultimate" for a while. Having a boyfriend was never all it was cracked up to be. It was just too much.

Chapter Twenty-Seven

After school, I hop off the bus, glad Dad's truck isn't here. When I get inside, the boys are in front of the TV, watching Sesame Street.

Charlie runs to me and hugs my legs. The twins are two years old.

"Daddy go wid suitcase," he says.

Do we even own a suitcase? What is he talking about? There's a noise coming from Mom and Dad's room and going in to check it out, I find Mom in a heap on the floor.

Standing with one hand on the door frame I ask, "Mom, what's wrong?"

"Your father left," she says, looking up at me, her eyes all red.

"What do you mean, *left*?" I walk over to her and squat down.

"He moved out. Packed his things. He's gone," she covers her face in her hands and resumes sobbing.

Inside me, the heavens open. A choir sings. My heart does a little jig. This is the best thing that could possibly happen. This is the answer to my prayers. Letting out a huge sigh of relief, my shoulders drop and suddenly Mom is *on me*. Her arms are like eight arms. She's heavy and thick and she's pushing me down to a sitting position on the floor. Her weight holds me down and she's slobbering into my neck.

"*She's gonna be so much better off*," I think to myself, patting her back.

She keeps blubbering away and suddenly I just want to smack her. After *everything,* she doesn't even wind up leaving him. *He* leaves *her?* She's a sniveling, little pathetic doormat. Stiff as a board I sit there with my stupid mother slobbering all over me, using me like one of Dad's old snot rags.

After a few minutes I can't take it anymore so I peel her off me and leave her there on the floor.

When I come out I notice all of Adam's stuff packed up by the door. He's decided to live with Dad. My stomach drops. I don't understand. Later, Mom tells me Adam feels sorry for Dad and doesn't want him to be all alone, and Mom's just letting him go, without a fight! She makes me sick.

Gramma Bonner is 87 now but she packs up her apartment of over 40 years and moves in with us to become full-time caretaker of the twins. It's so good to have Dad gone, to have Gramma here. No one's yelling at me. I don't have to constantly be on guard for someone spying on me. I do worry about Adam, living in a cheap apartment over a bar, with Dad.

Even though Gramma is old, she prepares all the meals and washes the dishes and sweeps the floor. At night, after working at CVS, and doing my homework, I lay my head in her lap and she strokes my hair as we watch Johnny Carson. A few months into my senior year in high school, for the first time ever, my grades shoot up, not just in English, but in everything.

Dad's new apartment is right over a bar in Irving. It isn't in our school district, so he has to drive Adam to school and lots of times he doesn't. After living with Dad for just a few months, Adam, who is smart as can be, drops out of high school. He gets a job as a laborer and soon gets his own apartment. It's a tiny room, located in between two garages in a row of storage units. It's dark and dreary and barely an apartment at all. He's got a mattress, some books and a guitar he's teaching himself how to play. He's just a teenager and when I go to visit, my heart aches at the thought of him being in this little shit hole all by himself. He has so much going for him, and I can't stand that he's dropped out of school at fifteen. I wish he'd come home, but Adam says "no" and never does live at Mom's house again.

He gets himself into a bit of trouble for a couple years, then falls in love with a born again Christian, who "saves him" from himself.

With Hilary away at school, it's just the twins, Mom, Gramma Bonner and me. For the first time ever I get to just do my school work, and have fun at my part time job, without worrying so much about everything at home. It's actually pretty peaceful.

***

Working at CVS is fun. Two senior boys from Irving are vying for my attention. They puff up their chests whenever they talk to me and insult each other if I'm within earshot.

"Uh, loser, could you hand me that box cutter?"

"Well, I would, but I was just about to use it. You're going to have to find another one, *homo*."

Technically, Dan is cuter. He's tall, with dark hair. He works out all the time and his body is all muscles, too much like Eric's. Rooting for the underdog, I give Luke most of my attention. He's shorter, a little softer, with light wavy hair.

One night, Mom had to go to work early and she called Dad to ask him to pick me up after my shift at CVS. Hardly ever do I see Dad anymore. I'm not thrilled about her calling him, but I do need a ride home. He agrees to pick me up.

He never shows. That's how I find myself walking down the shoulder of the highway in my mini-skirt and pumps, heading home in the dark. It's a three-mile walk. A car pulls up and slows down beside me. My heart starts beating fast, but then I see it's Luke. I'm so embarrassed.

"Do you need a ride?" he asks.

"No thanks," I say, acting like I always walk down the side of a two lane highway in my fuchsia pumps, after dark.

"C'mon," he says. "I won't bite."

Last year on our 11th grade field trip out to Dickenson Park, the school bus drove right by my house and one of the Andover kids said, "There's Janie's house!"

A boy from Baldwin laughed and said, "Yeah, right." He thought they were joking. He thought there was no way I lived in a dump like that. Laughing along, I never did tell him otherwise.

"C'mon," Luke said, smiling.

Hopefully he won't be able to see too much of my house in the dark. Tentatively, I climb into his little Chevy Citation and let him take me home. In my driveway, I smile and say, "Thanks," hopping out of the car quickly.

He rolls down his window and smiles, "See you tomorrow at work."

Noticing him checking out my legs in my mini-skirt as I walk toward the front door I feel relieved. He doesn't appear to be focusing on my *house* at all.

The next night I'm at CVS, ringing the cash register, catching glimpses of Luke every chance I get. CVS is decorated for the Christmas holidays and it's been very busy. People come in to buy wrapping paper and leave with carts full of stuff. I'm wearing a black and red sweater dress, black stockings, and red pumps and my outfit is having a crazy effect on Luke and Dan. They've been flirting with me extra hard all evening.

Halfway through my shift I get my 15-minute break. I buy some cheese & crackers and a *Mountain Dew* and just as I'm about to dip my red plastic stick into the tiny tub of orange cheese, Luke sneaks into the break room. He's wearing black corduroys and a white button down shirt with a thin black leather tie. Black dress shoes on his feet. He's got light brown, wavy hair, a biggish nose, and penetrating green eyes I somehow hadn't noticed 'til now.

With authority he looks at me and says, "Saturday….we're going skating."

A shiver goes down my spine.

Looking up from my cheese and crackers, my stomach flips but I try to act cool. "Oh….are we? You think so?" I say.

He lowers his head, and looking down at me where I sit, says, "We are."

Something about the way he just took control is thrilling.

Then, nearly as quick as he came in he turns and exits the room. The remaining eleven minutes of my break I sit there smiling, wondering if he meant ice or roller?

On roller skates I'm fine, but on ice skates I'm a mess. It doesn't matter though because it turns out Luke's been playing hockey since he was three and he can skate well enough for both of us. Even though he isn't a big guy, he holds me from behind and glides me all over the ice like it's nothing. Madonna's "Crazy For You" blares on the loudspeakers. My stomach feels all fluttery and my upper lip starts to twitch and I'm glad he's behind me so he can't see how nervous I am. He's wearing cologne and it smells good. After a while I relax and rest the back of my head on his chest and this is *really* nice. It feels so different than it ever felt with Eric. So thrilling!

We get hot chocolate at the snack counter and he won't let me pay. After, he takes me to his house and I meet his older sister and her boyfriend. Trish and Michael are so nice. Trish was an art major the first time through but now she's back in college studying to be an engineer. Michael works at an insurance company. They treat me like an old friend. When Luke's mom and dad come home, they're nice too. His dad's an IBM executive and his mom sells Avon from home.

From then on, if we're not at school or work, Luke and I are together. He's amazing. He gets straight A's and doesn't even have to study. After work, we eat handfuls of Christmas colored M & Ms while watching TV. Or, we go to Tony's Pizza for food. We kiss in the car when he drops me off and every moment with him is sweet.

His mom invites me for Christmas Eve dinner, and when I get there, she has presents for me too. Avon perfumes and lotions. I can't believe she thought of me and I thank her over and over. She has this whole big dinner made, with fancy napkins and a lace tablecloth. They have shrimp and roast beef and tons of appetizers. His mom has at least a dozen tins of homemade Christmas cookies in every flavor. My mom has to work tonight so she and Gramma and the boys were just going to have tomato soup and toast and I feel guilty about the dinner I'm having here at Luke's house.

For New Year's Eve, a girl from high school is having a formal party at her home. Kasey and I went shopping for dresses and here's what I found. It's a white satin Marilyn Monroe type dress. It's kind of a halter, and the neckline dips down to the waist but there's a thin sheer panel between the breasts so it isn't really naked, but looks it. I'm taking Luke to the party and I want to knock his socks off.

On New Year's Eve when I come downstairs in my dress, Mom and Gramma look shocked. They don't say anything, but I can tell by their faces they think I look like a total slut. I start to worry, but at this point what else am I gonna wear? Luke picks me up for the party and when I take off my coat all eyes are on me. Luke looks me up and down and puts his arm around me. He smiles proud and puffs up his chest a bit. The girls look down their noses at me and the boys all grin, and stare at my chest. After about five minutes I can't take it.

"I'm cold," I say and I ask Luke to get my coat. He does, and I cover up, but soon I ask Luke if we can just leave. He's more than happy to go since he doesn't know anyone here. He doesn't drink at all and he's not really into the party scene. He says his dad drinks enough for both of them.

We go back to Luke's house, and no one is home. They're all at a party down the street. In his room, he throws a towel over the lampshade to make the light dim. On a shelf above his desk is a statue of a cartoon baseball player, a hockey trophy, and a little boom box. He puts in a Lionel Richie CD and presses the power button.

We stand there kissing in the middle of his room. My arms are around his neck. His arms fall at my back, just above my waist. After a few minutes he stops. Looking in my eyes, he asks, "Have you ever?" then quickly looks down at the floor.

Should I tell him the truth? Will he think I'm a slut?

After a long pause, I nod. "Only with one boy," I say.

"Eric?" he asks.

I nod.

Luke looks relieved. I can't tell if he's relieved I'm not a virgin, or because I've only slept with one boy.

Lowering my head, I look up at him with just my eyes, "And you?"

"No," he shakes his head.

My hands slide to his chest and I gently push him back a little bit.

"I'm surprised," I say.

"It's not like I haven't had the opportunity," he says, quickly, cocking his head to the side, trying to sound cool.

I nod, "Of course you have."

"I just wanted to wait for the right person," he says. "I wanted it to be special," he almost whispers.

He kisses me for a long moment and then looks into my eyes. Then, leaning into my ear, he says softly, "I think you're what I've been waiting for." We have a little conversation about birth control and when I tell him I'm on the pill he hugs me hard and then unzips the back of my dress. As Lionel Richie belts out *Truly* on the boom box, it's over almost before it begins. He apologizes and I tell him not to worry about it. I'm not disappointed. I'm just happy to be here with him. Besides, Eric says I'm frigid anyway. We lay wrapped up in each other on his bed watching the digital clock on his desk. As it turns midnight, Luke kisses the top of my head and says, "I think I'm really going to like 1986."

Afterward, we get dressed and head to the party where his parents and sister are down the street.

"May I take your coat," the hostess asks.

"No thanks," I say. "I'm cold."

There is no way I'm letting Luke's parents see my slutty dress.

Luke and I sit squished together on a big comfy chair in his neighbor's rec room, watching the party. The music is loud and well-dressed drunk people buzz all around us. It's strange to see people who are drunk, but dressed nice. Drunk, but with nice houses. I feel stupid sitting here in my long wool coat, but no one seems to notice us. After a while, I feel Luke's head, heavy on my shoulder. He's asleep and he looks adorable. No one knows we just "did it" for the first time and I feel happy about our secret.

The next week, after work one night, and after going to Tony's for pizza, we head back to Luke's house to find everyone already in bed. Tiptoeing downstairs we make our way to the couch in the rec room.

I say something about my legs being tired from standing at the register for five hours in heels. Those heels and my little black mini-skirt drove Luke crazy all evening. Out of the corner of my eye, I kept noticing him checking me out. He slips off my shoes and starts rubbing my feet. Then my calves.

His touch is firm and fluid. He's massaging my calves and then goes right up my thigh and his fingers brush against my underpants before returning back down to my legs. He massages 'til my legs feel like putty and I'm relaxed and excited at the same time. He takes his time and when he's done with my legs he slides up my body.

He stands up and unbuckles his pants and he looks beautiful in the streetlight coming through the window. His shoulders are broad, his waist is slim. A line of fine golden hair goes all the way up his belly and then spreads out over his chest.

This time, when he's inside me, it's different. He's hitting just the right spots, over and over. We're taking our time, slow and steady, and then, *OH MY GOD! The ultimate. For real!* It feels good to know Eric was wrong. I hadn't been frigid. I just hadn't been ready.

After that, Luke and I become inseparable and it's "*the ultimate*," every time. We do it in the back of his car at the drive-in. We do it at night, out in the backyard, behind the above ground pool, getting our butts covered in mosquito bites. We do it at my house in my bedroom. We even did it at a party at his friend's house, in the coatroom on the floor between a bed and a wall. Sex with Luke makes me feel strong and powerful. I can't get enough of him, nor he of me.

It's not *all* about sex though. We crank dance music and act like fools in his basement. Prince sings "Kiss" and we shake our groove things and don't care how stupid we look. Centerville guys only listen to stuff like Lynyrd Skynyrd or Aerosmith. Eric only liked Neil Young and classic rock. Before Luke, I would have guessed only gay guys liked Prince. But here we are dancing our asses off to "Let's Go Crazy," Janet Jackson and Madonna. I've never had so much fun.

We go bowling with Trish and Michael every weekend and Trish becomes a dear friend. Luke is good at bowling. He's good at everything. At 17 he's already been made assistant manager at CVS. He always seems to get his way but he's so charming no one minds. It's Luke's world and I'm just lucky to be invited along for the ride.

At the end of the year, our senior proms wind up being one day apart. I spend every last dime I've earned at CVS on a beautiful lavender hoop dress. It rests off the shoulder and has tiny flowers down the bodice. For Luke's prom I borrow Jenna's red hoop dress from last year.

Luke's prom is first. We go out to dinner with a group of kids from his school and I know some of them from CVS. Everyone is in a good mood and it's fun. He drops me off home right after the dance and my feelings are hurt the next day when I find out he hit a post-prom party without me, but since I don't want to ruin *my* prom day, I let it go.

The next evening I'm all dressed up pretty and Luke is acting tired and not really into it. I don't have money to go out to dinner and he didn't offer to pay for *my* night so he just picks me up before the dance. As Mom snaps pictures, Bobby and Charlie keep crawling under my hoop skirt like it's a tent.

At my prom, Luke mopes. He doesn't really know anyone and doesn't want to dance. I stand on the sidelines with him, watching my senior year tick away and then I get mad. Right there, I decide he's not going to wreck my night. Kasey is out on the floor dancing with some of her brainiac friends so I leave Luke by himself and go join them.

Soon the floor opens up and everyone is in a big circle. One person gets in the middle, does a little something and then moves back out. Everyone is having fun, clapping, and then Luke is there, on the other side of the circle. He's dancing along, clapping, looking at me. I feel grateful he decided to join us.

After the prom there is a big party at one of my classmate's lake house but it's half an hour away and Luke doesn't want to go. I have no other way of getting there and it's too late to call anyone for a ride. He pulls into my driveway and a kiss in the car is followed by a long awkward pause. I thought he'd walk me to the door since it's a special night and I'm all dressed up, but suddenly I realize he's waiting for me to get out. Gathering up the crinolines of my fancy dress I step out of his car and walk to the front steps feeling let down and alone. Turns out, prom is just one big expensive disappointment.

On graduation day, Mom is pissed because Dad doesn't plan on coming. She's acting like she's mad for *me,* but it's really her trying to keep a hook dug into him. I couldn't care less whether he comes or not. In fact, I'd prefer he didn't. Mom and Gramma Bonner and Grandma Shea sit in the bleachers smiling and waving as I walk across the stage for my diploma.

That evening, Luke is off with friends from his school and he doesn't invite me. After spending all of high school with Eric and the last six months with Luke, I have no one to hang out with. It's a shitty day to realize you have no friends. Lindsay Martin put out an open invite to a pool party and I decide to go but when I get there it's just a very small tight group of her friends. Lindsay is friendly and warm but she's the hostess and she's buzzing around. No one else talks to me. I look at these people I've gone to high school with but none of them really know me and I don't know them at all. Sitting by the pool I've never felt more lonely.

I call home.

"But you've only been there a half hour," Mom says.

"There's a lot of drinking going on and I don't feel safe," I lie.

"I'll be right there," Mom says before hanging up.

Thanking Lindsay, I tell her I have another party to get to, "At one of *Luke's friend's.*"

Going home I spend graduation night with Gramma, eating chocolate ice cream and watching late night TV.

***

Luke and I spend the summer days in his pool, floating in the sun. Evenings, we work at CVS, stocking shelves, running the cash register. The older people who work there don't treat us like babies. The women, all mothers, talk about things like sex, and how rotten their kids are and they sometimes even swear out loud. Everyone jokes and laughs and somehow we get our work done all the while. CVS is like a big family.

When I'm not with Luke I feel like the same old nobody, but with him, it's different. With *him*, I feel like I can do anything. He expects me to get my driver's license, so I get my permit, take my test and pass it. Now he thinks I should go to college. Hilary is away at a two-year school, but *she's* smart. No one ever mentioned college to me before. Luke and all the other kids at CVS are planning to go to the community college next year, but just thinking about it is overwhelming. I wouldn't know where to begin.

At Luke's house after work tonight, his dad asks if he can talk with me. He leads me to the kitchen table and as I take a seat, Luke disappears.

Mr. Vincent has a small, runner's frame. He's skinnier than his son, and his nose is bigger but they have the same green eyes and sandy brown hair. He's some sort of big-wig at IBM and everyone knows two things about IBMers. They're smart, and they make a lot of money.

He sits across the table from me with a mug of beer, and a box of Cheez-Its. Mr. Vincent has a keg on tap at his house, just like at a bar, and he's always got a beer mug in his hand. It strikes me odd every time, to see someone normal drink beer. Someone with a good job and a nice four-bedroom split-level.

He holds out the Cheez-Its box to me.

"No thanks," I shake my head.

Setting the box down on the table, he takes a swill of beer.

My stomach squirms.

Where the hell is Luke and why did he leave me alone with his dad?

Setting his mug down hard he looks me in the eye.

"You're *too smart* not to go to college."

The words hover in the air over my head before searing their way into my brain.

My throat tightens.

"But how would I do it?" I say, almost in a whisper. "I don't have any money to pay for college."

234

"If you want to go, there are ways to finance it. Loans, grants. There really are no excuses."

"But...I don't even know how to apply. And I have no way to get there."

"Applying is easy. Don't worry about that. And to get there, you'll use the Chevette. All three of our kids used it, and now that Luke has his new car we don't need it. It's not fancy, but it will get you across town to G.C.C.."

"I couldn't take your car," I say.

He smiles, "We wouldn't get anything for it anyway."

He takes another swig of beer and when he sets his mug down he looks me straight in the eye.

"You're going to college," he repeats. "It would be a terrible waste if you didn't."

So, in July I had no intention of going to college. But now it's August, and here I am, registering along with all the other kids from CVS, as if I'd had a plan all along. My major will be communications.

Chapter Twenty-Eight

At Graham Community College, a girl named Vicki who I sort of know from cosmetology is dating one of Luke's new friends. Luke and Tim are in all the same engineering classes. Vicki is gorgeous. She's 5'2 like me, but she's thinner and curvier and she works in a clothes store so her outfits are always perfect. She's got crazy high cheekbones and white porcelain skin, huge blue eyes and thick wavy blonde hair down to her shoulders. She's also smart. She wants to be an archeologist. Every time I look at Vicki I want to have a little chat with God and ask Him a few questions about how things are doled out. Luke says she's no prettier than me, but he's just being nice and we both know it. The four of us become inseparable on campus.

Not knowing anything about college, the first couple of weeks are mostly play for me. Vicki and I skip class, find the engineering lab, and stand outside the door walking like Egyptians like the Bangles on MTV. I live to make Luke laugh. We also spend a lot of time in the cafeteria, hanging out.

Vicki tells me she's one of five kids in her family and most of them have different fathers. She's never met her father. He knows about her but has never wanted anything to do with her. My thought is one day he's going to find out how incredible she is and he'll be sorry. I was always jealous of Vicki at GOED. I thought with her looks, life must be perfect, but it isn't true. She quickly becomes like a sister to me.

One cold day halfway through our first semester, I'm walking across campus with Luke, and he's telling me how he might have messed up a problem on his calculus test. From there he starts talking about G.P.A.s. Listening silently, it takes me a couple of minutes to figure out what G.P.A. even stands for, but then he says something important.

"Only losers get below a 3.0."

Snatching up this piece of information I quickly do some research. I ask Vicki how she's doing, grades-wise. Turns out she expects to get at least a 3.5 GPA.

I'm expecting two Cs and the rest Bs...if I'm lucky.

I start cracking the books, but not in time for my grades to reflect it on my midterms. I tell Luke my grades are none of his business. After that I begin studying really hard. This is how I find out Luke is super attracted to smart girls. During breaks between classes we meet in the library and I always try to get there first. Putting on my reading glasses I act deeply absorbed in a book when he arrives. It works every time. The glasses just about kill him. My smart girl routine is working for me too. By the end of the semester I've managed to bring my G.P.A. *way* up.

***

The next semester, I get up the nerve to do something I've always wanted to do, sign up for a theater class. The director is Angelo D'Angelo and the first time I step into his world, I feel an electric buzz in the air. The amber lights are dim, giving the theater a soft, warm, cave-like feel. The students sit in the audience while Angelo D'Angelo stands on stage. Angelo is middle aged, tall and bald with dark hair around the edges. He's got dark eyebrows and a large Italian nose, with a mustache underneath. He wears baggy pants and a ratty old button down sweater. He's thin, and has big brown puppy dog eyes.

As students trickle in he greets each one with a big booming, "How 'ya doin?" His accent is New York-ish. Italian.

Students smile politely and look at him warily as they take their seats.

When everyone gets settled he introduces himself and tells us the deal. Show up prepared, try your best, you get an A. Then he makes each of us stand up and tell the group a few things about ourselves. I'm so nervous I could die. The prettiest girl in the class stands up. She's got long straight black hair and big green eyes. With her hands on her hips and her nose in the air she announces, "My name is Heather Majors, and I am *going* to be a professional actress in New York City."

There is no choice but to believe her.

When it's my turn I blurt out something about CVS, Luke and my little brothers. Sitting down, I feel like a country bumpkin fool.

A few classes in, Angelo asks us to sit in a circle. Students have to take turns getting in the middle and the rest of the group goes around one by one, stating a physical attribute they admire about that person.

"We all have something we can play up. Sometimes we get so used to the reflection in the mirror, we don't really see ourselves anymore," he says.

Sitting in the center of the circle is torture and I want to get up and run. People say they like my hair, my eyes, even my nose. When it's Heather Major's turn to say something to me, she pauses for a long time.

Maybe she can't find anything she likes about me.

I start to squirm.

Finally she smiles and says, "I'm totally jealous of her full lips."

As she says it, her hand goes up to cover her own mouth, but not before I notice Heather's lips are *thin*. I can't believe it. I never thought about my lips before and I *never* imagined someone as beautiful as Heather would be jealous of anything about *me*.

On a different day, Angelo has us taking turns doing our absolute silliest dance, across the stage. Everyone is being so dorky, but the weirder they get, the more everyone cheers. Waiting for my turn, I'm so nervous. But then, there I am, doing Jimmy Hendrix style air guitar across the stage. I'm crazy and free. Everyone whoops and claps and I can't remember ever laughing so hard. Angelo has opened up a door to a secret world, one I almost remember, where it's okay to play.

Another day, Angelo sends us all over campus to look at things from a different perspective. We're to get down and observe the underside of the drinking fountains and write down what we see. We're to spend some time standing on a desk and looking around from that vantage point.

"Open your minds," Angelo says. "The world isn't only what *you* see or how *you* see it."

Between classes, I start hanging out backstage. Angelo is always there, at the big long table, with a crowd of students surrounding him. He entertains them with his stories.

Every time someone walks in, his eyes light up and it's, "How ya doin! Welcome, welcome!"

The newcomer will fall into the group and he'll pick up the story in progress.

One rare day when I step back stage I find it's just Angelo. We sit in his office chatting and I don't know why, but suddenly I'm blabbering all about Dad leaving. About the twins. About Mom and Gramma who's almost 90, raising the boys. Angelo listens and when I'm done talking he digs around in his desk and hands me a form.

"You're here enough. I might as well put you to work," he says, handing me an application for a work-study.

Work-study means I help Angelo out backstage, answering phones, sending out fliers, etc. I get credit for school and a little money too.

At any given time when I show up for work, there are a handful of students backstage. We're all ages, and races. Many are new to the country and hardly speak English. We all have "work" studies, but mostly we sit around listening to Angelo tell his stories.

If we're in the middle of a stage production we work hard but Angelo doesn't make us do busy work if nothing is going on. More than once I've arrived backstage to find the lights dim and Angelo tiptoeing around covering up the tired immigrant students who are sprawled out asleep on various couches. He tucks old wool blankets over them, like a gentle godfather, giving them rest on their journeys. In Angelo D'Angelo's world it's okay to play, and it's also okay to rest.

Working at the theater, taking classes, working at CVS, and hanging out with Luke leaves little time for Bobby and Charlie. I feel so guilty not spending enough time with them. Dad hasn't been bothering to see them at all.

Luke doesn't want to hang out with my little brothers though. If Bobby and Charlie are around, he gets quiet and barely even looks at them. It's like he can't even see how cute they are. Luke doesn't mind if I want to spend time with them. He can always find something else to do. Seems I'm welcome in *his* world, but he has no interest in mine. Sometimes I get so mad at him, I can't even explain it. It's not like he cheats on me like Hilary's first boyfriend did to her. It's not like he's ever threatened me physically like her second boyfriend did to her. Luke really is a good guy. I guess I shouldn't get so mad.

***

It took her awhile, but Hilary has found someone good. Someone who treats her like a princess and they are getting married! She asks me to be her maid of honor and I say yes, though I have no idea what it entails.

I'm happy for my sister but I find out quickly with weddings, there are a lot of things to pay for. Besides my dress, and a gift, I have to chip in for the bridal shower. Luckily the groom's sister has pretty much taken over the details. She's trying to keep expenses down, but it's still a lot of money. I'm in college full-time, working part-time at CVS, and even with the little bit of extra money from my work-study, every last dime I earn is going toward my sister's wedding. I can barely afford gas to get to school. I am so stressed.

As if I need more to worry about, tonight after work at CVS I went to Luke's, and when I got home, Gramma was in her room, crying. She says the boys are out of control.

"I tell them they aren't allowed to jump all over the furniture. Next thing I know, your mother is letting them do it. I tell them they have to eat their vegetables. Next thing I know she doesn't make them."

She hangs her head and slowly shakes it side to side. It can't be easy taking care of two wild four-year-old boys when you're ninety.

Promising Gramma I'll talk to mom, I sit on the couch with her and rub liniment into her tired old feet.

The next day I try talking to Mom, but she blows me off. Nothing changes for Gramma. Mom doesn't back her at all. Between work, school, home, my sister's wedding, and worrying about Gramma, I don't know which way to turn.

A few nights later, I come in late and find Gramma is crying again. This time it's worse.

"Your mother is thinking about taking your father back," she says softly.

"WHAT?"

"I gave up my apartment," she says, her voice cracking, tears from her green eyes roll down the wrinkles in her face.

"Where will I live?" she asks.

Rage whips through my body.

Skipping my first class the next morning, I wait for Mom to get home from work. As soon as she walks in the door I pounce on her and Mom starts yelling, "It's none of your business. It doesn't concern you!"

"Doesn't concern me?" My voice is high and cracking. "Gramma has been crying her eyes out! She thinks she'll be out on the street. She gave up her apartment of 40 years! Her *apartment,* Mom! It doesn't *concern* me? You *know* he still drinks. You *know* he'll be awful to the boys. How can you even think of such a thing? HOW?"

"He isn't drinking *that much* anymore," she says softly, and then through clenched teeth she adds one more, "*It's none of your business,*" before stomping up the stairs to go to bed.

Gramma sits on her bed, head down, crying.

I hug her hard and tell her,

"Gramma, if he moves in here I'll get an apartment and you can come live with me. I promise."

Gramma shakes her head.

"You're 19 years old. You don't need to be taking care of a 90-year old lady."

"Gramma, I'm serious." I say.

"I will *never* live with him again."

I get to school in time for my second class and as I walk across campus I see Luke laughing and flirting with a girl he knows from high school. *His world is so fucking different than mine. He doesn't have a clue what I go through.*

The girl sees me out of the corner of her eye but Luke doesn't. She leans in and offers him a big hug, smiling smugly at me over his shoulder. He's all grins and his head tilts back in laughter. He hugs her back playfully, and as he does he lifts her off the ground. Later he'll act like I'm some sort of jealous loser when I ask him about it.

Fuck him. I turn around and walk fast toward the theater. When I get there, Angelo is getting his things together to leave. He looks at me and notes my tears, but doesn't ask specifics.

"You look wiped out," he says.

I slump down on the couch in his office and he shoves a stack of books off the other end and throws me a pillow. Angelo takes a wool blanket off a chair and pulls it over me. He walks over to his desk, and takes the phone off the hook. I hear his keys jingling in his pocket and the sound of him pulling his coat on.

"I have an appointment. Lock up when you leave," he says. Then, more gently, he adds, "Get some rest, kid."

With a lump of gratitude in my throat I whisper, "Thanks Ange."

"Fuh-get about it," I hear him say as he shuffles out the door.

When I wake up I've missed all my classes but if I hurry I can make it to CVS in time for my shift.

Mom and Dad try "working on things" for a while. She takes the boys to see him at his apartment a couple of times a week. Supposedly, she's told him he can't come back unless he stops drinking, though I'd bet a million dollars those words never passed her lips.

Dad's apartment is conveniently located right above a bar on Main Street in Irving. I drive by it everyday on my way to and from school. I've never been inside, but today I see Mom's car there and I stop because she owes me fifteen bucks and I want it back. When I walk in, the boys are playing on the floor in his living room and Mom and Dad are sitting together, all cozy on the couch. It makes me sick to see them like that. Bobby and Charlie jump all over me pulling at my legs and that's when I notice one of my paintings hanging on the wall in his living room.

She fucking gave him one of my paintings.

The next day, when I know he's at work, I take Mom's key, let myself in, and steal it back. No one ever mentions it.

A few weeks later, after one of their visits, Mom realized she left Bobby's teddy bear behind at Dad's apartment. She'd been gone all of twenty minutes, but when she walked back in she found Dad, on the couch, wrapped around a bar wench from downstairs.

It's the last we ever heard of my parents trying to "work it out." As my first year of college comes to a close, Gramma and I can finally let out our breath.

***

A couple of weeks before her wedding, Hilary invites me out to dinner at a fancy restaurant on a local golf course. She tells me to get whatever I want and I order the scallops. We sit and talk and she's being so nice. I'm proud to be out with her as a grown up and I order water to drink so she won't have to pay for a Coke. After dinner she surprises me with tickets to the Huey Lewis concert.

"I thought it would be fun," she says. "I want to show you how much I appreciate all you're doing for the wedding."

Hilary is an executive secretary at IBM now, and I guess maybe she's making some money to be able to afford all this.

Huey Lewis is all over the radio these days, "The Heart of Rock-n-Roll." I'm not really into him, but it's so *sweet* that she did this. The concert gets going and it's better than I ever imagined. The band stands in a semi-circle doing song after song, completely a cappella. At the concert, I feel closer to my sister than I ever have in my life. I'm so happy for her.

Hilary is a June bride. On her wedding day we get ready at Gramma Shea's house because it's cleaner and less cluttered than Mom's. The wedding party wears red. The dresses are okay. My hair turned out good but I feel fat. Bobby and Charlie are so stinkin' cute in their little black suits. They've got jackets and shorts with white knee socks. Red bow ties at their necks and shiny black shoes. Bobby poses proud in his dress up clothes. Charlie cries and begs to take his tie off. After pictures, Clyde looks happy and proud as he drives all the girls to the church in his Suburban.

Hilary is a delicate flower of a bride. I did her hair, pulling it up into a small bun on top of her head, with little loose dark ringlets framing her face. Sitting behind her in the back of the Suburban, I study the tiny embroidered flowers on her dress and marvel at her beauty. She looks like Snow White.

Hilary is getting married at the Episcopal Church, though we haven't gone there since Mom became Catholic. Good ole' Father Duncan is performing the service. He still looks like Jesus, but older. The music starts and the wedding party files in. Then, everyone stands as Dad and Hilary come walking down the aisle. She is happy, radiant. He beams with pride.

"What's he got to be proud of?" I think to myself.

My sister steps up toward the altar and hands me her flowers.

As Hilary and Craig make their vows, my throat gets tight. It's the sincerity in their voices. The promises they

246

make. The hope in their eyes. The church full of people, watching and praying for them.

After the ceremony, the whole wedding party drives around town, honking horns. By the time we get to the Elk's club I'm drunk on champagne, wobbling into the reception on the arm of Craig's best man, Smitty.

The reception hall is kind of like a school gym/cafeteria. There are lots of tables and a stage. All us girls in the wedding party decorated the place last night. With nice tablecloths and beautiful floral centerpieces, we actually managed to make it look kind of fancy. We didn't have the option of taking the big elk head off the wall, so we made the best if it by sticking the stem of a long red rose sideways into his mouth.

Smitty makes a nice toast and after dinner, the DJ calls Hilary and Dad out to the dance floor and they put on a little show dancing to, *Daddy's Little Girl*. The whole thing makes me want to puke. What a load of crap! He hasn't been any more of a parent to her than any of us, and look at them out there, acting like they have some amazing father/daughter bond. Getting up, I head toward the bathroom. I don't understand Hilary. She's never seemed to find Dad as disgusting as I do.

When the dance floor opens up, I grab Luke and we hit the floor. The DJ is great and the whole place is rockin' to The Knack's *My Sharona*! Next is *What I Like About You* by the Romantics. Luke is wearing his red shirt, black pants and red suspenders and we're having so much fun dancing!

During Eric Clapton's *Wonderful Tonight*, I lean my cheek on Luke's sweaty shoulder. Glancing up, I see the big Elk on the wall with the rose in its mouth. Closing my eyes I breathe Luke in and wonder if he'll ever want to marry me. Will anyone?

***

Hilary's wedding is over but Luke's oldest sister is in town making plans for hers. She lives with her fiancé in New Jersey and even though I've never met her, she's invited me to come over today and look at wedding plans with Trish and Luke's mom. Karen has light brown hair like Luke, and his green eyes too. She's funny and a little wild and I like her a lot. Listening to the details, I hear Trish mention something about her mom and dad paying for it all! Trish doesn't have to go broke being maid of honor and the bride doesn't have to pay for a thing! Karen is so nice. She includes me in the conversation, asks for my opinion and acts as if it really matters.

In August, Karen is a beautiful bride. The wedding reception is much fancier than Hilary's was. Luke and I dance the night away. It's a wonderful night but all the way home I feel sad.

All these weddings and Luke can't even say he loves me. He's been doing this stupid joke, saying I "*loaf*" you instead. Even when he writes me a note, he signs off, drawing a little cartoon loaf of bread instead of writing the actual word *love*. I'm sick of it.

Pulling the car into my driveway, he leans over to kiss me, then, looking up with his sweet little boy expression he says it. "I *loaf* you."

I swear to God I'm not in the mood for this crap.

"Luke, either you love me or you don't. If you don't, please just tell me and I'll be on my way. If you do….you gotta stop this *loaf* shit. If after all this time you can't even say the word, I think we have a big problem."

Luke lurches back as if I'd smacked him. "I love you," he mumbles, his lips in a tight line. His eyes stare down at his hands.

"Good," I say, stepping out of the car. I shut the door hard and walk up the path to my house.

Walking up the front steps I think to myself, *It's no proposal, but at least I got that much out of him.*

***

The fall semester started last week and I'm sitting on the floor in the living room, thumbing through my human biology flashcards. It's late, and Gramma is watching Johnny Carson on TV. I've studied all I can for my test tomorrow, so I'm mostly just hanging out with Gramma.

She sits on the couch with her throw blanket wrapped around her shoulders. Her white prayer book rests on the TV tray, along with her brown coffee cup, and her little dish of crystallized ginger. She keeps a tiny bite of it under her tongue at all times, saying it warms her blood, and wards off colds. The smell of camphor is all around because Gramma just rubbed liniment into her joints. Gramma acts so sweet and innocent. I'm always surprised she even gets it when Carson tells a risqué joke.

Even with four grown children for proof, Gramma acts like she's never had sex. One time when Adam and I were really little, she hit us with a metal spatula for looking at each other's privates in the bathtub. To this day I remember the shame and confusion, the sting of metal on wet skin. What she must have thought when

Mom was still in high school and got knocked up with Hilary!

My mind starts to wander. If Gramma left Mom's dad when Mom was a little girl, and now Mom is 40, that means Gramma hasn't had sex in over thirty years!

Gramma takes a sip of her coffee and chuckles at the TV, and just then, out of the corner of my eye, I see something in the air. It's black.

A bug?

Too big.

Did a bird get in? How?

The black thing flies in an arc across the front of the living room and circles back toward me. I've never seen a real one before but the shape of its wings is unmistakable. Around the room it goes again as my brain registers,

Oh my God! A bat.

Screaming, I drop to my knees, covering my head with my hands.

Oh my God. It's going to get stuck in my hair! It came out good today. I teased and sprayed it extra high.

Oh My God.

Looking up I see the bat fly into Gramma's room, where Bobby and Charlie are fast asleep. Mom moved their beds in there just last week, because they kept waking up scared in the night.

Oh my God! My little brothers! The bat is going to get them!

Flicking on the light I see the bat circling the room. The boys are rubbing their eyes and turning over in their beds.

"Bobby, wake up," I shake him. "Charlie, c'mon."

"Wuh?" He mumbles.

"There's a bat in the house and I want you to hide under your beds until we get it out. C'mon hurry up. It's all okay, but I you need to move, *now*!"

The bat is circle swooping just over my head. The boys are awake now and I thought they would be afraid, but they're excited and ready for adventure.

If only I were little like them and someone bigger would show up to take care of problems for me.

Glancing at Gramma, my stomach contracts. She's so old. So tiny. What could she possibly do? I'm the only one who's going to save us tonight and the thought pisses me off. Fathers are supposed to deal with stuff like this. If they can't do it, then mothers. Adam would know what to do, but he's not here.

My knees shake.

Crouching down low next to the boys' beds I try to think. I need to get the bat out the door. Maybe I can shoo it with a broom.

Oh God.

Bobby and Charlie look up at me grinning. No fear. I'm their hero and they've all the confidence in the world in my bat fighting abilities.

"Get me the broom!" I yell to Gramma.

Gramma shuffles from where she's standing in the bedroom doorway and heads into the kitchen. She comes back; her tiny frame wrapped in a white sheet draped over her head. A little wrinkled Mother Theresa clutching the stick of the broom in her gnarled arthritic hand where she holds the sheet together at her chin.

Grandma hands me the broom and then takes me under the sheet with her. We're a two-headed ghost swinging frantically at the bat, trying to shoo it out the door. Each swing of the broom causes the bat to circle

251

faster. Finally, exhausted, it lands on the wall above Charlie's bed.

It's hard to maneuver the broom with Grandma under the sheet so I tell her to go in the living room. She scoots out from under the sheet and does as she's told.

The way the bat just clings to the wall gives me the creeps. How does it stick? It hangs there upside down, breathing, and it seems to be looking right at me. Its eyes are shiny black bee-bees and its face looks like a tiny deranged evil pig whose snout has been punched upward.

Standing in the middle of the room, sheet over my head, I hold the broom up in the air, and wait for my nerve. I take two practice swings, gentle and easy and then the bat seals its fate by slowly spinning its head all the way around, Exorcist style.

It's Reagan.

A violent chill rips through my body and I bring the broom up directly over my head,

Mutherfucker!

Slamming the broom down hard on the wall, I only graze her. Reagan starts flying around the room even faster, then goes right out the bedroom door and through the living room with me chasing. She lands on the floor just inside the front door. She's breathing heavy.

With both hands I slowly bring the broom up over my head. Then, quick and solid, I slam it down on her hard.

"Ugh!" and again,

"Ugh!"and again,

"Ugh!"

The bat's blood spurts out on the entryway floor and I feel sick and guilty and sad and scared and I hate

Reagan for making me kill her. *Why couldn't you just leave me alone and stay outside where you belong?*

My hands are trembling. I open the front door and sweep her out of the house, I don't care where she goes. Leave her on the front steps? I don't care. The lawn? Whatever. Mom can deal with it. I've done *my* part. I shiver as I head back up the stairs. From the landing at the top of the steps I see Bobby and Charlie in the living room, dancing around in their pajamas. It's nighttime and they're awake and what a lucky break for them. They're doing karate chops pretending to be Teenage Mutant Ninja Turtles.

As I enter the living room I rest my hand on the back of the rocking chair. It's Gramma's rocker but it's *my* afghan draped over it. The afghan is green with white and yellow daises. I won it in a raffle when I was six, and the reason I loved it so much was because Hilary was sore she didn't win. Now I'm too old to gloat over winning a silly blanket, but touching it does give me a faint sense of joy.

It must be getting late.

I'm about to shout, "Okay guys, back to bed!" when I look down at the watch on my wrist, which is connected to my hand, which is resting on my afghan, which hangs on the back of Gramma's rocker. Inches away from my hand, I see two black spots.

Two more bats.

I am Michael Douglas! The bats are Glenn Close! We're in the final scene of *Fatal Attraction* when he thinks he's finally drowned the psychotic woman who's been threatening his family and she shoots up out of the bathtub, *alive!*

One bat? I did it. It nearly killed me, but I did it. Freaky *horror story* bats that keep on coming? I swear to God I'm going to have a nervous breakdown.

"Bobby and Charlie, back in your beds! Now!" I scream.

They finally seem a little afraid and scoot back into Gramma's bedroom. She shuts the door behind them and looks at me. She isn't scared, or mad, or even disgusted with me. What I see in her bright green eyes is compassion. Standing there trembling, just a foot away from two bats hanging on the back of the afghan, I honestly don't know what to do.

Gramma goes in the kitchen and I hear the door open to the back porch.

The bats don't move. They just hang there on my daisy afghan, looking at me with their beady black eyes.

I hear water running.

Trembling, *I hate Mom. I hate Dad. I hate this piece of shit house.*

Gramma heads into the living room lugging a heavy bucket.

I'm crying and my stomach hurts.

"Gramma...."

She nods, "I know."

Suddenly, without a word, she wads up the bats inside the afghan. Her stiff hands work fast as she stuffs the balled up blanket into the bucket of water.

She shuffles off through the kitchen, lugging her bucket and I hear the back door open and close again.

She washes her hands in the kitchen sink, then shuffles back into the living room, and says, winking at me, "That ought a take care of them, darlin.' Don't cha think?"

My gramma just drowned two bats with her bare hands.

She settles back down on the couch and pats the cushion next to her. I sit down and she pulls me in. After a minute I lay my head on her lap and she runs her fingers through my hair. It takes a long time, but finally I start to calm down. Her touch soothes me and I'm almost asleep when she busts out laughing at David Letterman.

In the morning, Mom walks in tired from work and I jump on her with the story from last night.

"Mom! We have to do something? We can't live like this!"

"What do you want me to do?" she snaps. "I don't have any money to pay an exterminator." She shrugs it off like it's not her problem.

I am so sick and tired of her bullshit. She hasn't asked Dad for a dime of child support in over two years. Imagining myself hurling my fist into her face I scream, "How convenient that *you* aren't the one home at night and you don't have to deal with it!"

She moves around me and stomps upstairs to bed.

I'm gonna move out, *I swear*! But where would I go? How would I finish school? And what about Bobby and Charlie? What about Gramma?

A week goes by with more bats visiting. When the exterminator finally comes he says thousands of bats had been calling our attic "home." I'm too ashamed to even tell Luke about it. He just doesn't get what I go through day to day.

***

Luke's been treating me like shit. He's always trying to make me jealous, flirting with other girls at work and at GCC. If I say anything he furrows his eyebrows and shakes his head looking disappointed and concerned. He denies anything is going on with any of them and acts like I'm pathetic and insecure.

He does the same thing when he points out celebrities on TV or gawks at beautiful women in restaurants.

"She's *hot,*" he'll say.

If I act hurt or even annoyed he gives me that "concerned" look. Never would I try to hurt his feelings like this.

Tonight at CVS he hardly spoke to me. I don't know what's going on. For two years we've been practically inseparable, and now it feels like I don't even know him.

After work we drive to the elementary school in Andover to talk. It's way out in the country and it will be private and quiet. It feels like he wants to break up with me. Silence fills the car on the way there.

At the school, we park and get out. He leans against the car and I face him. Reaching out I take his hands and feel relieved when he doesn't pull away. Our fingers, intertwined, carry on their own slow dance in the night air. Luke starts talking of things like transferring to a four-year college.

The future.

Are we too serious?

Are we too young?

He says his mom doesn't think he should be tied down to one girl.

My stomach hurts. Does she think I'm not good enough for him? Alternating between furious and deflated, I bow my head and look at our feet. My shoes are in between his shoes. Leaning forward, I press my body against his.

He says he loves me so much.

But should we break up now?

Will it be worse later?

Won't we just be more *attached*?

Looking up at his face, I see he's distraught. He looks in my eyes and somehow I actually feel sorry for him.

Luke is going places. He plans on going to Notre Dame in Indiana. Meanwhile I'm just a nobody from Centerville. He's never going to wind up with me. Even so, the thought of him breaking up with me tonight is more than I can bear. I offer him what I know he wants, while my heart sinks inside my chest.

"Luke, chances are we won't end up together, right?" I say, squeezing his hands.

He nods, tears welling in his eyes.

"But we love each other, right?"

Again he nods, looking down at our interlaced fingers.

Ducking down, I catch his eyes and ask, "Can't we just be *right now*?"

I won't ask for promises and he won't leave me tonight. I can't bear it if he breaks up with me tonight.

He pulls me in and hugs me long and tight.

We walk 20 paces out onto the soccer field and can no longer see the school because it's so foggy. A dim cast of streetlights from the parking lot gives off a golden glow. In the middle of the field we stop to kiss. He lies down on the grass and gently pulls me on top of him. Soon we're naked, our bodies warm in the clammy night air. A break in our kiss and I open my eyes and gasp at what I see.

"Luke, look." I whisper.

We're in the center of a circle. Immediately around us, the ground is a flat grassy field, but a hundred yards out is a puffy round wall of cloud. A white fortress. No one could ever get in. The world is the cloud and he is me and I am him and we are young and together we go beautifully on and on and there will never be another moment like this in all the world.

Don't leave me.

Don't leave me.

Please, don't leave me.

***

These last two years at GCC, Vicki and I have become super close. We're going out dancing tonight but the guys aren't coming with us. Luke doesn't drink at all (because his dad drinks too much)and he hates clubs. I'm glad he's not coming because he gets all irritated if I get even a little tipsy. He's Mr. Responsible, his family's designated driver.

In the parking lot of The Cheetah Lounge we sit in my Green Volkswagen Rabbit. Gramma gave me $600.00 to buy this car after Luke's old car finally died. The Rabbit is rusty and has a big dent in the side, which I've covered with a bumper sticker that looks like a giant Band-Aid. It gets a lot of laughs at school. Jill James taught me how to drive it and also how to park on a downward incline so I can pop the clutch when it fails to start, which is pretty often.

Earlier tonight, I talked Mom into buying us two four-packs of wine coolers. I lied and told her we'd be splitting the eight bottles among five girls but it's really just me and Vicki. Hilary's old ID will get me into The Cheetah Lounge, but I didn't want to push it in a well lit grocery store.

On the way to the club we listen to hip-hop on the college radio station and down three wine coolers each. After that, we're feeling good, and we get out of the car and head across the parking lot. The music is loud as it filters up to street level from The Cheetah Lounge downstairs. Waiting in line we act cool, checking out the other people coming and going. As I hand the bouncer Hilary's ID, I smile at him. He's all military looking with a buzz cut and taught muscles popping out of his tight T-shirt. I give him my best grin, lowering my head and looking up at him with big doe eyes. It's demure, with a hint of naughty. He responds with his own hungry smile, lowering his head and meeting my eyes. He presses the ID into my hand and holds it there a second.

Guys are so easy and stupid.

The bouncer, so suave with me, falls all over himself when Vicki presents her ID. It says she's *12* years older than she actually is, but he doesn't even question. She's so gorgeous, she has no need to resort to a fuck me smile.

The base beat thumps along with Salt & Pepa.

Push it. Push it good.

We walk down the flight of stairs, making our grand entrance into The Cheetah Lounge. The club is a big circle and everyone can see who's coming and going. The steps lead right to the dance floor.

In our heels and mini skirts, noses in the air, we walk down the steps and make an immediate left toward the bathrooms where we check our make-up and hair, then it's straight to the dance floor. A ledge with barstools encircles the dancing space and it's packed five people deep all around. The floor is shoulder to shoulder and it's steamy hot in here.

The bass beat is my heartbeat and my body is taken into the fold. Many eyes watch the floor but I dance alone. Moving, moving, I feel lifted. Arms above my head. Hips side-to-side, head shaking back and forth, feet moving, moving, twirling, bumping. Hands on my hips now, groovin' my shoulders, eyes closed. I'm one glint, one shimmer, one single part of the whole. Moving, moving, floating, floating. *Nothing is wrong.*

Song after song, so hot in here, and I hold my hair up off my neck with both hands, twirling, moving my hips. A guy behind me now, his breath on my neck and it's all right, we're moving together and then I twirl free of him and he nods and smiles as I go my own way; my own dance. I'm loose and powerful, beautiful, worthy, wild.

After the club closes, Vicki and I sit on a curb outside in the parking lot, drunk. Three wine coolers each and while we were in the club we also let some guys buy us more drinks.

"Vicki, you're my *best* friend," I tell her.

"*You*, Daka," she says. Daka is her nickname for me. She says it means friend. I can't remember in what language.

My head is spinning and I know I can't drive. Vicki can't either. After a while, the parking lot looks dark and spooky. We're downtown by ourselves and it's three in the morning.

Looking around, Vicki seems scared. She decides she's okay and gets into the driver's seat. I climb in the passenger's side. She turns the key in the ignition and the green VW Rabbit bucks forward, which almost makes me puke.

"Vicki, hit the clutch," I say, tightly gripping the handle above the passenger window.

"Which one is the clutch?" she asks. "I can't drive a stick."

Oh God. This is never going to work, but I'm gonna hurl. I simply cannot drive.

"Okay, I'll talk you through it," I slur.

On the third try a miracle occurs. Somehow she gets the footing and we're starting down the exit of the parking lot. The car is lurching along and with each jerk, my stomach flips, but at least we're heading home. She steers the car out onto Church St.

As we pick up speed, I rest my hand on the shifter and tell Vicki, "Hit the clutch! Hit the clutch!"

She does, and I shift. "Hit the gas!" I yell.

She hits the gas.

Now we're cruising down Franklin St. and I see a red traffic light up ahead.

If she stops now, she'll never get the footing again. I look around and then command her,

"Vicki, run it. No cars are coming just run the motherfucker."

Vicki runs the red light.

The rest of the lights are green.

We're almost to her road. One little turn and we're there.

"Don't stop, Vicki, just slow down and turn, hit the clutch. Hit the clutch!"

I downshift, and the Rabbit chokes the mile up her road in second gear, bucking to a stop in front of her driveway.

We make it inside and as I step into Vicki's room I grab a big decorative vase, dump it's dried flowers onto the floor and throw up into it.

In the morning I apologize a million times to Vicki for throwing up in her vase. Shame is all over me. Only losers drink so much they throw up. Only people like Dad.

She smiles and hugs me hard.

"Don't be silly Daka."

I'm grateful to have had her friendship over the last two years. She's so good to me. Leaving before her mom wakes up, I drive home feeling hung over, sick and full of self hate. Wondering what Luke would think I cringe, and decide he never needs to know I drank 'til I got sick. A worry hangs over me all the way home...what if I'm just like Dad?

***

Weeks go by and I don't drink a thing, but this weekend will be an exception. Mom's brother paid for her, Gramma and the boys to get on a plane and visit him in San Diego and that means I have the house to myself for one whole week of winter break. It's Saturday, and tonight I'm having a party. About a dozen friends from GCC are here and we're in the basement, hovering around the kerosene heater like a bon fire. We chipped in for a quarter keg and we're going to have so much fun! I've got the boom box plugged in and soon we're all dancing and it isn't cold anymore. Vicki's boyfriend Tim couldn't make it. Luke is here and even though he doesn't drink he looks like he's having fun. All our friends from CVS came. Me, Vicki, Rachel and Eileen start doing a dance to a song called *Doin' The Butt*. We're in a circle, laughing and taking turns shaking our backsides.

The music plays, "Sex-ay sex-ay, ain't nutt-in wrong if you wanna do the butt all night long."

We yell, "Rachel got a big old butt!"

Rachel screams, "Oh yeah?" and shakes it.

"Eileen got a big old butt!"

"Oh yeah?" Eileen sways her butt all slow and dramatic.

"Vicki got a big old butt!"

"Oh yeah!" Vicki works it.

"Janie got a big old butt!"

I turn my back, "that's right," and wiggle my ass for the girls.

The guys shake their heads, looking at us like we're crazy and we laugh 'til we cry.

After a while, I go upstairs to see if I can find something for us to eat. I'm looking through the fridge, but we've got nothing. In the cupboard, I find a couple bags of chips. I pour them in two big bowls and bring them downstairs. From the steps I can see the whole basement but I don't see Luke. He hates being around drunk people, but I don't think he would leave without saying good-bye.

At the bottom of the steps I hear a giggle and recognize it as Vicki's. *Good, maybe she knows where…?*

At the sight of them I drop the bowls. One lands flat, but the other makes a swirling sound as it spins round and round on the concrete floor. Potato chips scatter.

Luke and Vicki are all wrapped up in each other, playing a game of *Twister* in the little nook beneath the steps. Looking up at me they freeze, then Luke drops his position and Vicki laughs nervously. Turning around quick I stomp back up the stairs.

Thoughts of, "*They were just playing Twister*" and..."*I saw what I saw,*" alternate in my mind.

Stepping into Gramma's room, I shut the door, unplug the lamp, and it goes dark. Curling up into a ball on the far corner of her bed, I ask myself, "Why?" She can have anyone she wants. *Why* would she go after Luke?

My head aches.

Maybe he never really did love me? Maybe she was never really my friend? Maybe it was all in my head? Of course he would want her instead. The music stops downstairs and my head is spinning from all the beer I drank. Luke is calling my name but I don't respond. As his voice gets closer I roll toward the wall and make myself smaller. He's in the room now, rubbing his hand on the wall for the switch. He flicks it, but the light doesn't turn on.

"Janie?" he says softly. "Are you there?"

I'm barely breathing. I don't want to talk to him. He sits down on the bed, and feels around, just missing my body with his hand. It's very dark but I can see the outline of him. He leans forward and puts his elbows on his knees, his face in his hands.

"Oh God," he says, softly.

Nope, nope nope. I won't let him know I'm here. I hold my breath.

He sits for a long time and then gets up and walks out of the room.

The party is over. The house is quiet. I don't know where everyone went and I don't care. The two people I thought I could trust, I can't. My heart hurts and I just want to sleep and never wake up.

The next morning, Luke is at my house, denying anything was happening between him and Vicki. He gives me his practiced look that tells me I'm pathetic and insecure.

"We were playing *Twister*!" He says. "A *game*. What's the big deal?" His expression is worry, pity, disgust.

For the rest of winter break I don't call Vicki and she doesn't call me. When we get back to G.C.C. she acts like nothing ever happened. Maybe it *was* me. Maybe there truly was nothing going on. We go through our last semester and while everything seems the same, it isn't. With Luke, with Vicki, I keep a little part of myself locked away. No longer do I give them *everything*.

At the end of the year, I get a special tassel for graduating with honors. When I walk up to the podium, Luke and all his engineering friends cheer extra loud. Mom and both my grandmothers are in the audience, snapping pictures. No Dad per usual.

Over the summer, Luke and I are the same as ever. Vicki and I are back to normal. I'm sure I must have made big deal out of nothing. She's going to SUNY Fredonia in the fall. Her boyfriend Tim is going to Hamilton University. I'm going to SUNY Oswego and Luke is going to his dream school, Notre Dame in South Bend, Indiana.

Vicki is the first to leave and she sobs hysterically as she hugs me good-bye. Surprised by her strong reaction I say, "Vicki, we're just going away to school. No one is dying. Geesh! I'll see you every break. We'll talk on the phone, okay?"

She nods, hugs me and bursts out crying again.

Two nights before Luke leaves for Notre Dame, we finish our last shifts at CVS. As soon as we climb into the car, Luke loses it. He's sobbing and for Christ's sake! What's *with* everybody? I tell him, "It will all be the same. We'll see each other on breaks. It will be *fine.*"

Holding him, I run my fingers through his hair.

"I've barely ever left the town of Irving," he says. "I'm so scared. I feel like an idiot for crying."

"Shh....you're not an idiot," I say. "It's a lot to take in. A lot to think about."

I run my hand over his face, and stroke his forehead.

He says, "I'm going to miss you so much."

"We'll be *fine,*" I tell him.

"We're gonna write all the time and talk on the

phone. I'll be with you and you'll be with me. Always."

He looks up at me with gratitude and I love him so much. Nothing else matters. The flirting, Vicki, none of it. He loves me and I love him and I will never, ever abandon him.

After two years of being virtually inseparable at G.C.C., Vicki never did call me again. It would be a decade before I considered the possibility that it might have something to do with her, and not some heinous flaw in me.

Chapter Twenty-Nine

All my belongings fit into the back of Mom's car and SUNY Oswego is just two hours away. She helps carry my stuff up to the third floor and as soon as it's piled inside my dorm room, she's back downstairs ready to go. A quick hug and I'm watching the back of the white station wagon drive away. She doesn't look back. I wish she had looked back. Mom worked last night and she has to work again tonight. She hasn't slept yet today.

Inside, mothers are helping kids' hang things on the walls. Mothers are putting sheets on beds. Fathers stand around, trying to be helpful. Some pull carts with their kids' stuff in and out of elevators. All around me, parents linger just a little longer and it makes me feel worthless. My mom couldn't wait to take off.

My roommate is a big girl. You can see the desperation and neediness in her eyes as she agrees to let our neighbors fill up our little dorm fridge with beer, it is so obvious they are just using her.

"Do you want to come? They're having a party in Billy's room," she says, all giddy.

"No thanks, I want to finish unpacking."

Our dorm is co-ed and all evening, strange boys walk right in and head to the fridge.

"How ya doin?" they nod.

It's creepy, but I'm afraid of getting my new neighbors mad, so I smile and say, "Fine," even though I feel like crying.

Late at night, I lay in bed, looking at the moonlight, making stripes on my wall from the window blinds. My roommate is a loud snorer and I can smell the beer seeping out of her pores. Smells like Dad. Grabbing my keys and a roll of quarters I brought for laundry, I walk down three flights of stairs in my pajamas and sock feet and call Luke from a payphone in the lobby. Phone service isn't set up yet in our room and besides, I don't want to talk in front of *her*.

"Hello?" he answers, all groggy.

"Luke?" I start to cry.

"What's wrong? What time is it? What's going on?"

The concern in his voice sends me over the edge.

"I hate it here," I sob.

I tell him about the roommate and the beer. I tell him I'm never going to be okay here. I'm too ashamed to tell him about Mom leaving without a backward glance.

"It's going to be okay," he says.

"I hated it here the first couple of days too, but you're so great. People are going to love you. You'll be fine," he says.

"I miss you so much."

"I miss you too."

An operator comes on the line and tells me to put in more money. Forsaking my laundry, I stick more quarters in the slot.

"Tell me something happy," I say.

"Well, tonight I went to a candlelight mass held at the grotto here on campus. It was really cool. There were people playing guitars and it was just hard to explain. There's a statue of Mary and I felt, I just kind of felt ..."

"You felt God?" I smile.

"Yeah, I guess I did," he laughs.

"Did it feel like *nothing was wrong*?" I ask.

"Yeah. I guess it did."

"I love you," I smile dreamily into the phone.

"I love you too," he says.

Soon Luke and I are closer than ever. We talk on the phone every three days and at least twice a week he pours out his heart to me in letters. He writes of Notre Dame, of how he feels God around him and how he loves me and wants me to come visit him there. His letters keep me going, making me feel less alone.

All the good jobs were taken when I got to Oswego so I'm stuck working in the cafeteria. My stomach contracts every time the rugby team comes in. They treat me like shit. They're all rich boys, who probably couldn't get into better schools for poor grades. They bark out orders on how they want their sandwiches, and talk to me like I'm stupid.

Washing dishes and serving food here in the cafeteria, feels like the lowest of the low. Slapping their precious sandwiches together I make up my mind to find out if Oswego has any work-study programs.

When I visit the financial aid office, the counselor tells me my family income level is so low, I can receive grant money that will cover just about everything next semester. I might not even have to work. Beaming, I walk back to my dorm, holding a folder with the financial aid forms under my arm. *Finally,* being poor is going to pay off. By next semester, my dishwashing days will be behind me.

I ask Mom to send me her tax information so I can fill out the financial aid papers myself. They are complicated, and it takes me two full weeks to finish them between classes, dishwashing, and my other schoolwork. Finally, they're all set. Mom has one tiny part to fill out and then she just has to sign and mail them. Next semester, it's easy street!

One week before the deadline, I call her.

"Have you sent in my financial aid forms yet?"

"Not yet. I haven't had the time. They need special postage and I haven't been to the post office."

"Mom. It's really important. You have to send them in by the 15th."

"Okay, I'll get to it," she promises.

"Thanks Mom. Let me talk to Bobby and Charlie."

As much as I hate washing dishes, I *love* my classes at Oswego. I'm majoring in communications, with an emphasis on broadcasting. I even auditioned for a news anchor position at the college TV station and got it. I'm also taking classes in psychology, and political science. My political science professor is a young beautiful redhead. All the guys in class have a crush on her. She's smart and cool and really funny. The way she talks politics makes it exciting and interesting. My psychology teacher is nice too. Psychology is easy. It's basically just putting labels on things that are common sense.

When I'm not in class or working, or at the TV station, I'm in the library. I never knew how much I loved to study. Half the time I'm reading books that have nothing to do with my assignments but there are so many things to find out. I've fallen in love with learning and sometimes I swear I can feel my brain getting bigger from all I'm taking in. I read and read until my eyes cross. When I walk outside the library into Oswego's blustery snap, it feels like I'm stepping onto a different planet. Breathing in and out, my body contracts from the cold but my world expands as I push against the weather and walk to my dorm.

The day financial aid awards are to be announced, I practically skip into the office, ready to learn just how much money I'll be getting next semester.

The lady behind the desk says flatly, "We don't have your forms."

I make her check again, but they're not there.

Back at the dorm, my hands shake as I dial the phone.

Mom answers and I scream, "How could you not send in the forms? All you *fucking* had to do was send them in. I DID ALL THE WORK!"

"Don't swear at me," she snaps. "You have no idea what I'm going through here."

"I don't fucking care what you're going through. All you had to do was sign a Goddamn form, and you couldn't even do that for me? I never ask a thing of you and you couldn't do this simple God damn thing for me!"

Click.

My mother hangs up on me.

The rest of the semester I'm furious at Mom for screwing up my financial aide, but I'm also mad at Luke.

He insists on alternating who makes the calls even though his parents pay for *all* his living expenses. Here I am working my ass off, washing dishes, but every penny *I* earn goes toward talking to him. Luke's never had to struggle for anything in his life and I resent him for not having a clue how hard it is for me. But when he picks me up at Oswego at the end of the semester, I forget all that. He lifts me up and spins me around and it feels so good to have *someone* give a damn about me. We're close as ever, working at CVS, eating pizza, swimming in his pool. We go bowling with Trish and Michael, but this summer I realize I actually don't *like* bowling. I hate the way they all have their own balls and I have to stick my fingers into the sweaty holes a thousand other people have used. The smelly rental shoes are even worse. I hate the way Trish's long fingernails scrape inside her ball every time she throws it down the lane. I'd rather do just about anything than bowl but I don't have any money because I have to save it for school. All summer we do what Luke wants to do. He pays, so he gets to decide. It's the unwritten rule.

***

Senior year, I have a new roommate. Mary-Kathryn Meghan O'Brien is a Catholic redhead from Decatur, near my hometown. We even know a lot of the same kids. When we go out to happy hour, it's like we've known each other for years.

One day, while Mary-Kathryn's at class, I'm out of q-tips and I look in her top drawer to see if I can steal one. She's got q-tips and every other beauty supply you could imagine in there. I take one and stand there cleaning my ear, looking over the rest of the stuff in her drawer. Picking up a plastic tube with a prescription label on it, I read the instructions. *Apply to skin, once a day, for acne.* If the tube read "cure for cancer" I wouldn't be more astonished. A prescription product for acne? Glancing quick at the door, I take the tube and unscrew the top. I put a little dab on my finger and apply it to the blemishes under my bangs. The next day I do the same. By the third day, my acne is gone. As I look in the mirror at my clear skin I hear Dad's voice in my head, telling me acne is my own fault because I don't wash well enough. He can fuck off.

This semester I'm taking a women's studies class. My friend Kasey from high school is at Cornell, and she's into women's studies, so I figured, why not? The professor is older, probably in her sixties. She's a little heavyset, but very hip with her long flowy tops. She's published some books and I never really thought about the things she teaches before. About women being treated as less than men, I mean, except at home with Mom and Dad.

"What is feminism?" she writes on the board.

I have no idea.

I picture a woman in the 60's in go-go boots and straight long hair, walking down the sidewalk with a strong determined look on her face.

Everyone tosses in their own two cents about feminism and since I don't really know what it is, I say nothing.

The professor moves all over the room and it doesn't feel like a formal class but more like a discussion. There's a hippie looking girl to my right and she seems to know *everything* about feminism. The professor says male teachers get paid way more than female ones and men get promoted to jobs like principals much more often, even though they make up a smaller percentage of the workforce. I never thought about that before. I listen to the other student's comments about sex discrimination, the right to vote, and glass ceilings, and I wonder, *how do these kids know this stuff?*

The professor is in the back of the room, and as she walks down the aisle she stops at my desk, then pivots around quick to face me. "Okay Janie, bottom line…what is feminism?"

I gulp.

Thinking about all I've just heard, I pause, then say the first thing that pops into my head.

"Feminism is equal pay for equal work?"

She looks at me long and hard and I feel my face turn red.

Oh God, I'm so stupid.

She lights up and with a big smile she says, "You're succinct. I like that. Listen to this young woman. Janie is quiet, but there is a lot going on inside her brilliant mind."

I can't believe she said that about me.

She continues talking about how the person who controls the money has the power in a relationship.

I think about bowling. I'd rather do just about anything than bowl, but since I have no money, it's never up to me. I imagine myself sitting there on the bench in the bowling alley, with Luke and Trish and Michael, but wishing I were home with Bobby and Charlie. I wonder if *feminism* might also mean getting a say in how you spend your time?

***

The following semester, not only did my financial aid go through, I also got the easiest of work-studies at the art gallery on campus. All I have to do is sit at a desk and hit a clicker every time someone comes in, which isn't often. I'm saving all the money I make to go see Luke at

Notre Dame in the spring. He's going to pay for half my ticket. I should use this time to do homework, but mostly I just waste it, writing.

Sitting at the little desk, I write down all my thoughts and feelings in a pink notebook. Writing, with all this art around, is the time I feel God. I write and I write and I don't stop writing until my hand aches and there's a big dent in the middle finger of my left hand from the pen. Getting up, I wander the empty gallery, looking at all the paintings. The art clears my mind and eventually I'm propelled back to my notebook. When I'm done writing, I feel like all the bad things that have been building up in me are let out. I can breathe. I feel lighter. I feel relaxed, like *nothing is wrong*.

My roommate Mary-Kathryn doesn't have to work but even though her parents funnel money into a checking account for her, she's not spoiled. Her parents call every Sunday and at least one of her siblings calls during the week. She's the baby of four and her brothers and sister really seem to care about her. What is it like to have a family where the parents love and adore you? Where your siblings actually give a damn about you? If I ever have a family, it's going to be a good one, like Mary-Kathryn's. Luke is the only one who ever calls me, and only every *other* time.

In the spring, I'm on a plane to South Bend, Indiana. Luke paid for exactly half, and he's picking me up at the airport. It's my first airplane ride and as we descend into Fighting Irish territory, the pilot does a circle over the school and I see a big statue of The Virgin Mary. It looks like I could reach my hand right out of the plane and touch her but like my own mother, she ignores me, staring straight ahead.

Luke is there at the gate. He's got flowers. When we make eye contact we run toward each other full force. He picks me up and swings me around and it's just me and him and the rightness of his arms around me. Burying my face in his neck, I inhale the smell of him and he kisses the top of my head and when we come to, a crowd of travelers has stopped to watch us.

Luke takes me all over the beautiful Notre Dame campus. He shows me where he studies and where he loves to walk. Girls aren't allowed to stay in the men's dorms and it makes me nervous, but we sneak in and out of his private room and no one bothers us at all. It's the first time we're actually free to sleep in the same bed and hold each other all night. In the morning he stands behind me watching me do my make-up in the bathroom mirror. He puts his arms around me.

"You are *so beautiful*," he says, meeting my eyes in our reflections.

It's strange, because he never really said that before; not like that. It's always been, "You're hot." There's a big difference.

Luke is so kind while I'm here. So humble in his demeanor. Gone is the cocky hotshot he was at community college. Here, he is a small fish in a big pond and he knows it. In the evening, he takes me to Mass at the grotto. It's a little stone cave, all lit up with candles. Students sit on the ground and two guys are playing acoustic guitars. There is another statue of Mary and when I look at Luke in the glow of the candlelight, it's like God is resting a hand right there on his shoulder, lighting him up. He looks peaceful, and content.

The next night, we go to a Notre Dame football game. It's the Fighting Irish against Miami and I'm told at least a hundred times by Luke and other students what a privilege it is to sit in the student section since I don't actually go there. I get it. I'm not worthy of your stupid school. This game is evidently a big deal and somehow Luke finagled me a ticket. It's crowded and loud and when the coach comes out everyone starts chanting, "Lou! Lou! Lou!" forming "L's" with their thumb and forefingers and I just don't get it. People are screaming and jingling their keys. T-shirts for sale read "Catholics vs. Convicts."

It's a night game and as soon as the sun goes down I'm cold and bored. Sitting there with a million lunatics, I daydream about life after college. I want to get an apartment. I wonder what Bobby and Charlie are up to? I count the minutes 'til this game is over and can't wait to sneak back into Luke's dorm room to cuddle. I hate how we're wasting my last night here at a football game, but when Luke turns to me I smile and thank him for bringing me.

The next day I have to leave, but before I do we sit outside, on the grass under a giant tree. Luke looks at me, full of love in his eyes and a bolt of fear shoots through me. In that instant I know I will lose him. I don't belong here in these old stately buildings with their history, with these kids with all the money. With a sinking feeling I board the plane to go.

Back at Oswego, I go for long walks, listening to Billy Joel on my headphones. What if all this time with Luke, I've just been preparing him to be a really good husband for someone else? Someone prettier than me. Smarter than me. Someone rich. Someone who fits more nicely into his fancy picture. As I walk, the smell of dead fish fills the air, and the waves lap the cold rocks along the shore of Lake Ontario.

***

Senior year is winding down and Luke hasn't been calling me like usual. We're fighting. He's taking a job in Poughkeepsie after graduation. I don't come right out and say it, but I want him to ask me to join him. Instead, he says, "Poughkeepsie is just two hours from home. It will be easy to get together on the weekends."

After a long silence, he says, "We'll be fine. We managed the last two years long distance, didn't we?"

I play with the phone cord and stare at the wall in my dorm room.

In a big vacant field, SUNY Oswego has an annual party called Mud Fest. There are beer trucks and bands playing on stage, and as people get drunk, they start diving in the mud. By the end of the day if you aren't covered in mud, you're a target. Drunk off my ass, I'm standing with a group of friends when suddenly I'm dragged into the pit by a frat boy I sort of know. I wind up on crutches the next day with ligaments torn in my foot. I didn't even feel it happen. I don't tell Luke. Getting around campus on crutches was a bitch.

Out with Mary-Kathryn and friends another night, I'm drunk and "S*ure*, I'll walk home with you," I tell a frat boy named Mark. He's little, not much taller than me, and he's cute. He has a Brooklyn accent. We're laughing and Luke didn't call yesterday *or the day before* like he said he would, and fuck *him!* Who does he think he is anyway?

The frat house is quiet when we get there. Underneath my drunkenness, I get an uneasy feeling when I look around at all the guy stuff. We go to Mark's room, which is actually a big closet, with a sheet stapled to the doorway, which reminds me of Dad's spy curtain. We kiss a little and he offers me some sweatpants to sleep in and then leaves to use the bathroom. I use the bathroom next and it's filthy. When I get back, Mark's asleep on the bed. I think about leaving, but it's late and my buzz is wearing thin and I'm scared to walk all the way back to my dorm at night by myself. I lay on the bed next to Mark. He stirs, and then wraps his arms around me. With my eyes closed I see Luke's face. I miss him so much and I don't want him to break up with me. I'm sad and scared, but it feels so good to be held. Mark starts to kiss me behind the ear and I go with it. I turn around and kiss him back. Rolling over on top of him, my throat is tight as I commit to this, my first step toward letting Luke go.

At 6AM I wake up to Mark's snoring and start to panic. I've got to get out of here. I'm so embarrassed. I feel like one of those frat house groupies. What have I done? Tiptoeing out in Mark's sweats, I gather my shoes and jacket. There are guys sleeping here and there and I get a chill looking about me; all that testosterone in one place. Thank God none of them knew I was here.

Why did I even come here? I'm such a slut. I think of Luke asleep, all by himself at Notre Dame. Pure. He would never do this to me. But, we haven't talked in a week. What *is* he doing anyway?

The morning air feels good and cool and, in a way, I feel free. Maybe it doesn't *have to be* Luke? Maybe there are other people who might find me attractive. Birds are singing and I wonder if Mary-Kathryn worried about me last night. When I tiptoe in, she shoots up in bed.

"Where *were* you?" she says, holding her covers in front at her neck.

"I hooked up with Mark from the party," I say, kicking off my shoes.

"Hooked up?" she asks, sitting up straighter.

"Well not *hooked up*, hooked up. I just wound up crashing next to him on his bed," I lie.

"Oh," she says, and her eyes look down at the floor. She would never do something so stupid. So slutty.

Turning toward my dresser to take out a t-shirt I hear Mary-Kathryn yell,

"Ewwwww! What *is* that?"

"What?" I ask, looking back at her.

"The back of your sweats," her face is all twisted up like she smelled something disgusting.

Turning my body to look, there is a big brown globby stain on my butt. It looks like shit.

In horror, Mary-Kathryn and I look at each other, eyes popping out of our heads. I'm about to scream when I notice the distinct smell, of chocolate. There is melted chocolate all over the back of Mark's sweats.

"How the hell did I get chocolate all over my butt?" I ask.

Mary-Kathryn starts cracking up.

"Oh my God!" she says, flopping back on her bed laughing hysterically.

Cracking up, tears are streaming down my face when it occurs to me, "He's going to think I *shit* in his bed!"

Mary-Kathryn howls with laughter, and then says, "He'll *know* it was chocolate."

Pulling the sweats out far from my butt, I ask, "If you saw this, would *you* get down and sniff it to find out?"

The students in the next dorm room pound the wall because we're being so loud at 7AM. As I change my clothes, Mary-Kathryn gets up, walks to her desk, grabs a tissue, and dabs at her eyes.

Finally, we both hit our beds and sleep 'til lunch.

When Luke calls later I act like everything is normal. He says he's been really busy studying. The guilt tears me up inside, but I don't mention a thing about Mark. It's not like it meant anything.

Soon, school is almost over. Mark's fraternity is having a party and Mary-Kathryn convinces me to go. I see him, busy with his friends, and it's good, this "I don't know you" routine. I'm relieved. It seems our night of hooking up is behind us. Soon, me and my friends are drunk and we're on the dance floor having fun, when suddenly, I notice Mary-Kathryn swaggering through the crowd directly over to Mark who is putting out more plastic cups by the keg. She's waving her finger in his face, and her head is reared back. I run across the room, trying to stop whatever it is she's about to say, and catch up with her just in time to hear her slur..."And by the way......my room mate....did not ...*SHIT* in your bed." She staggers back a bit and gives Mark the evil stink eye.

His eyes light up. He looks at her, then to me.

"I KNOW!" He laughs. "It was some Easter candy my mom sent me. I'd been eating it in bed."

We all laugh and at least that much is clear. I'm able to retain a smidge of dignity. I may be a slut, but I *did not* shit anyone's bed.

Graduation is depressing. I've gained almost 20 pounds this semester with all the partying and the guilt.

I'm not looking forward to seeing Luke or worse, having Luke see me this fat. Mom and my Grammas and even Hilary attend the ceremony and take me out to a little fish stand everyone here raves about. I've wanted to go there for two years but never had any money to spend on something like fish and chips. Now that we're here, I don't know what the big deal was. The food isn't even that good. Sitting unhappily with my family, I stuff myself 'til the only thing I feel is my stomach hurting. With no fanfare, we pack up the station wagon with my things and head home with my Bachelor's degree from SUNY Oswego. On the way home, I sit in the back seat, running the strings of my Magna Cum Laude tassel through my fingers. I can't wait to get home to Bobby and Charlie.

Chapter Thirty

Bobby and Charlie have the room I used to share with Hilary. Mom is in Adam's old room and Gramma still has the bedroom downstairs that used to be my parent's. There is no longer any room for me in this house. Making a space in the basement, I do my best, stapling blankets to the wooden support beams for privacy. Like the kitchen, I have the brown wrap over pink insulation as my wallpaper. An old rusty metal wardrobe holds my clothes. A throw rug covers the area next to my bed on the concrete basement floor. Armed now with my Bachelor's degree in communications, I send out applications to all the TV and radio stations in the area.

A local TV station offers me an unpaid internship and I take it. They put me in charge of the teleprompter, and it's going great, until the sportscast one night.

I'm rolling right along, turning the dial on the machine that gives the handsome young anchor his script as he talks over a piece about high school hockey and then I get to thinking about Luke. He moves into his apartment in Poughkeepsie today. I wonder what's going to happen with us? Why hasn't he asked me to move there with him? Will I ever be good enough for him?

The sportscaster starts tripping over his words. I'm thinking, *whoa buddy, get it together*, and suddenly the director is ripping the teleprompter out of my hands and frantically flipping through to the right story. I was three behind. My heart beats fast and I super focus through the rest of the news. That night, I feel like such a failure about my mess up I can barely sleep.

After a month, I get a call from a program director at a local radio station. He wants to interview me for a job that actually pays.

The program director is Fred Nealon. He's a nice, middle-aged guy, probably in his forties. He reminds me of a gym teacher, all athletic and energetic as he tells me about the available position. I would be the new producer for the James Landon Show. I would actually be his *first* producer, since James has always done his phone calls and info gathering for himself. Fred takes me on a tour of the station and immediately, people are warning me about James Landon.

"He's arrogant," they say.

"He's a bear," they say.

"He's difficult to work with," they say.

I'm not scared. I've lived through my father. What can he do to me?

James Landon is a big heavyset guy with thick white hair and a big booming voice. He tells me to read through the papers, and if I see anything funny or interesting, I'm to schedule interviews. Coming in at 5AM, I grab a cup of coffee and start flipping through the local papers and *The USA Today*. This job is so much fun. I set up interviews, make calls, and patch them in to the studio.

James says, "I value your input. You're young, and what you find interesting will attract a whole new demographic."

I schedule an interview with a professional ice cream taster who sends us gallons and gallons of gourmet ice cream. I schedule an interview with the former Mayor of Irving, who is now working in the DC political scene. I schedule funny interviews and serious interviews and James talks just as easily with the locally famous as he does with little old ladies who call in to heckle him. He can talk to anyone and I learn so much. It seems the key is to really listen, and to enjoy whomever you're talking with. James and I laugh all morning, every morning. One weekend when Luke was home, James even picked us up in his limo and took us out to a fancy dinner with his wife at their country club.

"You're going places kiddo," he always says to me.

The only kind of bear James Landon is, is a big teddy bear. Like my theater director at G.C.C., Angelo D'Angelo, he's proof good men do exist.

***

Luke and I are seeing each other every other weekend, taking turns on who does the driving. If he had his way, I would drive down to Poughkeepsie every time. It doesn't matter to him one bit my car is falling apart and has no heat.

Last weekend, he had the nerve to complain I left hair on the bathroom floor after I'd used his shower to thaw myself out after my freezing two-hour drive to his apartment. It was my last nerve he stepped on and I informed him I would not be making the drive anymore in my dilapidated car. It wasn't fair. If he wanted to see me, he'd have to come up to Centerville.

In the spring, Hilary and Craig move to North Carolina for Craig's new job. I'm happy for her to be starting a new life, but sad because this is the first time I've ever felt close to her, and now she's gone. I take their little apartment. It is four tiny rooms; the upstairs in a house above a little old lady. It is carpeted, and has dark wood molding. Having a bedroom with actual walls is wonderful! No more insulation! There is an old claw foot tub, with a little ring around the top to hold a shower curtain. The kitchen is bright and yellow, and I have a little two-seater table. The floor slants a bit but I don't care because it's a real floor. No more concrete! The apartment is very cheap. Only $200 a month. The little old lady downstairs probably hasn't raised her rates in twenty years. I love having the place to myself and in the afternoons when I get home from work I lie on the couch with the sunshine filtering through the window, reading *Glam* and *Cosmo* magazines. I've been jogging again, and I feel strong, and slim, attractive and alive.

This month's *Glam* has an article about a self-defense class called "Model Mugging." There are pictures of women, beating the crap out of a male "mugger" who is really a professional martial artist, all dressed up in protective gear.

I flip the page and think to myself, "Wouldn't that feel good? To knock the shit out of someone but not really hurt them? To punch someone right in the face or kick them in the groin?" Smiling, I keep reading.

Each Model Mugging class is a group of women, learning to empower themselves by fighting through old traumas with a band of sisters, cheering them on.

A band of sisters. Imagine that.

Many women who take this class have been victims of sexual abuse.

Boy, that sucks. No wonder they want to learn to protect themselves.

The article has a quiz attached. I *love* magazine quizzes.

"Are you a Victim of Sexual Abuse?" it asks.

If you check yes to any of these questions, it's likely you have been sexually abused.

Well, I'm glad *I* wasn't sexually abused. No one's ever *raped* me.

I go down the list.

Check.

Check.

Check.

Check.

Check. *Five checks!*

For more information read this book, *The Courage to Heal* by Ellen Bass and Laura Davis.

Hey, why did I get five checks?

Sexual abuse.

I wasn't sexually abused, was I?

A tingle travels the length of my body and my stomach clenches. I shut the magazine quick.

Later, I drive to the bookstore. When I find it, I slip the book from the shelf. On the cover in purple letters is the title, *The Courage to Heal*. I open the book, then shut it quickly. I don't want anyone to see me with it. I don't want anyone to think *I* was sexually abused, because I wasn't.

The book is expensive and I don't have enough money. I leave the store, drive to an ATM and take out my last $30.00.

Back in the bookstore, I hold *The Courage to Heal* to my chest as I make my way to the register. My heart pounds. I don't want anyone seeing what I'm buying.

At the checkout, I'm praying the lady at the counter doesn't read the title. I despise the thought of her making assumptions about me. I don't know why I even want this book so much since I wasn't even sexually abused, but something deep inside propels me forward.

At the counter, I place the book face down and let my breath out when the cashier puts it in a bag without even bothering to glance at the title. In the car, I take the book out of the bag, and stare at the cover. The clock on the dashboard says 5:30 PM as I open *The Courage to Heal* and begin reading.

It says, if someone has made you uncomfortable by leering at you, spying on you, exposing themselves to you, exposing you to porn, touching your private areas (even just tickling), having sex in front of you……

Oh My God.

I was sexually abused.

Oh My God.

I think about Dad trying to plant a good night kiss on my privates when I was four. The spying. The leering. The constant talk of tits and ass, the too sexy movies on HBO, Dad sleeping sprawled out naked on his bed, exposing himself. Dad grabbing my breasts during tickle fights when I was starting to develop.

As I flip the pages, tears roll down my cheeks.

8:00PM, I'm still in the parking lot, reading by streetlight now. I'm nauseous and part of me feels deviant even reading this stuff. Like I'm somehow going to get in trouble.

Shutting the book I lay it on the seat next to me. Closing my eyes I say the words out loud.

"Sexual abuse."

That weekend I make an exception and drive down to Luke's apartment in Poughkeepsie. When we start being intimate, I keep thinking "sexual abuse" and I just can't get into it. Images of my father keep running through my head. I shove Luke off of me and roll on my side.

"Are you okay?" he asks.

"I think I was sexually abused," I blurt out.

He's silent for a long time and I wonder if he's going to pretend I didn't even say it.

I sit up on the side of his bed and he places his hand on my back. Finally, he says, "We're going to get you the help you need."

But Luke is a 22-year-old kid. I need more help than he could ever possibly give me. We never mention it again.

***

As the days go by I'm madder and madder at Dad and I decide to tell Mom once and for all. I want her to get angry too. Mom and I have been getting along great since I moved into my own apartment. Surely if she knows what he did was actual *sexual abuse*, she'll be on my side. Surely once she has the right information she'll stand up to that bastard once and for all.

I invite her over to my apartment and side-by-side, we sit on the floor, leaning back against the love seat. She has her hair cut short in a chin length bob, and is wearing a slightly ill fitting partial plate where her missing tooth belonged. It's better than a big gaping hole but I think the dentist could have done a better job. After some small talk, I get up my nerve.

"Mom. I need to tell you something."

Pausing, I run my hand back and forth over the little stretch of carpet in between us.

Finally I blurt out, "Dad sexually abused me."

I hold my breath and wait.

"What do you mean?" she asks, looking straight forward, out the window across the room from us.

"Well, there were only a couple of incidents where he actually touched me, but there were many more where he exposed me to pornography, walked around naked, exposed himself, constantly leered at me, *spied* on me. The spying was the worst. Mom, spying *is* sexual abuse. I've been reading a lot about it and all of that stuff is considered abuse. It isn't just rape or molestation."

Mom continues staring off in the distance, out my living room window.

"I wondered...," she says.

"You *wondered*?" I whisper, holding my breath, trying not to make her defensive. "Wondered *what?*"

"Well, the thought crossed my mind," she says, "but then I pushed it out as fast as it came in."

She smoothes her hands over her thighs.

"Mom, why didn't you do anything?" I ask.

"I guess I didn't want to believe it. It was too disgusting to even think about," she says.

She wondered? My heart sinks. She was right there for most of it. I flat out told her about the spying, *as it was happening*.

Okay...so that was then, this is now. Now she knows it was *abuse*. I wait for her to get mad. To stand up for me. To at least hold me and tell me she's sorry. I imagine her saying, "Let's call him."

I haven't spoke to Dad in almost a year, but I want us to join together, drive to his apartment, and confront his sorry ass.

There's a lump in my throat and I want to cry. I want to put my head on her lap and have her stroke my hair like Gramma does. I lean into her a little, but Mom, ever so slightly, moves away. She closes her eyes, then opening them again says softly, "I wonder if *I* was sexually abused?"

"What?" I pull back and look at her.

"Well, I didn't really know my father. Gramma left him when I was little, and I never really knew why. She wouldn't talk about it. She just packed us up and we moved in with Aunt Ellie, all in one day."

And Mom is off. Gone into her own thoughts, about her own childhood. Wherever she went, it's miles away from me. There will be no confrontation. *I get smaller.* No apologies. *Smaller still.* No comfort offered. *I almost disappear.*

The little girl inside me clenches her fists, and stamps her foot. Silently she screams, "*Mom! I just told you something about me! Can you please be here for me? I'm sorry if you were sexually abused. I really am, but you are the mother here. Please be my mother! Why won't you ever fucking be my mother?*"

Mom sits there on the floor, staring off into space, muttering to herself and all I can think is, *"She wondered......"*

My stomach is in knots and I just want her to leave.

When she finally goes, I lie in bed, crying. My whole life I convinced myself that even though we were poor, and even though my parents were rough around the edges, they truly loved me. They would be there if I really needed them. I believed it because I had to, but here in this room, in this tiny apartment, that fantasy is gone.

The door in my heart that slammed shut on my father years ago, now slams shut on Mom too. The slamming tears something and makes a permanent wound, like a leg being crushed by a heavy object. Pulling out, you lose the leg, but gain your freedom. If you survive you'll surely limp, but you'll no longer be bound. Someday with the right support you will walk, and maybe even run again.

I decide Hilary should know. She should know what I went through, what *we both* went through was actually sexual abuse. We have several phone conversations about it, about the spying, the leering, the pornography, all of it, and I think she's on my side, but finally she says, "I don't believe you were sexually abused."

I'm stunned.

"Dad was just inappropriate. He didn't molest you. He's got a perverted sense of humor, that's all."

Happy with her new husband and her new life, she makes it clear she doesn't want to hear it anymore. With a lump in my throat I hang up the phone, feeling like a fool for ever trusting her to talk about it.

Over the next several weeks my anger at Mom seeps out in every interaction with her. If it weren't for Bobby and Charlie I wouldn't care if I ever saw her again. Gramma doesn't understand. She thinks *I'm* the problem. She says I need to treat my mother with respect. She reminds me how hard Mom works. She tells me if *she* were Mom, she wouldn't let me step foot in the house, the way I talk to her.

Finally after one of her lectures I lose it, and yell, "Your precious daughter, who you can't stop defending was a horrible mother. She let a lot of things happen to me she shouldn't have, Gramma!"

Gramma looks me in the eye. She knows exactly what I mean. She looks shocked and disgusted, but quickly gains her composure.

"I don't care *what he did* to you, you can't live your whole life being ugly and angry!" she said.

Ugly and angry.

That's how she sees me.

The one person in the world I thought would love me no matter what.

***

It's been a month since I've seen Luke. Two weeks ago he didn't make the drive because he was "too tired" from stress at work. He's coming today and I try to ignore my feeling of dread by focusing on a project I want to do together. I'm painting my bedroom walls my favorite color, a sunny pale yellow. I didn't ask the landlord, but so what? I *need* something cheerful to counteract my heavy heart. I have not talked to mom, or Gramma or Hilary in a couple of weeks. Over the last few days I've pictured Luke and me here, painting. In my fantasy, we're getting ready for the real thing. Practicing for our own, grown up life, when we'll be painting the walls of our own home together. Maybe even the walls of a nursery one day. I so want to be part of a real family. A loving family.

When he gets to my apartment, Luke is distracted. He reluctantly agrees to help me paint, but breaks it down to his and hers tasks. He gets the roller. I get the trim. There is no flirting. No banter. He cranks out the paint on the walls quick and aggressive and when he's done with *his* part, I've still got tons to do. He puts the roller down, goes into the next room, and flips on the TV. The sound of the football game blares from the next room.

My heart literally aches in my chest. Mom, Hilary, Gramma, Luke. *Why doesn't anyone care about me?*

Dipping my brush into the buttery paint, I drag it along the trim. The lines from the bristles flow as I move the brush to the right, and a second swipe covers them up, leaving a shiny yellow glow. Dip, drag, dip, drag. Silent tears come, and I let them flow.

What is it about me that is so unlovable?

My chest feels so heavy I can barely breathe. My throat is tight. I wish I were dead. Pills. Run my car off a cliff. Injection. If I could get my hands on a lethal injection, that would be perfect. I'd go up in the woods behind mom's house, and lie on a blanket in the sunshine, and that would be it. I have no access to lethal injections though, so I put the idea aside. Hanging. I knew a kid who did that and it's so gruesome. I doubt I'd have the nerve. I don't have a gun. Carbon monoxide. I don't have a garage.

Dip, drag. Dip, drag.

Sunshine yellow walls.

Sadness slowly turns to anger, and it's,

FUCK YOU MOM!

FUCK YOU DAD!

FUCK YOU HILARY!

FUCK YOU GRAMMA!

Ugly and angry. That's me. Gramma is right.

Dip, drag.

My thoughts go to Luke in the next room.

Why aren't I enough for him?

*FUCK YOU LUKE AND YOUR FUCKING
FOOTBALL AND YOUR DREAMS OF A FANCY LIFE
WITH SOMEONE BETTER THAN ME.*

I decide right there I'd rather be alone than feel so lonely inside our relationship.

When I break up with him, he seems more relieved than sad.

Walking through the next couple of weeks, my stomach hurts. A tightness stays in my throat. It feels like I could cry at any second. I'm certain no one will ever love me again and I wonder if breaking up with Luke was a huge mistake. He didn't even try to talk me out of it.

At the radio station I do my job, all the while thinking about dying. Fantasies about the sweet relief of death keep me company through the days, evenings and especially at night. The world would be a better place without angry and ugly me. The only thing stopping me from taking action is the thought of Bobby and Charlie. I can't bear the thought of putting them through it. I can't bear having them haunted by my suicide the rest of their lives.

Sitting in my sadness one day after work, I am looking out the window, tears running down my cheeks. In my heart I believe my own mother would be relieved if I were dead. Her life would be easier if she didn't have to deal with me, or account for any of her mistakes. I'm going over it again. Why don't I matter to her? Why don't I matter to *anyone*?

It is a sunny afternoon. Trees sway in the breeze. Focusing on the fluttering leaves through my tears, the world goes blurry and my body starts to calm down. My breathing slows. I close my eyes and after a long time of just breath after breath, something changes. There it is. *Nothing is wrong.* Floating in this feeling, I am engulfed in peace. I am weightless. I am timeless. I am love. I am an innocent baby, held in the arms of God, and I do matter. To me.

***

The phone rings and it's Kasey from high school art class. Since graduating Cornell, she's been living in Washington, DC, working to raise money for women political candidates.

"One of our roommates has moved out and we need a replacement. Move here!" she says, all lighthearted and fun, and just like that, I agree.

Two weeks later I'm standing in Mom's driveway, my car packed full. The look of pain on Charlie's face as I hug him and Bobby good-bye will haunt me forever. It feels like I'm abandoning my baby brothers, and I am.

As much as the boys don't want me to leave, Mom can't wait to get rid of me. She and Gramma give me an envelope with $300.00 in it, money they can't really spare, and I give them quick obligatory hugs before getting in the car and turning the key in the ignition. A folder with James Landon's glowing references sits on the front seat beside me. The gravel crunches under my tires as I pull out of the driveway and onto the highway, passing The Rusty Nail as I head out of town.

Acknowledgements

This book could never have been written without the unconditional, unwavering love and support of my husband, Todd O'Neil. My darling you have healed me on so many levels and I thank you. Thank you to my children, who delight and amaze me every day with their kind and pure hearts.

Thank you to my mother, who supported me in telling my story. Thank you to my sister, and brothers. I realize putting myself out there, puts you out there, and I honor that your memories may be different from my own.

Thank you to my late grandmother Doris Wilson.

Thank you to Jennifer Lauck, my first writing mentor, for teaching me so much, and believing in me. Thank you to Monica Holloway for your time and advice and support.

Thank you Kathleen Connors, Carrie Link, Jenny Rough, Courtney Sheinmel, Kim Meisner, Jan C. Snow, Suzy Pafka, Kyra Anderson, Cindy Washabaugh, Amber Harris, Jerri Farris, Bryan Trandem, Amy Breau, Janet McSain, Michelle Casella, Cheryl Puzo Green, Lisa Baldwin, Angelo Zuccolo, John Leslie, and Robin Vieyra. Thank you Linda C., Stacy S., Bill S., and Rob V.

Thank you to my loyal blog readers. I love you all so much!

Thank you to the Source that holds the cosmos in order, for planting the seed of writing inside me. May I be a good steward.

And thank you to my Dad, who did better than his own father did. That's not nothing.

About the Author

Most of the places and all of the names have been changed in this book. The author used the pseudonym "Janie" in honor of the main character in her favorite novel, *Their Eyes Were Watching God*, by Zora Neale Hurston. She dedicates *Daughter of the Drunk at the Bar* to all the daughters, of all the drunks, at all the bars everywhere.

For more on Michelle O'Neil, check out her blogs, www.fullsoulahead.com, and www.daughterofthedrunkatthebar.blogspot.com.

Made in the USA
Charleston, SC
14 October 2013